TEXT BOOK OF PHARMACOLOGICAL AND TOXICOLOGICAL SCREENING METHODS - I

[According to latest syllabus of M. Pharm of Pharmacy Council of India]

Dr. Prabha Manjari

Assistant Professor

Dr Ram Manohar Lohia Awadh University,

Ayodhya (U.P.)

Mr. Vijay Kumar

Assistant Professor

Shree Ram College of Pharmacy,

Panchkula.

Ms. Sulakshana Pal Singh

Assistant Professor

Sharda School of Pharmacy,

Sharda University

Agra (U.P.)

Mrs. Swati Singh

Assistant Professor

BCDA College of Pharmacy &

Technology,

Hridaypur.

Mr. Subhadas Chatterjee

Assistant Professor

Sanaka Educational Trust's Group of

Institutions,

Malandighi, Durgapur.

NOTION PRESS

TEXT BOOK OF PHARMACOLOGICAL AND TOXICOLOGICAL SCREENING METHODS - I

NOTION PRESS

PREFACE

The authors feel great pleasure in presenting the first edition of the book "**Text book of Pharmacological and Toxicological Screening Methods - I**" for graduate and post graduate students. The present book on Text Book of **Pharmacological and Toxicological Screening Methods-I** has been written according to the syllabus of M. Pharm of Pharmacy Council of India and covers full course of the subject.

THE SALIENT FEATURES OF THE BOOK ARE:-

- *Easy to understand style of writing* which makes the book a self-study material.
- *Each new concept has been introduced through day-today problem of interest* to the students which makes the subject matter interesting.
- *The language of the book, on the whole, is lucid and easy to understand.*
- Wherever needed *neatly labeled figures have been drawn.*

The authors hope that the students, teachers and other readers will find the book interesting and to the point covering the course. We hope that the students will receive the book warmly.

I express a sincere thank you to the Management of Dr Ram Manohar Lohia Awadh University, Shree Ram College of Pharmacy, Sharda School of Pharmacy, Sharda University, BCDA College of Pharmacy & Technology and Sanaka Educational Trust's Group of Institutions for their support during the writing of this book.

Every effort is made to keep the book error free. The author will gratefully acknowledge the suggestions to improve the book to make it more useful.

Wishing our readers success in examination and life ahead. The authors feel that their efforts will be fully rewarded if the book serves the purpose for which it is written.

PHARMACOLOGICAL AND TOXICOLOGICAL SCREENING METHODS - I

CONTENTS

- Common laboratory animals:
    - Description of Common laboratory animals
    - Handling of Common laboratory animals
    - Applications of different species and strains of animals.
- Transgenic animals:
    - Transgenic animals in Laboratory Animals
    - Production of Transgenic animals in Laboratory Animals
    - maintenance of Transgenic animals in Laboratory Animals
    - applications Anaesthesia of experimental animals
    - Applications euthanasia of experimental animals.
- Maintenance and breeding of laboratory animals.
- CPCSEA guidelines to conduct experiments on animals
- Good laboratory practice.
- Bioassay
    - Principle of Bioassay
    - scope of Bioassay
    - limitations of Bioassay
    - methods of Bioassay

Preclinical screening of new substances for the pharmacological activity using in vivo, in vitro, and other possible animal alternative models.

- General principles of preclinical screening.
- CNS Pharmacology:
    - behavioural and muscle co-ordination,

- Extrapolation of in vitro data to preclinical

- Extrapolation of in preclinical to humans

CHAPTER - 1

LABORATORY ANIMALS

INTRODUCTION:

An introduction to laboratory animals encompasses various aspects related to the use of animals in scientific research. Here's a detailed overview covering the key points:

1. **Definition and Purpose**: Laboratory animals refer to animals used in scientific research, experimentation, and testing. They are utilized across various scientific disciplines for studying diseases, testing the safety and efficacy of drugs, understanding biological processes, and advancing medical knowledge.

2. **Types of Laboratory Animals:**
   a. **Mice and Rats**: Among the most commonly used due to their small size, fast reproduction, and genetic similarity to humans.
   b. **Guinea Pigs:** Often used in studies related to respiratory diseases and immunology.
   c. **Rabbits:** Valuable for studies in cardiovascular research, eye diseases, and reproductive biology.
   d. **Non-human Primates:** Used in research requiring complex cognitive or physiological functions due to their genetic similarity to humans.
   e. **Fish, Birds, and Amphibians**: Used in various fields such as developmental biology, toxicology, and neuroscience.

3. **Ethical Considerations**: The use of laboratory animals raises ethical concerns regarding animal welfare, pain, and suffering. Researchers and institutions must adhere to strict ethical guidelines and regulations to ensure the humane treatment of animals and minimize their discomfort.

4. **Regulatory Framework**: Most countries have regulatory bodies and laws governing the use of laboratory animals. These regulations aim to ensure the

ethical treatment of animals, the scientific validity of research, and the safety of researchers.

5. **Housing and Care**: Laboratory animals are typically housed in specialized facilities designed to provide optimal environmental conditions, including temperature, humidity, lighting, and ventilation. Proper care and husbandry practices are essential to maintain the health and well-being of the animals.

6. **Use in Research**: Laboratory animals are used in a wide range of research applications, including basic research to understand fundamental biological processes, drug discovery and development, toxicity testing, and the development of medical treatments and therapies.

7. **Alternatives to Animal Testing**: Efforts are ongoing to develop alternative methods to reduce, refine, or replace the use of animals in research. These include in vitro models, computer simulations, tissue engineering, and epidemiological studies.

8. **Role of Animal Welfare Organizations**: Various organizations advocate for the ethical treatment of laboratory animals and work to promote alternatives to animal testing. They also engage in public education and outreach to raise awareness about animal welfare issues.

9. **Transparency and Reporting**: Researchers are encouraged to maintain transparency in their use of laboratory animals by accurately reporting methods, results, and the rationale for using animals in their research. This transparency helps ensure scientific rigor and accountability.

10. **Continuing Debate and Evolution**: The use of laboratory animals remains a topic of debate and evolving ethical standards. Scientists, ethicists, policymakers, and animal welfare advocates continue to engage in dialogue to balance the need for scientific advancement with ethical considerations and animal welfare concerns.

COMMON LABORATORY ANIMALS

A. Description of Common laboratory animals:

Here's a detailed description of some of the most common laboratory animals used in scientific research:

1. **Mice (Mus musculus):**
   a. **Description**: Mice are small rodents with a typical length of 2.5 to 4 inches and weigh between 20 to 40 grams. They have large, rounded ears, long tails, and a pointed snout. Mice exhibit a wide range of coat colors and patterns.
   b. **Characteristics:** Mice are prolific breeders, have a short gestation period (about 19-21 days), and reach sexual maturity quickly. They are genetically similar to humans, making them valuable for studying various diseases and genetic conditions.
   c. **Uses**: Mice are widely used in biomedical research for studying genetics, immunology, cancer, neuroscience, and drug development. They are particularly popular for creating genetically modified strains to model human diseases.

2. **Rats (Rattus norvegicus):**
   a. **Description:** Rats are larger than mice, typically measuring 9 to 11 inches in length and weighing between 200 to 500 grams. They have long tails, large ears, and a more robust build compared to mice.
   b. **Characteristics:** Rats are social animals that exhibit complex behaviors, making them useful for behavioral studies. They have a longer lifespan compared to mice and are easier to handle in some experimental settings.
   c. **Uses:** Rats are utilized in various areas of research, including behavioral neuroscience, toxicology, physiology, and pharmacology. They are commonly used to study addiction, obesity, hypertension, and neurological disorders.

3. **Guinea Pigs (Cavia porcellus):**

a. **Description:** Guinea pigs are small rodents native to South America, weighing between 700 to 1200 grams and measuring around 8 to 10 inches in length. They have a stocky build, short legs, and no tail.

b. **Characteristics:** Guinea pigs are docile and social animals, making them easy to handle and suitable for behavioral studies. They have a unique requirement for dietary vitamin C, as they cannot synthesize it endogenously.

c. **Uses:** Guinea pigs are commonly used in immunology, allergy, and infectious disease research. They are particularly valuable for studying respiratory diseases, such as asthma and tuberculosis, due to similarities in their respiratory anatomy and immune system to humans.

4. **Rabbits (Oryctolagus cuniculus):**

   a. **Description:** Rabbits are small mammals with a slender body, long ears, and fluffy tail. They vary in size depending on the breed, with domestic rabbits typically weighing between 2 to 5 kilograms.

   b. **Characteristics:** Rabbits have a well-developed cardiovascular system, making them useful for cardiovascular research and studies involving vascular interventions. They are also commonly used for ocular research due to their large eyes.

   c. **Uses:** Rabbits are employed in various research areas, including cardiovascular physiology, ophthalmology, reproductive biology, and toxicology. They are often used to assess the safety and efficacy of medical devices and surgical procedures.

These common laboratory animals play crucial roles in advancing scientific knowledge across diverse fields of research. Understanding their characteristics and suitability for specific research applications is essential for designing and conducting experiments effectively.

B. Handling of Common laboratory animals:

Handling laboratory animals requires care, skill, and adherence to ethical guidelines to ensure the well-being of the animals and the reliability of research results. Here's a detailed overview of the handling procedures for some common laboratory animals:

1. Mice and Rats:

1. **Housing:** Mice and rats are typically housed in cages with bedding material for comfort. The cages should provide adequate space, ventilation, and enrichment to promote natural behaviors. Animals are often housed in groups to reduce stress.

2. **Handling**: When handling mice and rats, it's important to approach them calmly and confidently to minimize stress. Grasp them gently but firmly by the base of the tail or around the body, taking care to support their weight. Avoid lifting them by the tail alone, as this can cause injury.

3. **Restraint**: Restraint techniques may be necessary for certain procedures, such as injections or blood sampling. Restraint devices, such as tubes or restrainers, can be used to immobilize the animal safely while minimizing stress.

4. **Training:** Some research protocols may involve training mice and rats for specific tasks, such as maze navigation or operant conditioning. Positive reinforcement techniques, such as food rewards, can be used to encourage desired behaviors.

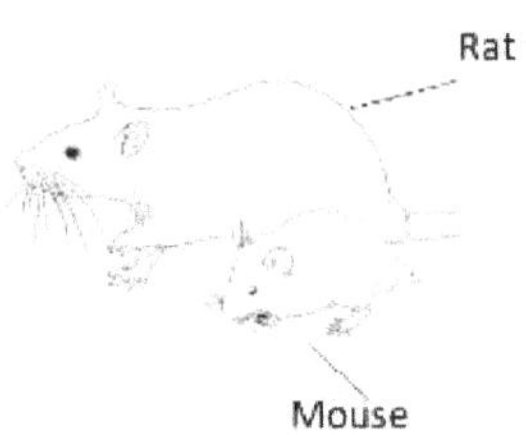

2. Guinea Pigs:

1. **Housing:** Guinea pigs are typically housed in cages with solid floors to prevent foot injuries. They require a diet rich in vitamin C, as they are unable to synthesize it endogenously. Like mice and rats, they benefit from social housing and enrichment.

2. **Handling:** Guinea pigs should be handled gently and supported securely to prevent injury. Grasp them around the body with one hand, supporting the hindquarters, while the other hand supports the chest and forelimbs. Avoid lifting them by the scruff of the neck, as this can cause distress.

3. **Restraint:** Restraint may be necessary for procedures such as injections or examinations. Guinea pigs can be restrained manually or placed in a towel or restrainer to immobilize them safely while minimizing stress.

4. **Health Monitoring**: Guinea pigs are prone to certain health issues, such as respiratory infections and dental problems. Regular health checks, including examination of the eyes, ears, teeth, and coat, are essential for early detection and treatment of any issues.

GUINEA PIG

3. Rabbits:

1. **Housing:** Rabbits require larger enclosures than mice, rats, and guinea pigs to allow for hopping and stretching. Their housing should provide

adequate space, ventilation, and opportunities for exercise and enrichment.

2. **Handling:** When handling rabbits, it's important to approach them calmly and avoid sudden movements. Grasp them gently but securely around the body, supporting the hindquarters to prevent injury to the spine.

3. **Restraint:** Restraint may be necessary for procedures such as injections, blood sampling, or examinations. Rabbits can be restrained manually or placed in a towel or restrainer to immobilize them safely while minimizing stress.

4. **Health Monitoring**: Rabbits are susceptible to various health issues, including dental problems and gastrointestinal stasis. Regular health checks, including examination of the teeth, eyes, ears, and feces, are essential for early detection and treatment of any issues. Monitoring the health of a rabbit involves a combination of observation, regular veterinary check-ups, and preventive care. Here are some tips for keeping tabs on your rabbit's health:

- Observation: Keep an eye on your rabbit's behavior and appearance. Changes in appetite, activity level, grooming habits, and waste elimination can be indicators of health issues.

- Regular Veterinary Check-ups: Schedule routine check-ups with a veterinarian who is experienced in treating rabbits. They can assess your rabbit's overall health, provide vaccinations if necessary, and address any concerns you may have.

- Diet and Nutrition: Ensure your rabbit's diet is appropriate and well-balanced. Provide plenty of fresh hay, high-quality rabbit pellets, and fresh vegetables. Avoid giving too many treats, as this can lead to obesity and other health problems.

- Hydration: Make sure your rabbit always has access to fresh water. Dehydration can be a serious issue for rabbits.

- Dental Health: Check your rabbit's teeth regularly for signs of overgrowth or dental problems. Dental issues are common in rabbits and can affect their ability to eat and groom themselves properly.

- Grooming: Regularly groom your rabbit to prevent matting and to check for any signs of skin problems, parasites, or injuries.

- Housing and Environment: Ensure your rabbit's living space is clean, spacious, and free from hazards. Provide opportunities for exercise and mental stimulation.

RABBIT

C. Applications of different species and strains of animals:

Different species and strains of laboratory animals are utilized in a wide range of research applications across various scientific disciplines. Here's a detailed overview of the applications of some common laboratory animals:

1. **Mice (Mus musculus):**

   a. **Applications:**

      i. **Genetics and Genomics**: Mice are extensively used for studying gene function, inheritance patterns, and genetic variation. Genetically engineered mouse models, including knockout, knock-in, and transgenic mice, are valuable for investigating the role of specific genes in development, disease, and behavior.

ii. **Immunology:** Mice are used to study immune system function, including immune cell development, activation, and response to pathogens. They are valuable for modeling autoimmune diseases, infectious diseases, and immune deficiencies.

iii. **Cancer Research**: Mice are commonly used to study cancer biology, tumor development, metastasis, and the efficacy of anticancer therapies. Genetically engineered mouse models of cancer can mimic human disease progression and help identify novel therapeutic targets.

iv. **Neuroscience**: Mice are employed to study brain development, neurobiology, and neurological disorders. Transgenic and knockout mouse models are used to investigate the molecular mechanisms underlying neurodegenerative diseases, psychiatric disorders, and neurodevelopmental disorders.

2. **Rats (Rattus norvegicus):**
   a. **Applications:**
      i. **Behavioral Research**: Rats are widely used in behavioral studies to investigate learning, memory, cognition, and social behavior. They are valuable for studying addiction, depression, anxiety, and other behavioral disorders.

      ii. **Cardiovascular Research**: Rats are commonly used to study cardiovascular physiology, hypertension, heart failure, and ischemic heart disease. Various rat models, including spontaneously hypertensive rats (SHR) and myocardial infarction models, are employed to investigate the pathophysiology of cardiovascular diseases.

iii. **Toxicology:** Rats are used in toxicology studies to evaluate the safety of chemicals, drugs, and environmental contaminants. They are valuable for assessing acute and chronic toxicity, carcinogenicity, and reproductive toxicity.

iv. **Surgical Models**: Rats are frequently used in surgical research to develop and refine surgical techniques, test medical devices, and study wound healing. Rat models of stroke, spinal cord injury, and traumatic brain injury are widely used in neuroscience and regenerative medicine research.

3. **Guinea Pigs (Cavia porcellus):**
   a. **Applications:**
      i. **Respiratory Research**: Guinea pigs are commonly used to study respiratory diseases, including asthma, chronic obstructive pulmonary disease (COPD), and tuberculosis. They are valuable for investigating airway inflammation, bronchial hyperreactivity, and immune responses to respiratory pathogens.

      ii. **Allergy and Immunology**: Guinea pigs are used to study allergic reactions, hypersensitivity responses, and immune modulation. They are employed in models of allergic rhinitis, allergic asthma, and contact dermatitis to investigate immune mechanisms and test potential therapeutics.

      iii. **Infectious Disease Research**: Guinea pigs are utilized as animal models for studying infectious diseases caused by bacteria, viruses, and parasites. They are particularly valuable for researching tuberculosis, syphilis, and streptococcal infections due to their susceptibility to these pathogens.

      iv. **Wound Healing:** Guinea pigs are used in wound healing studies to investigate tissue repair mechanisms, wound closure rates, and the efficacy of wound care treatments. They are valuable for assessing the effects of various interventions on wound healing outcomes.

4. **Rabbits (Oryctolagus cuniculus):**
   a. **Applications:**
      i. **Ophthalmology:** Rabbits are commonly used in ophthalmic research to study eye anatomy, physiology, and diseases. They are valuable for investigating corneal wound healing, glaucoma, cataracts, and retinal degeneration.
      ii. **Cardiovascular Research**: Rabbits are utilized in cardiovascular studies to investigate atherosclerosis, thrombosis, and vascular interventions. They are employed in models of hypercholesterolemia, hypertension, and myocardial infarction to study disease mechanisms and test therapeutic interventions.
      iii. **Reproductive Biology**: Rabbits are used in reproductive research to study fertility, pregnancy, and embryonic development. They are valuable for investigating gamete biology, embryo implantation, and reproductive disorders.
      iv. **Toxicology and Drug Testing**: Rabbits are employed in toxicology studies to evaluate the safety of drugs, chemicals, and medical devices. They are valuable for assessing systemic toxicity, reproductive toxicity, and ocular irritation potential.

These are just a few examples of the diverse applications of different species and strains of laboratory animals in scientific research. Each species offers unique advantages and characteristics that make them suitable for specific research questions and experimental approaches.

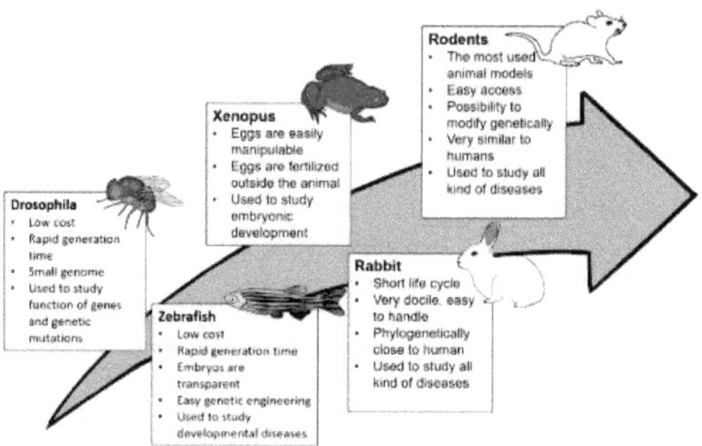

TRANSGENIC ANIMALS

A. Transgenic animals in Laboratory Animals:

Transgenic animals are a crucial tool in biomedical research, allowing scientists to study gene function, disease mechanisms, and potential treatments. Here's a detailed overview of transgenic animals in laboratory research:

1. **Definition:**

   a. Transgenic animals are organisms that have had foreign genes introduced into their genome through genetic engineering techniques. These foreign genes, or transgenes, are typically introduced to study gene function, model human diseases, or produce biologically active molecules.

2. **Creation of Transgenic Animals:**

   a. Transgenic animals are created using various techniques, including:

      i. **Pronuclear microinjection: This** involves injecting foreign DNA directly into the pronucleus of a fertilized egg. The DNA integrates randomly into the genome of the developing embryo.

      ii. **Embryonic stem cell (ESC) technology**: ESCs are isolated from early embryos and genetically modified in vitro using gene targeting techniques. The modified ESCs are then injected into blastocysts to generate chimeric animals, which can transmit the transgene to their offspring.

   iii. **Viral vectors:** Viral vectors, such as retroviruses or lentiviruses, can be used to deliver transgenes into the genome of target cells or embryos.

   iv. **CRISPR/Cas9 technology**: CRISPR/Cas9 allows for precise genome editing by introducing targeted mutations or inserting transgenes into specific genomic loci.

3. **Applications of Transgenic Animals:**

   a. **Functional Genomics:** Transgenic animals are valuable for studying gene function and regulation. By introducing transgenes that overexpress or knock out specific genes, researchers can investigate the effects on phenotype, behavior, and disease susceptibility.

   b. **Disease Modeling**: Transgenic animals are used to model human diseases, including cancer, neurodegenerative disorders, cardiovascular diseases, and metabolic disorders. These models help researchers understand disease mechanisms, identify therapeutic targets, and test potential treatments.

   c. **Drug Discovery and Development**: Transgenic animals are employed in preclinical drug testing to evaluate the safety and efficacy of novel therapeutics. They provide valuable insights into drug metabolism, pharmacokinetics, and toxicology.

   d. **Biomedical Research**: Transgenic animals are used to produce biologically active molecules, such as hormones, growth factors, antibodies, and enzymes, for biomedical research and therapeutic applications. Transgenic animal models are also used to study gene therapy approaches for treating genetic diseases.

4. **Examples of Transgenic Animal Models:**

a. **Alzheimer's disease:** Transgenic mouse models expressing mutant forms of amyloid precursor protein (APP) and presenilin genes develop amyloid plaques and cognitive deficits similar to Alzheimer's disease.

b. **Cancer:** Transgenic mice engineered to overexpress oncogenes or lack tumor suppressor genes develop spontaneous tumors, providing valuable models for studying cancer initiation, progression, and metastasis.

c. **Diabetes:** Transgenic mice expressing human insulin genes or lacking insulin-producing pancreatic beta cells are used to study diabetes mellitus and test novel therapies, such as insulin replacement and islet transplantation.

d. **Cystic Fibrosis:** Transgenic pigs expressing mutant cystic fibrosis transmembrane conductance regulator (CFTR) gene mutations mimic the lung and gastrointestinal manifestations of cystic fibrosis in humans.

5. **Ethical Considerations:**

a. The creation and use of transgenic animals raise ethical considerations related to animal welfare, genetic manipulation, and potential unintended consequences. Researchers and institutions must adhere to ethical guidelines and regulatory frameworks to ensure the humane treatment of animals and responsible use of genetic technologies.

Transgenic animals play a vital role in advancing our understanding of gene function, disease mechanisms, and potential treatments in biomedical research. Their creation and use require careful consideration of ethical, scientific, and regulatory factors to ensure the integrity of research and the welfare of the animals involved.

B. Production of Transgenic animals in Laboratory Animals:

The production of transgenic animals involves the introduction of foreign genes, known as transgenes, into the genome of an organism using genetic engineering techniques. Here's a detailed overview of the steps involved in producing transgenic animals in laboratory research:

1. **Design of Transgene:**
   a. The first step in producing transgenic animals is designing the transgene, which typically consists of the gene of interest (the gene being introduced into the animal) along with regulatory elements necessary for its expression, such as promoters and enhancers.
   b. The transgene may also include selectable markers, such as antibiotic resistance genes, to facilitate the identification of transgenic animals during the selection process.

2. **Vector Construction:**
   a. The transgene is inserted into a vector, which is a DNA molecule used to carry the transgene into the target organism's genome. Common vectors used for transgenesis include plasmids and viral vectors.
   b. The transgene is typically inserted into the vector using recombinant DNA technology, which involves cutting the vector and the transgene with restriction enzymes and ligating them together.

3. **Delivery of Transgene:**
   a. There are several methods for delivering the transgene into the target organism's genome, depending on the species and the desired outcome:
      i. **Pronuclear Microinjection**: In this method, the transgene is injected directly into the pronucleus of a fertilized egg using a fine glass needle. The injected embryos are then implanted into a surrogate mother's uterus for development.
      ii. **Embryonic Stem Cell (ESC) Technology**: ESCs are isolated from early embryos and cultured in vitro. The transgene is

introduced into the ESCs using gene targeting techniques, such as homologous recombination. The modified ESCs are then injected into blastocysts, which are implanted into surrogate mothers to generate chimeric animals.

iii. **Viral Vectors:** Viral vectors, such as retroviruses or lentiviruses, can be used to deliver transgenes into the genome of target cells or embryos. The viral vector containing the transgene is injected into embryos, and the infected embryos are implanted into surrogate mothers for development.

4. **Screening and Selection:**

   a. After the delivery of the transgene, screening and selection methods are used to identify animals that have successfully incorporated the transgene into their genome. Common screening methods include polymerase chain reaction (PCR) analysis of genomic DNA, fluorescence microscopy (for transgenes containing fluorescent protein markers), and Southern blot analysis.

   b. Animals that test positive for the presence of the transgene are further bred to establish stable transgenic lines with the desired genetic modification.

5. **Characterization and Validation:**

   a. Once stable transgenic lines are established, they are characterized and validated to ensure that the transgene is expressed as intended and has the desired phenotype.

   b. Characterization may involve analyzing the expression levels of the transgene using techniques such as quantitative PCR or Western blotting, as well as assessing the phenotypic effects of the transgene through physiological, biochemical, and behavioral assays.

   c. Validation studies may also involve comparing transgenic animals to wild-type animals or other relevant controls to confirm the specificity and relevance of the transgenic model to the research question being addressed.

6. Ethical Considerations:

a. The production of transgenic animals raises ethical considerations related to animal welfare, genetic manipulation, and potential unintended consequences. Researchers and institutions must adhere to ethical guidelines and regulatory frameworks to ensure the humane treatment of animals and responsible use of genetic technologies.

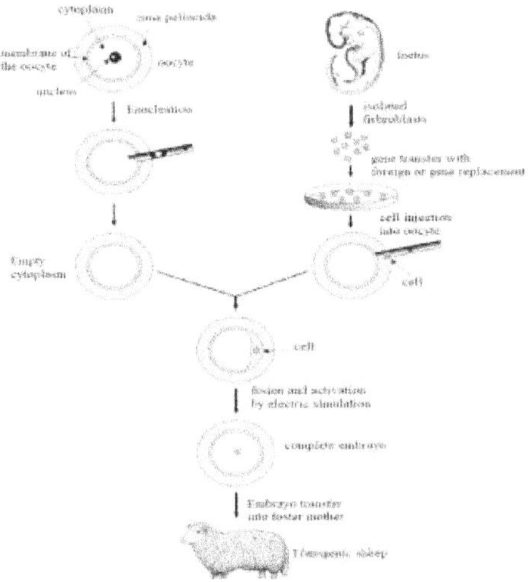

C. Maintenance of transgenic animals in laboratory animals:

Maintaining transgenic animals in laboratory settings involves careful management to ensure their well-being, genetic integrity, and suitability for research purposes. Here's a detailed overview of the maintenance procedures for transgenic animals:

1. Housing:

a. Transgenic animals are typically housed in specialized facilities designed to meet their specific needs. Housing conditions should provide adequate space, ventilation, temperature, humidity, and lighting to promote the health and well-being of the animals.

b. Animals are often housed in individual cages or group-housing systems, depending on species-specific requirements and research protocols.

c. Housing environments may include enrichment items, such as nesting material, toys, or hiding places, to promote natural behaviors and reduce stress.

2. Health Monitoring:

a. Regular health monitoring is essential for detecting and preventing diseases and ensuring the welfare of transgenic animals.

b. Health checks may include visual observation of behavior and appearance, as well as physical examination of key indicators such as body weight, coat condition, and posture.

c. Veterinary care, including routine health screenings, vaccinations, and treatment of illnesses or injuries, should be provided as needed.

3. Breeding Management:

a. Breeding transgenic animals requires careful planning and management to maintain genetic integrity and produce offspring with the desired genotype.

b. Breeding strategies may involve mating transgenic animals with wild-type animals to generate heterozygous or homozygous offspring with the transgene of interest.

c. Controlled breeding programs may be implemented to maintain specific genetic lines and phenotypic characteristics over multiple generations.

4. Genetic Monitoring:

a. Regular genetic monitoring is essential for verifying the presence and stability of the transgene in transgenic animals.

b. Techniques such as polymerase chain reaction (PCR), fluorescence in situ hybridization (FISH), or Southern blot analysis may be used to detect and characterize the transgene in genomic DNA samples.

c. Genetic monitoring helps ensure the integrity of transgenic lines and identify any genetic alterations or unintended mutations that may affect research outcomes.

5. Record Keeping:

a. Accurate record keeping is crucial for documenting the pedigree, genotype, health status, and experimental history of transgenic animals.

b. Detailed records should be maintained for each animal, including identification numbers, birth dates, breeding history, genetic modifications, and experimental interventions.

c. Electronic databases or laboratory information management systems (LIMS) may be used to organize and manage animal records efficiently.

6. Ethical Considerations:

a. The maintenance of transgenic animals raises ethical considerations related to animal welfare, genetic manipulation, and the use of animals in research.

b. Researchers and institutions must adhere to ethical guidelines and regulatory frameworks to ensure the humane treatment of transgenic animals and minimize any potential harm or suffering.

D. Applications Anaesthesia of experimental animals:

Anesthesia is a critical component of experimental procedures involving laboratory animals, ensuring their welfare by minimizing pain and distress during invasive or potentially uncomfortable manipulations. Here's a detailed overview of the applications of anesthesia in experimental animals:

1. Surgical Procedures:

a. Anesthesia is essential for surgical interventions, including tissue biopsies, organ transplantation, and implantation of medical devices. It allows researchers to perform precise surgical manipulations while preventing pain and distress in the animal.

b. Common surgical procedures performed under anesthesia include abdominal surgeries, orthopedic procedures, and neurosurgical interventions.

2. Imaging and Diagnostic Procedures:

a. Anesthesia is often required for imaging studies, such as magnetic resonance imaging (MRI), computed tomography (CT), and positron emission tomography (PET). It ensures immobility and reduces motion artifacts during imaging acquisition.

b. Diagnostic procedures, such as endoscopy, bronchoscopy, and ultrasound, may also require anesthesia to facilitate examination and sample collection.

3. Behavioral Experiments:

a. Anesthesia is used in behavioral experiments to immobilize animals during data collection or to induce specific behavioral states for study. For example, anesthesia may be used to induce sleep or sedation for studies on sleep physiology or circadian rhythms.

b. Anesthesia can also facilitate the handling and manipulation of animals during behavioral assays, such as fear conditioning or cognitive tests.

4. Pain Management:

a. Anesthesia is often combined with analgesia (pain relief) to manage postoperative pain and discomfort in animals undergoing surgical procedures. Multimodal analgesic protocols may include local anesthetics, opioids, non-steroidal anti-inflammatory drugs (NSAIDs), and other pain-relieving medications.

b. Effective pain management is essential for promoting postoperative recovery, reducing stress, and improving the welfare of experimental animals.

5. **Experimental Manipulations:**

   a. Anesthesia may be used to facilitate experimental manipulations that require immobilization or temporary loss of consciousness. This includes procedures such as blood collection, injections, catheterization, and physiological measurements.

   b. Anesthesia allows researchers to perform these manipulations safely and effectively while minimizing the potential for stress, pain, or injury to the animal.

6. **Species-Specific Considerations:**

   a. Different species of laboratory animals may have unique requirements and responses to anesthesia. Anesthetic protocols must be tailored to the species, age, weight, and health status of the animals.

   b. Some species, such as rodents and non-human primates, may require specialized anesthesia delivery systems or monitoring equipment to ensure optimal anesthesia depth and safety.

7. **Ethical Considerations:**

   a. The use of anesthesia in experimental animals raises ethical considerations related to animal welfare, pain management, and the refinement of experimental procedures.

   b. Researchers and institutions must adhere to ethical guidelines and regulatory requirements to ensure that anesthesia is used appropriately and that the welfare of animals is prioritized throughout the research process.

D. Applications euthanasia of experimental animals:

Euthanasia, the humane and intentional ending of an animal's life, is a necessary component of laboratory animal research to minimize pain and suffering, particularly at the conclusion of studies or when animals are no longer needed for research purposes. Here's a detailed overview of the applications of euthanasia in experimental animals:

1. **Study Endpoints:**
   a. Euthanasia is often performed when animals reach the endpoint of a study, as defined by the experimental protocol. This may be based on predetermined criteria such as tumor size, disease progression, or experimental duration.
   b. Ending the study with euthanasia allows researchers to collect tissues and samples for analysis and to examine the effects of the experimental intervention on the animal's physiology, pathology, or behavior.

2. **Health and Welfare Concerns:**
   a. Euthanasia is employed when animals develop severe or untreatable health problems that compromise their welfare or quality of life. This includes conditions such as terminal illnesses, severe injuries, or chronic pain that cannot be alleviated through medical intervention.
   b. Humane euthanasia prevents animals from experiencing prolonged suffering and distress and allows them to be euthanized in a controlled and painless manner.

3. **Breeding Management:**
   a. Euthanasia may be used as part of breeding management programs to control the size and composition of animal colonies. Excess animals, offspring with undesirable genetic traits, or animals with genetic modifications that are no longer needed for research may be euthanized to maintain colony health and genetic integrity.

b. Euthanasia also prevents overcrowding in animal facilities and ensures that resources are allocated efficiently to support the welfare of remaining animals.

4. **Experimental Procedures:**

   a. Euthanasia may be performed as part of experimental procedures to collect tissues, organs, or biological samples for research purposes. This includes terminal studies in which animals are euthanized to harvest tissues for histological, biochemical, or molecular analysis.

   b. The timing and method of euthanasia must be carefully planned to minimize potential confounding factors and to ensure that tissues are collected in a consistent and reproducible manner.

5. **Regulatory Compliance:**

   a. Euthanasia practices in laboratory animal research are subject to regulatory oversight and must comply with ethical guidelines and institutional policies. Regulatory bodies such as institutional animal care and use committees (IACUCs) or animal ethics committees review and approve euthanasia protocols to ensure that they meet legal and ethical standards.

   b. Researchers and animal care staff must be trained in euthanasia techniques and procedures to ensure that euthanasia is performed humanely and in accordance with established guidelines.

6. **Species-Specific Considerations:**

   a. Different species of laboratory animals may require species-specific euthanasia methods and techniques. For example, rodents may be euthanized using methods such as carbon dioxide (CO_2) inhalation or cervical dislocation, while larger animals may require intravenous injection of euthanasia agents.

b. The choice of euthanasia method should consider factors such as animal size, anatomy, behavior, and the availability of equipment and expertise.

7. **Psychological Impact:**

   a. Euthanasia can have emotional and psychological impacts on researchers, animal care staff, and other individuals involved in laboratory animal research. Providing support, counseling, and training on coping strategies and ethical decision-making can help mitigate the psychological stress associated with euthanasia.

8. **Ethical Considerations:**

   a. The decision to euthanize animals in laboratory research raises ethical considerations related to animal welfare, scientific integrity, and the justification of research goals. Euthanasia should be performed only when necessary, based on scientific and ethical considerations, and in accordance with established guidelines and regulations.

By applying euthanasia judiciously and compassionately, researchers and animal care staff can uphold ethical standards and ensure the welfare of laboratory animals while advancing scientific knowledge and discovery.

MAINTENANCE AND BREEDING OF LABORATORY ANIMALS

Maintaining and breeding laboratory animals involves a series of comprehensive procedures to ensure their health, welfare, and suitability for research purposes. Here's a detailed overview of the maintenance and breeding of laboratory animals:

1. **Housing:**

   a. Laboratory animals are typically housed in specialized facilities designed to meet their specific needs. Housing conditions should provide adequate space, ventilation, temperature, humidity, and lighting to promote the health and well-being of the animals.

b. Animals are often housed in individual cages or group-housing systems, depending on species-specific requirements and research protocols.

c. Housing environments may include enrichment items, such as nesting material, toys, or hiding places, to promote natural behaviors and reduce stress.

2. Nutrition:

a. Providing appropriate nutrition is essential for the health and well-being of laboratory animals. Diets should be formulated to meet the specific dietary requirements of each species, including nutrient composition, energy content, and dietary supplements.

b. Nutritional requirements may vary depending on factors such as age, sex, reproductive status, and health status. Regular monitoring of food consumption and body weight can help ensure that animals receive adequate nutrition.

3. Health Monitoring:

a. Regular health monitoring is essential for detecting and preventing diseases and ensuring the welfare of laboratory animals.

b. Health checks may include visual observation of behavior and appearance, as well as physical examination of key indicators such as body weight, coat condition, and posture.

c. Veterinary care, including routine health screenings, vaccinations, and treatment of illnesses or injuries, should be provided as needed.

4. Breeding Management:

a. Breeding laboratory animals requires careful planning and management to maintain genetic integrity, produce offspring with the desired genotype, and control population size.

b. Breeding strategies may involve selecting breeding pairs based on desired traits or genetic characteristics, monitoring reproductive cycles, and managing mating schedules.

c. Controlled breeding programs may be implemented to maintain specific genetic lines and phenotypic characteristics over multiple generations.

5. **Genetic Monitoring:**

a. Regular genetic monitoring is essential for verifying the genetic composition and integrity of laboratory animal colonies.

b. Techniques such as polymerase chain reaction (PCR), fluorescence in situ hybridization (FISH), or genetic sequencing may be used to detect and characterize genetic mutations, polymorphisms, or transgenic modifications in animals.

c. Genetic monitoring helps ensure the genetic quality and reproducibility of research results and facilitates the management of breeding programs.

6. **Record Keeping:**

a. Accurate record keeping is crucial for documenting the pedigree, genotype, health status, and experimental history of laboratory animals.

b. Detailed records should be maintained for each animal, including identification numbers, birth dates, breeding history, genetic modifications, and experimental interventions.

c. Electronic databases or laboratory information management systems (LIMS) may be used to organize and manage animal records efficiently.

7. **Ethical Considerations:**

a. The maintenance and breeding of laboratory animals raise ethical considerations related to animal welfare, genetic manipulation, and the use of animals in research.

b. Researchers and institutions must adhere to ethical guidelines and regulatory requirements to ensure that animals are housed, bred, and used responsibly and humanely.

CPCSEA GUIDELINES TO CONDUCT EXPERIMENTS ON ANIMALS

The CPCSEA (Committee for the Purpose of Control and Supervision of Experiments on Animals) is an Indian regulatory body that oversees the ethical use and welfare of animals in scientific research. The guidelines set forth by CPCSEA provide standards and regulations for the humane and ethical treatment of animals used in experimentation. Here are the key aspects of CPCSEA guidelines for conducting experiments on animals:

1. **Institutional Animal Ethics Committee (IAEC):**

   a. Every institution conducting experiments on animals must establish an Institutional Animal Ethics Committee (IAEC) accredited by CPCSEA.

   b. The IAEC is responsible for reviewing and approving research protocols involving animals, ensuring compliance with CPCSEA guidelines, and overseeing the welfare of animals used in experiments.

2. **Experimental Protocols:**

   a. Researchers must submit detailed experimental protocols to the IAEC for review and approval before conducting experiments on animals.

   b. Protocols should include information on the purpose of the study, experimental procedures, justification for the use of animals, species and number of animals to be used, housing and husbandry conditions, anesthesia and analgesia protocols, methods of euthanasia, and plans for monitoring and minimizing pain and distress.

c. The Committee for the Purpose of Control and Supervision of Experiments on Animals (CPCSEA) in India provides guidelines and regulations for conducting experiments on animals. These guidelines aim to ensure ethical treatment and minimize the pain and suffering of animals used in scientific research. Here's an outline of the general experimental protocols as per CPCSEA guidelines:

- Ethical Approval: Before conducting any experiments involving animals, researchers must obtain ethical approval from an Institutional Animal Ethics Committee (IAEC) or the CPCSEA.

- Animal Procurement: Animals should be sourced from registered breeders or suppliers who comply with CPCSEA guidelines. The transportation and housing of animals should meet specified standards to ensure their welfare.

- Housing and Care: Animals should be housed in appropriate facilities that provide adequate space, ventilation, temperature, and lighting. They should receive proper nutrition, clean water, and enrichment to ensure their well-being.

- Health Monitoring: Regular health monitoring of animals should be conducted to ensure they are free from diseases or health issues that could affect the validity of experimental results.

- Anesthesia and Analgesia: Anesthesia and analgesia should be administered to minimize pain and distress during experimental procedures. The choice of anesthetic and analgesic agents should be appropriate for the species and the nature of the procedure.

- Experimental Procedures: Experimental procedures should be carefully designed to minimize pain, suffering, and distress to the animals involved. Researchers should consider alternatives to invasive procedures whenever possible.

- Euthanasia: If euthanasia is necessary, it should be carried out in a humane manner, using approved methods that minimize pain and distress.

- Record Keeping: Detailed records should be maintained for each experimental procedure, including the number of animals used, their source, housing conditions, experimental procedures performed, and any adverse events or outcomes.

- Reporting: Researchers should accurately report their methods and findings in scientific publications, including details of ethical approval, animal welfare measures, and adherence to CPCSEA guidelines.

- Training and Education: Researchers and animal care personnel should receive appropriate training in animal handling, care, and experimental procedures to ensure compliance with CPCSEA guidelines and the highest standards of animal welfare.

3. **Animal Welfare:**
   a. Animals used in experiments must be treated humanely and provided with appropriate care, housing, and husbandry to ensure their welfare.
   b. Housing facilities should meet standards for space, ventilation, temperature, humidity, lighting, and sanitation to promote the health and well-being of animals.
   c. Animals must have access to food and water ad libitum, unless withholding food or water is necessary for the experimental protocol and approved by the IAEC.

4. **Anesthesia, Analgesia, and Euthanasia:** The Committee for the Purpose of Control and Supervision of Experiments on Animals (CPCSEA) in India

provides specific guidelines regarding anesthesia, analgesia, and euthanasia for laboratory animals to ensure their welfare and minimize pain and distress during experimental procedures. Here's an overview:

a. Anesthesia:
- Anesthesia should be administered to minimize pain and distress during surgical and other procedures that may cause pain or discomfort to the animals.
- The choice of anesthetic agents should be based on factors such as the species of animal, the nature and duration of the procedure, and the health status of the animal.
- Anesthesia should be administered by trained personnel following appropriate protocols, and the animals should be carefully monitored during anesthesia to ensure their safety.

b. Analgesia:
- Analgesia (pain relief) should be provided to animals before, during, and after procedures that are likely to cause pain or discomfort.
- The choice of analgesic agents should be based on the species of animal, the type and severity of pain, and any contraindications or potential side effects.
- Analgesia should be administered by trained personnel according to established protocols, and the animals should be monitored for signs of pain or distress.

c. Euthanasia:
- Euthanasia should be performed in a humane and compassionate manner to minimize pain and distress to the animals.
- The choice of euthanasia method should be based on factors such as the species of animal, the size and age of the animal, and the purpose of euthanasia.

- o Approved methods of euthanasia may include overdose of anesthetic agents, physical methods (such as cervical dislocation or decapitation), or other humane techniques.
  - o Euthanasia should be performed by trained personnel following established protocols, and the animals should be carefully monitored to ensure death is achieved quickly and painlessly.
- d. Training and Certification:
  - o Personnel responsible for administering anesthesia, analgesia, and euthanasia should receive appropriate training and certification to ensure they are competent in performing these procedures safely and effectively.
  - o Training programs should cover topics such as anesthesia techniques, pain assessment, drug administration, and euthanasia methods, as well as ethical considerations and animal welfare guidelines.

Adherence to these guidelines is essential to ensure the ethical treatment of laboratory animals and compliance with regulatory requirements. Researchers and laboratory personnel should familiarize themselves with the specific recommendations and requirements outlined in the CPCSEA guidelines relevant to anesthesia, analgesia, and euthanasia for laboratory animals.

5. Species-Specific Considerations:

- a. Researchers must consider the species-specific needs, behaviors, and physiology of animals when designing experimental protocols and providing care and enrichment.
- b. Special considerations may be necessary for the housing, handling, and management of different species of animals to ensure their welfare and minimize stress.

6. Training and Oversight:

a. Researchers, animal care staff, and personnel involved in handling and conducting experiments on animals must receive appropriate training in animal care, handling, anesthesia, analgesia, euthanasia, and ethical principles.

b. Institutions must provide oversight and monitoring of animal research activities to ensure compliance with CPCSEA guidelines and regulations.

7. Reporting and Documentation:

a. Researchers must maintain detailed records of experimental procedures, animal welfare assessments, anesthesia and analgesia protocols, and adverse events.

b. Institutions are required to submit annual reports to CPCSEA summarizing the number and species of animals used in experiments, the nature of experiments conducted, and measures taken to ensure animal welfare and compliance with CPCSEA guidelines.

Overall, the CPCSEA guidelines aim to promote the ethical and humane use of animals in scientific research while ensuring the validity and reliability of research outcomes. Compliance with CPCSEA guidelines is essential for obtaining approval to conduct experiments on animals and for maintaining accreditation of institutional animal research programs.

GOOD LABORATORY PRACTICE

Good Laboratory Practice (GLP) refers to a set of principles and standards established to ensure the quality, integrity, and reliability of non-clinical laboratory studies, including those involving laboratory animals. GLP guidelines provide a framework for conducting research in a manner that promotes accuracy, consistency, and transparency in data generation and reporting. Here's a detailed overview of GLP in laboratory animals:

1. Regulatory Framework:

a. GLP regulations are typically enforced by government agencies responsible for regulating the safety and efficacy of products such as pharmaceuticals, agrochemicals, and medical devices.

b. In many countries, GLP compliance is a legal requirement for conducting non-clinical studies intended for submission to regulatory authorities for product approval or registration.

2. **Key Principles:**

   a. GLP encompasses several key principles that govern the conduct of non-clinical laboratory studies, including:

      i. Compliance with applicable regulations and guidelines.

      ii. Implementation of standardized operating procedures (SOPs) for all aspects of study conduct.

      iii. Validation and maintenance of analytical methods, equipment, and facilities.

      iv. Documentation of study procedures, data, and results in a complete, accurate, and traceable manner.

      v. Quality assurance (QA) oversight to ensure adherence to GLP standards and identify and address deficiencies or discrepancies.

3. **Study Design and Conduct:**

   a. GLP requires the use of well-defined study protocols that outline the objectives, procedures, methods, and acceptance criteria for each study.

   b. Animal studies conducted under GLP must adhere to standardized protocols for housing, husbandry, handling, dosing, sampling, and observation.

   c. SOPs must be developed and followed for all aspects of animal care, experimental procedures, data collection, and record-keeping.

4. **Facilities and Equipment:**

a. GLP-compliant facilities must meet specific requirements for laboratory design, construction, maintenance, and cleanliness.

b. Animal housing areas must provide appropriate environmental conditions, including temperature, humidity, lighting, and ventilation, to ensure the health and welfare of animals.

c. Equipment used in animal studies, such as cages, feeding systems, anesthesia machines, and laboratory instruments, must be validated, calibrated, and maintained according to SOPs.

5. **Personnel Training:**

a. Personnel involved in GLP studies, including researchers, technicians, veterinarians, and support staff, must receive appropriate training and education in GLP principles, study protocols, animal care, and experimental procedures.

b. Training records must be maintained to document the qualifications and competency of personnel involved in GLP studies.

6. **Quality Assurance:**

a. GLP studies are subject to QA oversight to ensure that they are conducted in compliance with GLP standards and regulatory requirements.

b. QA personnel are responsible for conducting audits, inspections, and reviews of study documentation, facilities, equipment, and procedures to verify compliance and identify any deviations or deficiencies.

c. QA audits may be conducted internally by the study sponsor or externally by regulatory agencies or independent auditing organizations.

7. **Data Management and Reporting:**

a. GLP requires the collection, recording, and retention of all raw data, documentation, and study records generated during the conduct of a study.

b. Data must be documented in a manner that is clear, complete, accurate, and traceable, with appropriate controls to prevent data manipulation or falsification.

c. Study reports must be prepared in accordance with GLP requirements and include detailed descriptions of study objectives, methods, results, statistical analyses, conclusions, and any deviations or discrepancies encountered during the study.

By adhering to GLP principles and standards, researchers can ensure the reliability, integrity, and regulatory compliance of non-clinical laboratory studies involving laboratory animals. GLP-compliant studies provide valuable data for assessing the safety, efficacy, and quality of products intended for human or animal use, while also promoting animal welfare and ethical conduct in scientific research.

BIOASSAY

A. Principle of Bioassay:

Bioassay, also known as biological assay, is a technique used to measure the potency, effectiveness, or concentration of a substance by its effect on living organisms. In laboratory animals, bioassays are commonly used to evaluate the pharmacological, toxicological, or physiological effects of drugs, chemicals, hormones, toxins, or other biological substances. Here's a detailed overview of the principles of bioassay in laboratory animals:

1. Quantitative Measurement:

a. Bioassays aim to quantitatively measure the biological response elicited by a test substance. This response may include changes in physiological parameters, biochemical markers, tissue morphology, behavior, or mortality rates.

b. The magnitude of the biological response is proportional to the concentration or dose of the test substance, allowing researchers to establish dose-response relationships and determine potency or effectiveness.

2. Standardization:

a. Bioassays require standardization of experimental conditions, including the selection of appropriate animal models, experimental protocols, dosing regimens, and outcome measures.

b. Standardization ensures consistency and reproducibility of results across different experiments and laboratories, allowing for reliable comparisons between test substances or experimental conditions.

3. Selection of Animal Models:

a. The choice of animal model for a bioassay depends on factors such as the biological target of interest, species-specific responses, availability of animals, ethical considerations, and regulatory requirements.

b. Commonly used laboratory animal species in bioassays include mice, rats, guinea pigs, rabbits, dogs, and non-human primates, each with specific advantages and limitations.

4. Dose-Response Relationship:

a. Bioassays characterize the dose-response relationship between the concentration or dose of the test substance and the biological response observed in animals.

b. Dose-response curves are constructed to visualize the relationship between increasing doses of the test substance and the corresponding magnitude of the biological effect, allowing determination of the potency, efficacy, or toxicity of the substance.

5. Statistical Analysis:

a. Statistical methods are employed to analyze bioassay data, including determination of mean values, standard deviations, confidence intervals, and significance levels.

b. Parametric and non-parametric statistical tests may be used to compare experimental groups, assess dose-response relationships, and determine the statistical significance of observed differences.

6. **Reference Standards:**

   a. Bioassays often use reference standards or control substances with known potency or activity levels for comparison with test substances.

   b. Reference standards serve as benchmarks for assessing the sensitivity, specificity, accuracy, and precision of the bioassay and for establishing potency or concentration units.

7. **Validation and Quality Assurance:**

   a. Bioassays require validation to demonstrate the reliability, accuracy, and reproducibility of results. Validation studies assess assay precision, linearity, specificity, sensitivity, and robustness under defined experimental conditions.

   b. Quality assurance measures, including adherence to Good Laboratory Practices (GLP) and documentation of experimental procedures, data, and results, ensure the integrity and reliability of bioassay data.

B. Scope of Bioassay:

The scope of bioassay in laboratory animals is broad and encompasses various applications across pharmacology, toxicology, physiology, and biomedical research. Here's a detailed overview of the scope of bioassay in laboratory animals:

1. **Drug Discovery and Development:**

   a. Bioassays are extensively used in drug discovery and development to evaluate the pharmacological properties of new chemical entities (NCEs) or potential drug candidates.

   b. Pharmacodynamic bioassays assess the physiological effects of drugs on target tissues or systems in laboratory animals, providing information on potency, efficacy, mechanism of action, and therapeutic potential.

c. Pharmacokinetic bioassays measure the absorption, distribution, metabolism, and excretion (ADME) of drugs in animals, helping to optimize drug formulations, dosing regimens, and routes of administration.

2. **Toxicology and Safety Assessment:**

a. Bioassays play a crucial role in toxicology and safety assessment by evaluating the adverse effects of chemicals, environmental pollutants, pesticides, food additives, and pharmaceuticals on living organisms.

b. Acute toxicity bioassays determine the lethal dose (LD50) or lethal concentration (LC50) of a substance in laboratory animals, providing information on its acute toxicity and potential hazards.

c. Subchronic and chronic toxicity bioassays assess the cumulative effects of repeated or prolonged exposure to a substance over time, identifying potential organ toxicity, carcinogenicity, reproductive toxicity, and developmental toxicity.

3. **Endocrine Disruption:**

a. Bioassays are used to assess the endocrine-disrupting effects of chemicals on hormone systems in laboratory animals, including disruption of hormone synthesis, secretion, transport, receptor binding, and signaling pathways.

b. Endocrine bioassays measure changes in hormone levels, reproductive parameters, sexual development, and other endocrine-related endpoints in response to chemical exposure, helping to identify potential risks to human and animal health.

4. **Biomedical Research:**

a. Bioassays are employed in biomedical research to investigate physiological processes, disease mechanisms, and therapeutic interventions in laboratory animals.

b. Disease models are developed using bioassays to mimic human diseases such as cancer, diabetes, cardiovascular disorders, neurodegenerative diseases, autoimmune diseases, and infectious diseases, allowing researchers to study disease pathogenesis, progression, and treatment strategies.

c. Efficacy bioassays evaluate the therapeutic efficacy of drugs, biologics, gene therapies, cell therapies, vaccines, and other interventions in animal models of disease, providing preclinical evidence to support clinical translation and drug approval.

5. **Environmental Monitoring:**

a. Bioassays serve as sensitive and cost-effective tools for environmental monitoring and biomonitoring by assessing the health and ecological impacts of environmental contaminants on living organisms.

b. Environmental bioassays measure physiological, biochemical, and behavioral endpoints in sentinel species or bioindicator organisms exposed to contaminated environments, providing early warning signs of environmental pollution and ecosystem health.

6. **Regulatory Compliance:**

a. Bioassays are conducted to meet regulatory requirements and standards established by government agencies for product safety, environmental protection, and public health.

b. Regulatory bioassays are designed to generate data required for product registration, risk assessment, hazard identification, safety evaluation, and regulatory approval, ensuring that products meet established safety and efficacy criteria before market authorization.

C. limitations of Bioassay:

While bioassays in laboratory animals are invaluable tools for assessing the potency, efficacy, toxicity, and physiological effects of substances, they also have several limitations that researchers must consider. Here are detailed explanations of some of these limitations:

1. **Species Differences:**
   a. Laboratory animals may not always accurately represent human physiology and response to substances. Species-specific differences in metabolism, pharmacokinetics, pharmacodynamics, and receptor specificity can lead to discrepancies between animal and human responses.
   b. Translating findings from animal bioassays to human outcomes requires careful consideration of species differences and validation in human studies.

2. **Ethical Concerns:**
   a. Conducting bioassays in laboratory animals raises ethical concerns related to animal welfare, pain and distress, and the use of animals in research. Ethical considerations may limit the types of experiments that can be performed and require researchers to adhere to strict regulations and guidelines for animal care and use.
   b. Researchers must prioritize the ethical treatment of animals and consider alternatives to animal experimentation whenever possible.

3. **Limited Predictive Value:**
   a. The predictive value of animal bioassays for human outcomes is often limited due to species differences, variability in experimental conditions, and the complexity of biological systems.
   b. While animal studies can provide valuable insights into the biological effects of substances, they may not always accurately predict human responses or clinical outcomes. Human variability, genetic factors, and

environmental influences can further complicate extrapolation of animal data to humans.

4. High Costs and Time Requirements:

a. Conducting bioassays in laboratory animals can be costly and time-consuming, requiring resources for animal acquisition, housing, husbandry, veterinary care, experimental procedures, and data analysis.

b. Longitudinal studies, chronic toxicity assessments, and large-scale experiments may require significant time and financial investment, limiting the feasibility of certain types of research.

5. Small Sample Sizes:

a. Bioassays in laboratory animals often involve relatively small sample sizes due to practical constraints such as space limitations, cost considerations, and ethical concerns.

b. Small sample sizes can limit the statistical power of experiments and increase the risk of Type I or Type II errors, reducing the reliability and generalizability of study findings.

6. Inherent Variability:

a. Biological variability within and between animal populations can affect the reproducibility and consistency of experimental results. Factors such as age, sex, genetic background, housing conditions, diet, and handling procedures can contribute to variability in study outcomes.

b. Researchers must account for and minimize sources of variability through proper experimental design, randomization, blinding, and statistical analysis.

7. Limited Scope of Endpoints:

a. Bioassays often focus on a limited set of endpoints or biomarkers to assess the biological effects of substances. While these endpoints may provide valuable information on specific aspects of toxicity, pharmacology, or physiology, they may not capture the full spectrum of potential effects or mechanisms of action.

b. Integrated approaches combining multiple endpoints and omics technologies may help overcome this limitation by providing a more comprehensive assessment of substance effects.

Despite these limitations, bioassays in laboratory animals remain essential tools for scientific research, regulatory decision-making, and product development. By acknowledging and addressing these limitations, researchers can optimize the design, conduct, and interpretation of animal bioassays to maximize their scientific value and relevance.

D. Methods of Bioassay:

Bioassays in laboratory animals encompass a variety of methods used to evaluate the biological effects of substances on living organisms. These methods are essential for assessing potency, efficacy, toxicity, and physiological responses to drugs, chemicals, hormones, toxins, and other biological agents. Here's a detailed overview of some common methods of bioassay in laboratory animals:

1. Acute Toxicity Testing:

a. Acute toxicity tests determine the lethal dose (LD50) or lethal concentration (LC50) of a substance by administering escalating doses to animals and observing mortality or toxic effects over a short duration (usually 24 to 72 hours).

b. Common animal models used in acute toxicity testing include mice, rats, guinea pigs, and rabbits. The test substance is typically administered via oral gavage, inhalation, dermal application, or intravenous injection.

c. Acute toxicity tests provide valuable information on the acute toxic effects, hazard classification, and initial safety assessment of substances.

2. **Subchronic and Chronic Toxicity Testing:**

   a. Subchronic and chronic toxicity tests evaluate the cumulative effects of repeated or prolonged exposure to a substance over weeks to months.

   b. Animals are dosed daily or intermittently with the test substance for a specified duration, and a comprehensive battery of toxicological endpoints is assessed, including clinical signs, body weight changes, organ weights, histopathology, hematological and biochemical parameters, and functional observations.

   c. These tests provide data on systemic toxicity, target organ toxicity, carcinogenicity, reproductive toxicity, developmental toxicity, and other long-term effects.

3. **Pharmacological Bioassays:**

   a. Pharmacological bioassays assess the pharmacological effects of drugs, hormones, neurotransmitters, and other bioactive substances in laboratory animals.

   b. Animal models are used to study specific physiological responses or pharmacodynamic endpoints, such as analgesia, sedation, muscle relaxation, cardiovascular effects, respiratory effects, gastrointestinal effects, and behavioral changes.

   c. Pharmacological bioassays help characterize the potency, efficacy, mechanism of action, and therapeutic potential of substances.

4. **Biological Assay of Hormones and Growth Factors:**

   a. Biological assays are used to measure the biological activity or potency of hormones, growth factors, cytokines, and other biologically active substances.

b. Animal models or cell-based assays are employed to assess the physiological effects of hormones on target tissues or biological responses, such as hormone secretion, receptor activation, cell proliferation, differentiation, or gene expression.

c. Hormone bioassays are used in endocrinology, reproductive biology, neurobiology, and drug development to evaluate hormone function and activity.

5. **Immunological Bioassays:**

a. Immunological bioassays evaluate the immunomodulatory effects of drugs, vaccines, antibodies, cytokines, and immunomodulators in laboratory animals.

b. Animal models are used to study immune responses, including antibody production, cellular immune responses, cytokine production, immune cell activation, and inflammation.

c. Immunological bioassays help assess the immunogenicity, efficacy, safety, and mechanism of action of immunomodulatory substances.

6. **Behavioral Assays:**

a. Behavioral assays assess the effects of substances on animal behavior, cognition, motor function, sensory perception, and mood.

b. Animal models are used to study specific behaviors or behavioral endpoints, such as locomotor activity, anxiety, depression, learning and memory, social interaction, and drug-seeking behavior.

c. Behavioral assays provide insights into the neuropharmacological effects, psychoactive properties, and potential side effects of drugs and other substances.

7. **Genotoxicity and Mutagenicity Testing:**

a. Genotoxicity and mutagenicity tests assess the potential of substances to induce genetic damage or mutations in laboratory animals.

b. Animal models, such as rodents and Drosophila fruit flies, are used to study chromosomal aberrations, micronucleus formation, gene mutations, DNA damage, and other genotoxic effects following exposure to test substances.

c. Genotoxicity and mutagenicity testing are important components of safety assessment and regulatory evaluation for drugs, chemicals, pesticides, and environmental contaminants.

8. Pharmacokinetic Studies:

a. Pharmacokinetic studies evaluate the absorption, distribution, metabolism, and excretion (ADME) of drugs and chemicals in laboratory animals.

b. Animal models are used to assess pharmacokinetic parameters, such as bioavailability, plasma concentration-time profiles, tissue distribution, metabolism rates, and elimination half-life.

c. Pharmacokinetic studies provide insights into drug absorption, distribution, metabolism, and excretion kinetics, helping to optimize drug formulations, dosing regimens, and routes of administration.

These are just a few examples of the diverse methods of bioassay in laboratory animals. Depending on the specific research objectives, experimental requirements, and regulatory considerations, researchers may employ a combination of these methods to evaluate the biological effects of substances and generate data for scientific research, drug development, safety assessment, and regulatory decision-making.

Multiple-Choice Questions (MCQs)

1. What is the primary purpose of using laboratory animals in scientific research?

A) Entertainment

B) Cosmetic testing

C) Studying diseases and drug efficacy

D) Breeding exotic animals

2. Which animal is commonly used for cardiovascular studies and ocular research?

    A) Guinea pigs

    B) Rabbits

    C) Mice

    D) Fish

3. What is a significant ethical consideration in using laboratory animals?

    A) Cost-effectiveness

    B) Time efficiency

    C) Animal welfare and minimizing discomfort

    D) Ease of availability

4. What type of housing condition is crucial for laboratory animals?

    A) Colorful environments

    B) Adequate space and controlled environment

    C) Outdoor access

    D) Minimalistic designs

5. Which animal is NOT typically used for genetic studies?

    A) Mice

    B) Rats

    C) Non-human primates

    D) Rabbits

6. Which technology is used to create transgenic animals?

    A) PCR

    B) CRISPR/Cas9

    C) Southern blotting

    D) Flow cytometry

7. What is the primary use of rats in scientific research?

   A) Immunology only

   B) Behavioral studies and pharmacology

   C) Cosmetic testing

   D) Only genetic modification studies

8. Why are guinea pigs particularly valuable in respiratory disease studies?

   A) They are small and easy to handle

   B) Similar respiratory anatomy to humans

   C) They reproduce quickly

   D) They are inexpensive

9. What does CPCSEA stand for?

   A) Committee for the Purpose of Control and Supervision of Experiments on Animals

   B) Central Protocol for Scientific and Ethical Control of Animal Experiments

   C) Council for the Prevention of Cruelty to Science Experiment Animals

   D) Central Panel for Control and Supervision of Experiments on Animals

10. Which method is NOT used in the creation of transgenic animals?

   A) Pronuclear microinjection

   B) Embryonic stem cell technology

   C) Random mutagenesis

   D) Viral vectors

11. What role do bioassays play in drug development?

   A) Packaging only

   B) Evaluating pharmacological properties

   C) Advertising only

   D) Distribution logistics

12. Which animal is most commonly used in toxicology studies?

   A) Rabbits

B) Guinea pigs

C) Rats

D) Birds

13. Which regulatory body reviews experimental protocols involving animals in India?

   A) FDA

   B) CPCSEA

   C) WHO

   D) IACUC

14. What is essential for breeding transgenic animals?

   A) High-cost facilities only

   B) Genetic monitoring

   C) Minimal genetic variation

   D) Large populations

15. Which of the following is NOT a focus of the CPCSEA guidelines?

   A) Ensuring scientific validity

   B) Maintaining minimal documentation

   C) Animal welfare

   D) Compliance with ethical standards

16. What is the significance of CRISPR/Cas9 in laboratory research?

   A) It is used for cleaning cages

   B) It allows for precise genome editing

   C) It is a type of animal feed

   D) It monitors animal health

17. What is the least likely use of mice in research?

   A) Immunology studies

   B) Cancer research

   C) Studying large animal physiology

   D) Neuroscience

18. What does GLP stand for in laboratory settings?

   A) General Laboratory Procedure

   B) Good Laboratory Practice

   C) Global Laboratory Protocol

   D) Generalized Legal Parameters

19. What is a primary concern when using anesthesia in experimental animals?

   A) Enhancing color perception

   B) Ensuring immobility for procedures

   C) Increasing environmental awareness

   D) Enhancing sensory perception

20. What is the purpose of euthanasia in laboratory animal management?

   A) To train new researchers

   B) To prolong studies indefinitely

   C) To end an animal's life humanely when necessary

   D) To promote animal breeding

Short Answer Type Questions (Subjective)

1. What are laboratory animals primarily used for in scientific research?

2. List three types of laboratory animals commonly used and the specific studies they are used for.

3. What are the main ethical considerations in the use of laboratory animals?

4. Describe the type of regulatory framework that governs the use of laboratory animals.

5. What is meant by the term "alternative to animal testing"?

6. Why is housing and care critical for laboratory animals?

7. Explain the role of animal welfare organizations in the context of laboratory animals.

8. What is the significance of transparency and reporting in experiments involving laboratory animals?

9. What are some common diseases or conditions studied using mice?

10. Why are rats considered suitable for behavioral studies?

11. Describe how guinea pigs are used in immunology research.

12. What type of research commonly involves rabbits?

13. Define what transgenic animals are and why they are important in research.

14. Describe the technique of pronuclear microinjection in the creation of transgenic animals.

15. What are the applications of CRISPR/Cas9 technology in the production of transgenic animals?

16. Explain the process and importance of screening and selection in producing transgenic animals.

17. What ethical considerations must be taken into account when maintaining transgenic animals?

18. How is anesthesia used in experimental procedures involving laboratory animals?

19. Discuss the conditions under which euthanasia is considered necessary in laboratory animal research.

20. What are the key principles of Good Laboratory Practice (GLP) as it relates to laboratory animals?

Long Answer Type Questions (Subjective)

1. Discuss the ethical implications of using laboratory animals in biomedical research and the measures taken to address these concerns.

2. Explain the roles of different laboratory animals in biomedical research, focusing on their specific contributions to advancements in medical science.

3. Describe in detail the housing and care requirements for laboratory animals, emphasizing the importance of environmental conditions.

4. Evaluate the impact of regulatory frameworks on ensuring the ethical treatment of laboratory animals and the validity of scientific research.

5. Discuss the advantages and limitations of using transgenic animals in research, including examples of specific disease models.

6. Outline the steps involved in the creation of transgenic animals using embryonic stem cell technology and the challenges associated with this technique.

7. Provide a comprehensive overview of the applications of anesthesia in research involving experimental animals, including specific types of procedures.

8. Analyze the role of euthanasia in laboratory animal management, discussing ethical considerations and methods used.

9. Describe the process and criteria for establishing and maintaining transgenic animal lines in research settings.

10. Discuss the significance of pharmacokinetic studies in drug development and how laboratory animals are utilized to assess drug metabolism and distribution.

Answer Key

1. (C) Studying diseases and drug efficacy

2. (B) Rabbits

3. (C) Animal welfare and minimizing discomfort

4. (B) Adequate space and controlled environment

5. (D) Rabbits

6. (B) CRISPR/Cas9

7. (B) Behavioral studies and pharmacology

8. (B) Similar respiratory anatomy to humans

9. (A) Committee for the Purpose of Control and Supervision of Experiments on Animals

10. (C) Random mutagenesis

11. (B) Evaluating pharmacological properties

12.(C) Rats

13.(B) CPCSEA

14.(B) Genetic monitoring

15.(B) Maintaining minimal documentation

16.(B) It allows for precise genome editing

17.(C) Studying large animal physiology

18.(B) Good Laboratory Practice

19.(B) Ensuring immobility for procedures

20.(C) To end an animal's life humanely when necessary

CHAPTER - 2

PRECLINICAL SCREENING

INTRODUCTION:

Preclinical screening of new substances for pharmacological activity is a crucial stage in drug development, where potential therapeutic compounds are rigorously tested to determine their efficacy, safety, and pharmacokinetic properties before advancing to clinical trials in humans. This process involves a variety of methodologies, including in vivo (within a living organism) and in vitro (outside a living organism) studies, as well as alternative animal models where applicable. Here's a detailed introduction to each aspect:

In Vivo Studies:

In preclinical drug development, in vivo studies play a crucial role in evaluating the safety, efficacy, pharmacokinetics, and pharmacodynamics of potential drug candidates in living organisms. These studies involve the administration of the drug candidate to animal models to assess its biological effects and potential therapeutic benefits. Here's an overview of in vivo studies commonly conducted in preclinical screening:

Acute Toxicity Studies:

a. Acute toxicity studies are conducted to determine the potential adverse effects of a drug candidate following a single exposure at various dose levels. These studies typically involve the administration of escalating doses of the drug to animals, followed by observation of acute toxic effects such as mortality, changes in behavior, clinical signs of toxicity, and gross pathological findings. The results of acute toxicity studies help establish the maximum tolerated dose (MTD) and inform dose selection for subsequent studies.

Repeated Dose Toxicity Studies:

a. Repeated dose toxicity studies are conducted to evaluate the potential adverse effects of a drug candidate following repeated or prolonged exposure over an extended period. These studies involve the administration of the drug to animals daily or intermittently for several weeks or months, followed by comprehensive assessment of systemic toxicity, organ toxicity, histopathological changes, and biochemical alterations. Repeated dose toxicity studies provide valuable information on the safety profile of the drug candidate and help identify target organs for toxicity.

Pharmacokinetic Studies:

a. Pharmacokinetic studies are conducted to investigate the absorption, distribution, metabolism, and excretion (ADME) of a drug candidate in vivo. These studies involve administering the drug to animals via various routes of administration (e.g., oral, intravenous, subcutaneous) and analyzing blood and tissue samples to quantify drug concentrations over time. Pharmacokinetic parameters such as bioavailability, half-life, clearance, and volume of distribution are determined to assess the drug's pharmacokinetic profile and inform dosing regimens for subsequent studies.

Pharmacodynamic Studies:

a. Pharmacodynamic studies are conducted to assess the biological effects of a drug candidate in vivo, including its mechanism of action, therapeutic efficacy, and dose-response relationship. These studies involve administering the drug to animals and measuring relevant pharmacodynamic endpoints such as physiological changes, biochemical markers, biomarker expression, tissue function, or disease progression. Pharmacodynamic studies provide insight into the drug's mechanism of action and its potential therapeutic benefits in vivo.

Safety Pharmacology Studies:

a. Safety pharmacology studies are conducted to evaluate the potential effects of a drug candidate on vital physiological functions, including cardiovascular, respiratory, central nervous system, and renal function. These studies involve assessing the drug's impact on parameters such as heart rate, blood pressure, respiratory rate, electrocardiography (ECG), and neurological function in animal models. Safety pharmacology studies help identify potential safety concerns and guide the design of clinical trials to monitor these effects in humans.

Efficacy Studies:

a. Efficacy studies are conducted to assess the therapeutic efficacy of a drug candidate in relevant disease models or experimental paradigms. These studies involve administering the drug to animal models of disease and evaluating its effects on disease progression, symptomatology, biomarker expression, histopathological changes, or survival outcomes. Efficacy studies provide evidence of the drug's effectiveness in vivo and support its advancement to clinical trials for further evaluation in human subjects.

In vivo studies are essential for characterizing the safety and efficacy profile of a drug candidate in living organisms and guiding decision-making in preclinical drug development. These studies help identify potential safety concerns, optimize dosing regimens, understand the drug's mechanism of action, and provide evidence of therapeutic efficacy, ultimately supporting the transition of promising candidates into clinical development.

In Vitro Studies:

In preclinical drug development, in vitro studies are conducted to assess the biological activity, mechanism of action, and safety profile of potential drug candidates using isolated cells, tissues, or biological molecules in controlled laboratory conditions. These studies provide valuable insights into the pharmacological properties and potential therapeutic benefits of drug candidates before advancing to in vivo testing. Here's an overview of common in vitro studies conducted in preclinical screening:

Cell Viability and Cytotoxicity Assays:

a. Cell viability and cytotoxicity assays are conducted to assess the effects of a drug candidate on cell viability, proliferation, and survival using cultured cells. These assays utilize various techniques such as MTT (3-(4,5-dimethylthiazol-2-yl)-2,5-diphenyltetrazolium bromide), MTS (3-(4,5-dimethylthiazol-2-yl)-5-(3-carboxymethoxyphenyl)-2-(4-sulfophenyl)-2H-tetrazolium), or LDH (lactate dehydrogenase) assays to measure cell metabolic activity, mitochondrial function, membrane integrity, or apoptotic/necrotic cell death following exposure to the drug candidate. Cell viability and cytotoxicity assays help determine the concentration-dependent effects of the drug on cell health and inform dose selection for subsequent studies.

Cellular Pharmacology Assays:

a. Cellular pharmacology assays are conducted to evaluate the effects of a drug candidate on specific cellular targets, pathways, or biological processes relevant to disease pathology. These assays utilize cell-based models or reporter systems to assess parameters such as receptor binding, enzyme inhibition, signal transduction, gene expression, protein synthesis, or cellular function in response to drug treatment. Cellular pharmacology assays provide mechanistic insights into the drug's mode of action and help identify potential therapeutic targets or biomarkers for further investigation.

Enzyme Inhibition Assays:

a. Enzyme inhibition assays are conducted to assess the ability of a drug candidate to inhibit specific enzymes involved in disease pathogenesis or physiological processes. These assays typically involve measuring the enzymatic activity of a purified enzyme or enzyme-containing cell lysate in the presence of varying concentrations of the drug candidate. Enzyme inhibition assays help characterize the potency, selectivity, and mechanism of action of the drug candidate and guide the design of subsequent studies to evaluate its therapeutic potential.

Binding Affinity Assays:

a. Binding affinity assays are conducted to assess the interaction between a drug candidate and its molecular target, such as receptors, transporters, or ion channels. These assays utilize techniques such as radioligand binding, surface plasmon resonance (SPR), or fluorescence polarization to measure the binding affinity, kinetics, and specificity of the drug for its target protein. Binding affinity assays help elucidate the molecular interactions underlying drug-receptor binding and provide quantitative data to support structure-activity relationship (SAR) analysis and lead optimization.

ADME (Absorption, Distribution, Metabolism, Excretion) Assays:

a. ADME assays are conducted to assess the pharmacokinetic properties of a drug candidate, including its absorption, distribution, metabolism, and excretion characteristics. These assays utilize in vitro models such as cell monolayers, tissue slices, or metabolic enzyme systems to predict drug behavior in vivo. ADME assays provide valuable information on factors influencing drug bioavailability, tissue distribution, metabolic stability, and elimination kinetics, helping optimize drug candidates for improved pharmacokinetic profiles and reduced toxicity.

Safety Pharmacology Assays:

a. Safety pharmacology assays are conducted to evaluate the potential effects of a drug candidate on vital physiological functions, including cardiovascular, respiratory, central nervous system, and renal function. These assays utilize in vitro models such as isolated tissues, organ preparations, or cellular systems to assess drug-induced changes in specific physiological parameters. Safety pharmacology assays help identify potential safety concerns and guide the design of subsequent in vivo studies to further evaluate these effects in living organisms.

In vitro studies are essential for characterizing the biological activity, mechanism of action, and safety profile of potential drug candidates in a controlled laboratory setting. These studies provide valuable mechanistic insights, inform lead optimization, support candidate selection, and guide decision-making in preclinical drug development. However, it's important to note that in vitro results may not always translate directly to in vivo efficacy or safety, and therefore, a comprehensive preclinical evaluation combining in vitro and in vivo studies is necessary to fully assess the potential of a drug candidate before advancing to clinical trials.

Alternative Animal Models:

Alternative animal models are utilized in preclinical screening to address ethical concerns, improve translatability to human physiology, and overcome limitations associated with traditional animal models. These alternative models encompass a range of organisms, including non-mammalian species, genetically modified organisms, and invertebrate species, which offer unique advantages for studying specific aspects of drug efficacy, safety, and mechanisms of action. Here's a detailed overview of alternative animal models commonly used in preclinical screening:

1. **Non-Mammalian Models:**
   a. **Zebrafish (Danio rerio):** Zebrafish are widely used in preclinical research due to their rapid development, transparency during embryonic stages, and genetic tractability. They offer advantages for studying vertebrate development, organogenesis, and genetic disorders. Zebrafish models have been employed to assess drug toxicity, cardiotoxicity, neurotoxicity, and behavioral effects, as well

as to investigate disease mechanisms and drug efficacy in various therapeutic areas.

b. **Fruit Flies (Drosophila melanogaster):** Fruit flies are genetically tractable organisms with well-characterized genetics and relatively simple nervous systems, making them valuable models for studying neurodegenerative diseases, developmental disorders, and drug metabolism. Fruit fly models have been used to screen for potential therapeutic compounds, elucidate disease mechanisms, and identify genetic modifiers of drug response.

c. **Caenorhabditis elegans (C. elegans):** C. elegans is a nematode worm with a simple nervous system, transparent body, and well-defined anatomy, making it an ideal model for studying developmental biology, neurobiology, and aging. C. elegans models have been utilized to investigate neurodegenerative diseases, aging-related disorders, and drug metabolism, as well as to screen for novel drug candidates and study drug toxicity.

2. **Genetically Modified Models:**

a. **Transgenic Mice:** Transgenic mice are genetically modified to express specific genes or mutations associated with human diseases, making them valuable models for studying disease pathogenesis, drug efficacy, and therapeutic interventions. Transgenic mouse models have been used to study cancer, neurodegenerative diseases, cardiovascular disorders, metabolic disorders, and infectious diseases, as well as to evaluate gene therapy approaches and pharmacological interventions.

b. **Knockout Mice:** Knockout mice are genetically engineered to lack specific genes of interest, allowing researchers to study the effects of gene deletion on phenotype, physiology, and disease susceptibility. Knockout mouse models have been instrumental in elucidating gene function, identifying therapeutic targets, and investigating drug mechanisms of action in various disease contexts.

c. **Patient-Derived Xenografts (PDX):** Patient-derived xenograft models involve transplanting human tumor tissues into immunodeficient mice to create in vivo models of human cancer. PDX models maintain the histological and genetic characteristics of the original tumor, making them valuable tools for studying tumor biology, drug response, and personalized medicine. PDX models have been used to evaluate anticancer therapies, identify biomarkers of drug response, and optimize treatment regimens for individual patients.

3. **Invertebrate Models:**

a. **Sea Urchins:** Sea urchins are marine invertebrates with transparent embryos and well-characterized developmental processes, making them useful models for studying embryonic development, cell signaling, and toxicology. Sea urchin embryos have been employed to assess drug toxicity, teratogenicity, and developmental defects, as well as to screen for potential therapeutic compounds targeting specific signaling pathways.

b. **Planarians:** Planarians are flatworms with remarkable regenerative abilities and relatively simple nervous systems, making them attractive models for studying regeneration, neurobiology, and behavior. Planarian models have been used to investigate neurodegenerative diseases, psychiatric disorders, and drug-induced behavioral changes, as well as to screen for compounds with neuroprotective or neuroregenerative properties.

Alternative animal models offer complementary approaches to traditional mammalian models, providing unique advantages for addressing specific research questions, reducing reliance on higher vertebrates, and accelerating preclinical drug discovery and development. By leveraging the strengths of alternative models alongside conventional animal models, researchers can gain deeper insights into disease mechanisms, identify novel therapeutic targets, and optimize drug candidates for clinical translation. Additionally, the use of alternative animal models contributes to the ethical and sustainable conduct of preclinical research while enhancing the robustness and reproducibility of scientific findings.

Overall, preclinical screening of new substances for pharmacological activity involves a comprehensive approach combining in vivo, in vitro, and alternative animal models to evaluate safety, efficacy, and mechanism of action, laying the groundwork for successful drug development.

GENERAL PRINCIPLES OF PRECLINICAL SCREENING

Preclinical screening plays a pivotal role in drug development, serving as the bridge between initial compound discovery and clinical trials in humans. It aims to assess the safety, efficacy, pharmacokinetics, and pharmacodynamics of a potential therapeutic agent before it can be tested in humans. Here are the general principles of preclinical screening in detail:

1. **Safety Assessment:**
    a. **Toxicology Studies**: Evaluate the potential toxicity of the compound through acute, subacute, and chronic toxicity studies in animal models.
    b. **Genotoxicity Studies**: Assess the compound's ability to damage genetic material, usually conducted using in vitro tests like the Ames test and in vivo tests like the micronucleus assay.
    c. **Carcinogenicity Studies**: Determine if the compound has carcinogenic potential through long-term exposure studies in animal models.

d. **Reproductive Toxicity Studies**: Investigate the effects of the compound on fertility, pregnancy, and offspring development.

2. **Efficacy Evaluation:**

   a. **Disease Models**: Use relevant animal models or in vitro systems that mimic the disease or condition the drug aims to treat.

   b. **Endpoint Measurement**: Define specific endpoints relevant to the disease or condition, such as tumor size reduction, symptom relief, or biochemical markers.

   c. **Dose-Response Relationship**: Determine the optimal dose range for therapeutic efficacy while minimizing adverse effects.

3. **Pharmacokinetic Assessment:**

   a. **Absorption:** Measure the rate and extent of absorption of the compound after administration via various routes (e.g., oral, intravenous, topical).

   b. **Distribution:** Evaluate the distribution of the compound within tissues and organs to assess its bioavailability and potential for accumulation.

   c. **Metabolism:** Determine the metabolic fate of the compound, including identification of metabolites and assessment of metabolic stability.

   d. **Excretion:** Study the elimination of the compound and its metabolites from the body, mainly through urine and feces.

4. **Pharmacodynamic Studies:**

   a. **Mechanism of Action**: Investigate how the compound interacts with its target molecules or pathways to produce therapeutic effects.

   b. **Biomarker Analysis**: Identify relevant biomarkers that can be used to monitor the compound's pharmacodynamic effects in preclinical and clinical settings.

c. **Tolerance and Dependence**: Assess the development of tolerance or dependence with prolonged use of the compound.

5. **Formulation Development:**

   a. **Stability Studies**: Evaluate the chemical and physical stability of the compound in various formulations and storage conditions.

   b. **Dosing Form Selection**: Optimize the formulation to achieve the desired pharmacokinetic profile, dosing regimen, and patient compliance.

6. **Regulatory Compliance:**

   a. **Good Laboratory Practice (GLP):** Ensure that preclinical studies are conducted in compliance with GLP regulations to guarantee the reliability and integrity of the data.

   b. **Regulatory Guidance**: Adhere to regulatory guidelines provided by agencies such as the FDA (Food and Drug Administration) or EMA (European Medicines Agency) regarding preclinical study design, conduct, and reporting.

7. **Data Interpretation and Decision Making:**

   a. **Risk-Benefit Assessment**: Evaluate the balance between the potential benefits of the compound and its associated risks based on preclinical data.

   b. **Go/No-Go Decision**: Make informed decisions on whether to proceed to clinical trials based on the preclinical findings, considering safety, efficacy, and feasibility factors.

Overall, preclinical screening involves a comprehensive evaluation of the safety, efficacy, pharmacokinetics, and pharmacodynamics of a potential therapeutic compound to support its progression through the drug development pipeline. This process requires interdisciplinary collaboration among scientists from various fields, including toxicology, pharmacology, medicinal chemistry, and regulatory affairs, to ensure thorough assessment and interpretation of preclinical data.

CNS PHARMACOLOGY

A. Behavioral and muscle coordination:

Behavioral and muscle coordination are intricate processes regulated by the central nervous system (CNS), involving complex interactions between neurons, neurotransmitters, and various brain regions. Pharmacology studies focusing on CNS aim to understand how drugs affect these processes, either therapeutically or as side effects. Here's a detailed overview:

Behavioral Pharmacology:

1. Behavioral pharmacology examines how drugs influence behavior, cognition, and emotion. It involves studying the effects of drugs on various behavioral paradigms in animal models and humans. Key aspects include:
   a. **Animal Models:** Researchers use animal models to assess behaviors relevant to human conditions, such as anxiety, depression, addiction, and schizophrenia. Common animal tests include the elevated plus maze, forced swim test, and conditioned place preference.
   b. **Drug Effects on Behavior**: Drugs can alter behavior in multiple ways. For example, anxiolytics reduce anxiety-like behaviors, antidepressants alleviate depressive symptoms, and psychostimulants increase locomotor activity.
   c. **Neurotransmitter Systems**: Different neurotransmitter systems in the CNS modulate behavior. For instance, serotonin regulates mood, dopamine influences reward processing and motor activity, and GABAergic signaling modulates anxiety and relaxation.
   d. **Therapeutic Applications**: Behavioral pharmacology helps identify drugs with therapeutic potential for psychiatric disorders and

neurological conditions. For example, selective serotonin reuptake inhibitors (SSRIs) are used to treat depression and anxiety disorders.

Muscle Coordination and CNS Pharmacology:

1. Muscle coordination involves the synchronized activation of muscles to produce smooth and precise movements. The CNS plays a crucial role in coordinating muscle activity, primarily through the motor cortex, basal ganglia, cerebellum, and brainstem. Pharmacological studies focus on understanding how drugs affect muscle coordination, including:

    a. **Motor Cortex:** The motor cortex initiates and controls voluntary movements. Drugs that modulate neurotransmitter activity in this region can influence muscle coordination. For example, dopaminergic medications are used to manage motor symptoms in Parkinson's disease.

    b. **Basal Ganglia**: The basal ganglia regulate motor planning, execution, and inhibition. Dysfunction in this circuitry can lead to movement disorders such as Parkinson's disease and Huntington's disease. Pharmacological interventions target neurotransmitter systems within the basal ganglia to alleviate symptoms.

    c. **Cerebellum:** The cerebellum fine-tunes motor movements and maintains balance and posture. Drugs that affect neurotransmission in the cerebellum can impact muscle coordination. For example, alcohol impairs cerebellar function, leading to ataxia and impaired coordination.

    d. **Neuromuscular Junction**: Drugs can influence muscle coordination by targeting the neuromuscular junction, where motor neurons synapse with muscle fibers. Neuromuscular blockers are used during surgical procedures to induce muscle relaxation.

Clinical Implications:

1. Understanding the pharmacology of behavior and muscle coordination has clinical implications for treating neurological and psychiatric disorders. Pharmacological interventions can alleviate symptoms, improve quality of life, and enhance functional outcomes for patients. However, drugs targeting the CNS may also produce adverse effects, including sedation, cognitive impairment, and motor dysfunction.

In summary, behavioral and muscle coordination in CNS pharmacology involve studying how drugs affect behavior, cognition, emotion, and motor function. Through preclinical and clinical research, pharmacologists aim to develop novel treatments for neurological and psychiatric disorders while minimizing adverse effects on behavior and motor coordination.

B. CNS stimulants and depressants:

In CNS pharmacology, drugs are classified based on their effects on the central nervous system (CNS) as stimulants or depressants. These drugs have distinct mechanisms of action and produce opposing effects on neuronal activity and behavior. Here's a detailed overview of CNS stimulants and depressants:

CNS Stimulants:

1. CNS stimulants increase neuronal activity and arousal, leading to heightened alertness, wakefulness, and increased energy levels. They exert their effects primarily by enhancing the release or inhibiting the reuptake of neurotransmitters such as dopamine, norepinephrine, and serotonin. Key CNS stimulants include:

   a. **Amphetamines:** Drugs like amphetamine and methamphetamine increase the release of dopamine and norepinephrine from presynaptic neurons, leading to increased arousal, attention, and euphoria. They are used clinically to treat attention deficit hyperactivity disorder (ADHD) and narcolepsy.

b. **Methylphenidate**: Methylphenidate (e.g., Ritalin) also enhances dopamine and norepinephrine activity but primarily by blocking their reuptake. It improves attention and focus and is commonly prescribed for ADHD.

c. **Cocaine**: Cocaine blocks the reuptake of dopamine, norepinephrine, and serotonin, leading to increased alertness, euphoria, and energy. It has a high potential for abuse and addiction.

d. **Modafinil and Armodafinil**: These wakefulness-promoting agents enhance dopamine and norepinephrine transmission but have a different mechanism of action compared to traditional stimulants. They are used to treat narcolepsy, sleep apnea, and shift work sleep disorder.

2. Clinical uses of CNS stimulants include the treatment of ADHD, narcolepsy, and certain cases of depression that are unresponsive to other medications. However, they can also have significant side effects, including insomnia, anxiety, hypertension, and addiction.

CNS Depressants:

1. CNS depressants, also known as sedatives or tranquilizers, reduce neuronal activity and produce calming, sedative, or hypnotic effects. They act primarily by enhancing the inhibitory neurotransmitter gamma-aminobutyric acid (GABA) or by blocking excitatory neurotransmission. Key CNS depressants include:

a. **Benzodiazepines**: Drugs like diazepam (Valium), alprazolam (Xanax), and lorazepam (Ativan) enhance the effects of GABA by binding to benzodiazepine receptors on GABA receptors. They are used to treat anxiety disorders, insomnia, and seizures.

b. **Barbiturates**: Barbiturates such as phenobarbital and secobarbital also enhance GABA activity but through a different mechanism. They are less commonly used today due to their high risk of dependence, overdose, and respiratory depression.

c. **Alcohol:** Ethanol, the active ingredient in alcoholic beverages, enhances GABAergic transmission and inhibits glutamate receptors, leading to sedation, relaxation, and disinhibition. Chronic alcohol use can lead to dependence, tolerance, and withdrawal syndrome.

d. **Opioids:** Opioids like morphine, oxycodone, and hydrocodone produce analgesic and sedative effects by binding to opioid receptors in the CNS. They are used to relieve pain but can also cause respiratory depression, sedation, and euphoria. Opioid abuse has become a significant public health concern.

2. Clinical uses of CNS depressants include the treatment of anxiety disorders, insomnia, seizures, and alcohol withdrawal. However, they carry a risk of tolerance, dependence, overdose, and withdrawal symptoms, especially with prolonged use or misuse.

In summary, CNS stimulants and depressants exert opposing effects on neuronal activity and behavior. Stimulants increase arousal and alertness by enhancing excitatory neurotransmission, while depressants produce sedative and calming effects by enhancing inhibitory neurotransmission. Understanding the pharmacology of these drugs is crucial for their appropriate clinical use and for managing their potential side effects and risks of abuse.

C. Anxiolytics:

Anxiolytics are a class of drugs used to treat anxiety disorders by reducing feelings of fear, worry, and tension. They act primarily on the central nervous system (CNS) to modulate neurotransmitter activity and promote relaxation. Here's a detailed overview of anxiolytics in CNS pharmacology:

Benzodiazepines:

1. Benzodiazepines are among the most commonly prescribed anxiolytics. They enhance the inhibitory effects of gamma-aminobutyric acid (GABA), the primary inhibitory neurotransmitter in the CNS, by binding to specific benzodiazepine receptors on GABA-A receptors. This leads to increased chloride ion influx, hyperpolarization of neurons, and ultimately, a reduction in neuronal excitability. Key benzodiazepines used as anxiolytics include:
   a. Alprazolam (Xanax)
   b. Diazepam (Valium)
   c. Lorazepam (Ativan)
   d. Clonazepam (Klonopin)
2. Benzodiazepines are effective for short-term management of acute anxiety symptoms but are associated with risks of tolerance, dependence, and withdrawal symptoms with long-term use. They are often prescribed for panic disorder, generalized anxiety disorder (GAD), and social anxiety disorder.

Buspirone:

1. Buspirone is a non-benzodiazepine anxiolytic that acts as a partial agonist at serotonin 5-HT1A receptors and as an antagonist at dopamine D2 receptors. Its exact mechanism of action in anxiety is not fully understood, but it is believed to modulate serotonin and dopamine neurotransmission in the CNS. Buspirone is used for the treatment of GAD and has a slower onset of action compared to benzodiazepines.

Selective Serotonin Reuptake Inhibitors (SSRIs):

1. While primarily used as antidepressants, SSRIs such as sertraline (Zoloft), fluoxetine (Prozac), and paroxetine (Paxil) are also effective in treating certain anxiety disorders. SSRIs block the reuptake of serotonin in the synaptic cleft, leading to increased serotonin levels in the brain. This modulation of serotonin neurotransmission is thought to alleviate symptoms

of anxiety. SSRIs are commonly used to treat panic disorder, social anxiety disorder, and obsessive-compulsive disorder (OCD).

Serotonin-Norepinephrine Reuptake Inhibitors (SNRIs):

1. SNRIs like venlafaxine (Effexor) and duloxetine (Cymbalta) are another class of antidepressants that are also used to treat anxiety disorders. These drugs inhibit the reuptake of both serotonin and norepinephrine, leading to increased levels of both neurotransmitters in the synaptic cleft. SNRIs are particularly effective in treating generalized anxiety disorder (GAD).

Beta-Blockers:

1. While primarily used to treat hypertension and cardiac arrhythmias, beta-blockers such as propranolol (Inderal) are sometimes used off-label to manage symptoms of performance anxiety (stage fright). Beta-blockers reduce the physiological symptoms of anxiety, such as rapid heart rate and trembling, by blocking the effects of adrenaline (epinephrine) on beta-adrenergic receptors in the body.

Anxiolytics play a crucial role in the management of anxiety disorders and can significantly improve the quality of life for individuals affected by these conditions. However, it's important to use them judiciously, considering their potential for side effects, drug interactions, and risks of tolerance and dependence, particularly with long-term use of benzodiazepines. Treatment with anxiolytics should be guided by a healthcare professional and may involve a combination of pharmacotherapy, psychotherapy, and lifestyle modifications.

D. Anti-psychotics:

Antipsychotic medications, also known as neuroleptics, are a class of drugs used to manage symptoms of psychosis, including hallucinations, delusions, and disorganized thinking, commonly associated with schizophrenia and related psychotic disorders. Here's a detailed overview of antipsychotics in CNS pharmacology:

First-Generation Antipsychotics (Typical Antipsychotics):

1. First-generation antipsychotics were the first medications developed to treat psychosis and have been in clinical use since the 1950s. They primarily act by blocking dopamine D2 receptors in the brain, thereby reducing dopamine neurotransmission, which is thought to be involved in the pathophysiology of psychosis. Key first-generation antipsychotics include:

   a. Chlorpromazine (Thorazine)

   b. Haloperidol (Haldol)

   c. Fluphenazine (Prolixin)

   d. Thioridazine (Mellaril)

   e. Perphenazine (Trilafon)

2. First-generation antipsychotics effectively alleviate positive symptoms of psychosis (such as hallucinations and delusions) but have limited efficacy against negative symptoms and cognitive impairment. They are associated with a higher risk of extrapyramidal side effects (e.g., dystonia, akathisia, parkinsonism), tardive dyskinesia, and hyperprolactinemia.

Second-Generation Antipsychotics (Atypical Antipsychotics):

1. Second-generation antipsychotics were developed in the latter half of the 20th century as newer alternatives to first-generation agents. Unlike typical antipsychotics, they have a broader pharmacological profile, targeting multiple neurotransmitter systems beyond just dopamine. While they also block dopamine receptors, they also antagonize serotonin receptors, particularly 5-HT2A receptors, and some have affinity for other neurotransmitter receptors. Key second-generation antipsychotics include:

   a. Clozapine (Clozaril)

   b. Risperidone (Risperdal)

   c. Olanzapine (Zyprexa)

   d. Quetiapine (Seroquel)

   e. Aripiprazole (Abilify)

    f. Ziprasidone (Geodon)

    g. Paliperidone (Invega)

    h. Asenapine (Saphris)

    i. Lurasidone (Latuda)

2. Second-generation antipsychotics are associated with a lower risk of extrapyramidal side effects compared to first-generation agents, but they may still cause metabolic side effects such as weight gain, dyslipidemia, and insulin resistance. Clozapine, in particular, is effective in treatment-resistant schizophrenia but requires close monitoring due to the risk of agranulocytosis.

Third-Generation Antipsychotics (Partial Dopamine Agonists):

1. Third-generation antipsychotics represent a newer class of agents that aim to provide the efficacy of antipsychotics while minimizing side effects. Aripiprazole (Abilify) is the prototypical third-generation antipsychotic. It acts as a partial agonist at dopamine D2 receptors, meaning it has both agonist and antagonist properties depending on dopamine levels. Aripiprazole is associated with a lower risk of metabolic side effects but may still cause akathisia and other extrapyramidal symptoms.

Antipsychotic medications are essential for managing psychosis and reducing the severity of symptoms in schizophrenia and related disorders. Treatment with antipsychotics should be individualized based on the patient's symptoms, comorbidities, and tolerability. Close monitoring for side effects and regular follow-up with a healthcare provider are essential for optimizing treatment outcomes and minimizing adverse effects. Additionally, antipsychotic medications are often used in conjunction with psychosocial interventions such as therapy and support programs to address the holistic needs of individuals with psychotic disorders.

E. Anti-epileptics:

Anti-epileptic drugs (AEDs), also known as anti-seizure or anticonvulsant medications, are a class of medications used to manage and prevent epileptic seizures, which are abnormal electrical discharges in the brain. These drugs work by stabilizing neuronal excitability and inhibiting the abnormal electrical activity that leads to seizures. Here's a detailed overview of anti-epileptic drugs in CNS pharmacology:

Sodium Channel Blockers:

1. Sodium channel blockers are among the oldest and most commonly used class of AEDs. They work by reducing the excessive neuronal firing that can lead to seizures. These drugs primarily block voltage-gated sodium channels, thereby preventing the rapid influx of sodium ions that triggers neuronal depolarization. Examples include:
    a. Phenytoin (Dilantin)
    b. Carbamazepine (Tegretol)
    c. Lamotrigine (Lamictal)
    d. Oxcarbazepine (Trileptal)
    e. Topiramate (Topamax)
2. Sodium channel blockers are effective in treating partial seizures and generalized tonic-clonic seizures but may have limited efficacy against absence seizures. They can also cause side effects such as dizziness, drowsiness, ataxia, and cognitive impairment.

Calcium Channel Blockers:

1. Calcium channel blockers primarily inhibit the influx of calcium ions into neurons, thereby reducing neuronal excitability and neurotransmitter release. These drugs are particularly effective in treating absence seizures. Examples include:

a. Ethosuximide (Zarontin): Used as a first-line treatment for absence seizures.

b. Valproic acid (Depakene, Depakote): While primarily a sodium channel blocker, valproic acid also inhibits calcium channels and is effective against multiple seizure types, including absence seizures.

2. Calcium channel blockers may cause gastrointestinal upset, weight gain, and liver toxicity, particularly with long-term use of valproic acid.

GABAergic Drugs:

1. Gamma-aminobutyric acid (GABA) is the primary inhibitory neurotransmitter in the brain. Drugs that enhance GABAergic neurotransmission increase inhibitory tone and reduce neuronal excitability, making them effective in controlling seizures. Examples include:

a. Benzodiazepines: While primarily used as anxiolytics, benzodiazepines like diazepam (Valium) and lorazepam (Ativan) are also used as rescue medications to abort acute seizures.

b. Clonazepam (Klonopin): Effective in treating absence seizures and myoclonic seizures.

c. Gabapentin (Neurontin) and Pregabalin (Lyrica): These drugs modulate calcium channels and enhance GABAergic neurotransmission. They are used to treat partial seizures and neuropathic pain.

2. GABAergic drugs may cause drowsiness, dizziness, and cognitive impairment, particularly at higher doses.

Glutamate Receptor Antagonists:

1. Glutamate is the primary excitatory neurotransmitter in the brain. Drugs that block glutamate receptors can reduce neuronal excitability and prevent seizure propagation. One example is:

a. Perampanel (Fycompa): A non-competitive antagonist of the AMPA subtype of glutamate receptors. It is used to treat partial-onset seizures and generalized tonic-clonic seizures.

2. Perampanel may cause dizziness, drowsiness, and behavioral changes, including aggression and irritability.

Potassium Channel Modulators:

1. Potassium channel modulators stabilize neuronal membranes and reduce excitability by enhancing potassium efflux. One example is:

a. Ezogabine (Potiga): Enhances potassium channel activity and is used to treat partial seizures.

2. Ezogabine may cause urinary retention, cognitive impairment, and QT prolongation.

Novel Mechanisms:

1. Some newer AEDs target novel mechanisms of action, such as synaptic vesicle protein 2A (SV2A) or the sodium channel subtype Nav1.7. Examples include:

a. Levetiracetam (Keppra): Binds to SV2A and modulates neurotransmitter release. It is used to treat partial seizures and myoclonic seizures.

b. Lacosamide (Vimpat): Enhances slow inactivation of Nav1.7 sodium channels. It is used to treat partial seizures.

2. These newer agents may offer improved efficacy and tolerability compared to traditional AEDs.

Anti-epileptic drugs are essential for managing epilepsy and reducing the frequency and severity of seizures. Treatment should be individualized based on the type of seizures, the patient's age, comorbidities, and medication tolerability. Close monitoring for efficacy and side effects is necessary, and adjustments to medication regimens may be required over time. Additionally, patients with epilepsy should receive education and support to optimize their treatment outcomes and quality of life.

F. Nootropics:

Nootropics, also known as smart drugs or cognitive enhancers, are a class of substances that purportedly enhance cognitive function, including memory, concentration, creativity, and motivation. While the term "nootropic" was coined by Romanian psychologist and chemist Dr. Corneliu E. Giurgea in the 1970s, the concept of cognitive enhancement has been studied for decades. Here's a detailed overview of nootropics in CNS pharmacology:

Mechanisms of Action:

1. Nootropics exert their effects through various mechanisms of action, which may include:

    a. **Enhancing Neurotransmission**: Some nootropics modulate neurotransmitter systems in the brain, such as increasing acetylcholine levels (important for memory and learning) or enhancing dopamine and norepinephrine activity (associated with mood and motivation).

    b. **Improving Cerebral Blood Flow**: Certain nootropics increase blood flow to the brain, delivering more oxygen and nutrients to neurons, which can enhance cognitive function.

    c. **Protecting Neurons**: Nootropics may have neuroprotective properties, helping to shield neurons from damage caused by oxidative stress, inflammation, or excitotoxicity.

    d. **Enhancing Synaptic Plasticity**: Some nootropics promote synaptic plasticity, the ability of synapses to strengthen or weaken over time in response to activity, which is crucial for learning and memory.

    e. **Reducing Brain Fog**: Nootropics may alleviate feelings of mental fatigue or brain fog, enhancing mental clarity and focus.

Common Nootropics:

1. There are numerous substances that are considered nootropics, each with its own mechanism of action and purported cognitive benefits. Some of the most commonly used nootropics include:

    a. **Caffeine:** Found in coffee, tea, and energy drinks, caffeine is a stimulant that can enhance alertness, focus, and cognitive performance.

    b. **L-theanine**: Found in green tea, L-theanine is an amino acid that may promote relaxation and reduce stress and anxiety without causing sedation.

    c. **Bacopa monnieri**: An herb used in traditional Ayurvedic medicine, bacopa monnieri has been studied for its potential to enhance memory and cognitive function.

    d. **Ginkgo biloba**: Derived from the leaves of the ginkgo tree, ginkgo biloba is believed to improve memory and cognitive function by increasing blood flow to the brain.

    e. **Omega-3 fatty acids**: Found in fatty fish and fish oil supplements, omega-3 fatty acids may support cognitive function and reduce the risk of age-related cognitive decline.

    f. **Modafinil:** A wakefulness-promoting agent used to treat narcolepsy, modafinil has also been used off-label as a cognitive enhancer to improve alertness and cognitive function.

    g. **Racetams (e.g., piracetam):** A class of synthetic compounds that includes piracetam, racetams are believed to enhance cognitive function by modulating neurotransmitter systems in the brain.

    h. **Lion's mane mushroom**: This mushroom contains compounds called hericenones and erinacines, which may stimulate nerve growth factor (NGF) production, potentially supporting cognitive function and nerve regeneration.

Safety and Efficacy:

1. While some nootropics have shown promising results in animal studies or small-scale human trials, the evidence for their efficacy and safety in healthy individuals is often limited. Moreover, the long-term effects of regular nootropic use are not well understood. It's essential to approach the use of nootropics with caution and to consult with a healthcare professional before starting any new supplement regimen, especially if you have underlying health conditions or are taking medications.

Ethical Considerations:

1. The use of nootropics for cognitive enhancement raises ethical questions regarding fairness, autonomy, and potential risks. There are concerns about the unequal access to cognitive enhancement, the pressure to use cognitive enhancers in competitive environments, and the potential for unintended consequences on society as a whole.

In summary, nootropics represent a diverse class of substances that are purported to enhance cognitive function. While some individuals may experience benefits from certain nootropics, the evidence for their efficacy and safety is often limited. It's essential to approach the use of nootropics with caution, to prioritize evidence-based approaches to cognitive enhancement, and to consider the broader ethical implications of cognitive enhancement in society.

DRUGS FOR NEURODEGENERATIVE DISEASES LIKE

A. Parkinsonism:

Parkinsonism refers to a group of neurological disorders characterized by movement abnormalities such as tremors, bradykinesia (slowness of movement), rigidity, and postural instability. The most common cause of Parkinsonism is Parkinson's disease, but other conditions such as drug-induced Parkinsonism, vascular Parkinsonism, and atypical parkinsonian syndromes (e.g., multiple system atrophy, progressive supranuclear palsy) can also present with similar symptoms. Pharmacological treatment for Parkinsonism primarily focuses on managing symptoms and improving quality of life. Here's a detailed overview of drugs used in the management of Parkinsonism, particularly Parkinson's disease:

Levodopa/Carbidopa (Sinemet):

1. Levodopa is the most effective medication for relieving the motor symptoms of Parkinson's disease. Levodopa is converted to dopamine in the brain, replenishing dopamine levels depleted in Parkinson's disease. Carbidopa is often co-administered with levodopa to inhibit the peripheral conversion of levodopa to dopamine, allowing more levodopa to reach the brain and reducing peripheral side effects such as nausea and hypotension. Sinemet is a combination product containing levodopa and carbidopa.

Dopamine Agonists:

1. Dopamine agonists directly stimulate dopamine receptors in the brain, mimicking the action of dopamine. They are commonly used as adjunctive therapy to levodopa or as monotherapy in early Parkinson's disease. Dopamine agonists can be classified into two main categories:
    a. **Non-Ergot Dopamine Agonists**: Examples include pramipexole (Mirapex), ropinirole (Requip), and rotigotine (Neupro).
    b. **Ergot Dopamine Agonists**: Examples include bromocriptine (Parlodel) and pergolide (no longer available in many countries due to safety concerns).
2. Dopamine agonists may be associated with side effects such as nausea, dizziness, hallucinations, and impulse control disorders.

Monoamine Oxidase Type B (MAO-B) Inhibitors:

1. MAO-B inhibitors block the enzyme monoamine oxidase type B, which metabolizes dopamine in the brain. By inhibiting MAO-B, these drugs increase dopamine levels in the brain, helping to alleviate Parkinson's

symptoms. Examples include selegiline (Eldepryl, Zelapar) and rasagiline (Azilect).

Catechol-O-Methyltransferase (COMT) Inhibitors:

1. COMT inhibitors prolong the duration of levodopa's action by inhibiting the enzyme catechol-O-methyltransferase, which metabolizes levodopa in the peripheral tissues. By reducing levodopa metabolism, COMT inhibitors increase levodopa availability in the brain. Examples include entacapone (Comtan) and tolcapone (Tasmar).

Anticholinergics:

1. Anticholinergic medications can help alleviate tremor and dystonia in Parkinson's disease by blocking the effects of acetylcholine, which is in excess relative to dopamine in the brain. Examples include trihexyphenidyl (Artane) and benztropine (Cogentin). Anticholinergics are generally used as adjunctive therapy and are less commonly prescribed due to their side effects, including cognitive impairment and worsened motor symptoms.

Amantadine:

1. Amantadine is an antiviral medication that also has mild anti-Parkinsonian effects. Its precise mechanism of action in Parkinson's disease is not fully understood, but it is believed to enhance dopamine release and inhibit dopamine reuptake. Amantadine may be used to alleviate dyskinesias associated with long-term levodopa therapy or as adjunctive therapy for Parkinson's symptoms.

Surgical Interventions:

1. In advanced cases of Parkinson's disease that are refractory to medical therapy, surgical interventions such as deep brain stimulation (DBS) or lesioning procedures (e.g., pallidotomy, thalamotomy) may be considered to alleviate motor symptoms and improve quality of life.

It's important to note that while medications can effectively manage the motor symptoms of Parkinsonism, they do not slow the progression of the disease.

Additionally, individual response to medications can vary, and a personalized approach to treatment is essential. Close monitoring by a healthcare provider is necessary to optimize medication regimens, manage side effects, and adjust treatment as the disease progresses.

B. Alzheimers:

Alzheimer's disease is a progressive neurodegenerative disorder characterized by cognitive decline, memory loss, and impairment of daily functioning. While there is currently no cure for Alzheimer's disease, pharmacological treatments aim to alleviate symptoms, slow disease progression, and improve quality of life for affected individuals. Here's a detailed overview of drugs used in the management of Alzheimer's disease:

Cholinesterase Inhibitors:

1. Cholinesterase inhibitors are the mainstay of pharmacological treatment for Alzheimer's disease. They work by inhibiting the enzyme acetylcholinesterase, which breaks down acetylcholine, a neurotransmitter involved in memory and cognitive function. By increasing acetylcholine levels in the brain, cholinesterase inhibitors help to enhance cholinergic neurotransmission and alleviate symptoms of Alzheimer's disease. Commonly prescribed cholinesterase inhibitors include:

    a. **Donepezil (Aricept)**: Donepezil is the most widely used cholinesterase inhibitor and is approved for all stages of Alzheimer's disease. It is available in both immediate-release and extended-release formulations.

    b. **Rivastigmine (Exelon)**: Rivastigmine is available as an oral medication or as a transdermal patch and is approved for mild to moderate Alzheimer's disease.

c. **Galantamine (Razadyne)**: Galantamine is also approved for mild to moderate Alzheimer's disease and is available in immediate-release and extended-release formulations.

2. Cholinesterase inhibitors can help improve cognitive function, delay institutionalization, and enhance activities of daily living in individuals with Alzheimer's disease. However, they are not effective in all patients and may only provide modest benefits.

NMDA Receptor Antagonist:

1. Memantine (Namenda) is an N-methyl-D-aspartate (NMDA) receptor antagonist that is approved for moderate to severe Alzheimer's disease. Memantine works by blocking excessive activation of glutamate receptors, which can contribute to neuronal damage and cognitive decline in Alzheimer's disease. Memantine helps regulate glutamate levels in the brain and may help improve cognitive function, behavior, and activities of daily living in some individuals with Alzheimer's disease. It can be used alone or in combination with cholinesterase inhibitors.

Combination Therapy:

1. In some cases, combination therapy with both a cholinesterase inhibitor and memantine may be considered, especially in individuals with moderate to severe Alzheimer's disease who do not respond adequately to monotherapy with either drug alone. The rationale behind combination therapy is to target multiple neurotransmitter systems involved in Alzheimer's pathology and to potentially achieve synergistic effects in managing symptoms.

Symptomatic Treatments:

1. In addition to disease-modifying therapies, symptomatic treatments may be prescribed to manage specific symptoms associated with Alzheimer's disease. These may include:

a. **Antidepressants:** Selective serotonin reuptake inhibitors (SSRIs) or other antidepressants may be prescribed to manage depression, anxiety, or behavioral symptoms such as agitation or aggression.

b. **Antipsychotics:** Atypical antipsychotic medications may be used cautiously to manage severe behavioral disturbances such as hallucinations, delusions, or aggression. However, their use is associated with an increased risk of adverse events, including stroke and mortality, particularly in elderly patients with dementia.

It's important to note that while pharmacological treatments can help alleviate symptoms and improve quality of life for individuals with Alzheimer's disease, they do not halt or reverse the underlying neurodegenerative process. Additionally, individual responses to medication can vary, and treatment decisions should be individualized based on factors such as disease severity, symptom profile, comorbidities, and medication tolerability. Close monitoring by a healthcare provider is essential to optimize treatment outcomes and adjust therapy as needed over time.

C. Multiple sclerosis:

Multiple sclerosis (MS) is a chronic autoimmune disease of the central nervous system (CNS) characterized by inflammation, demyelination, and neurodegeneration. The treatment of MS aims to reduce the frequency and severity of relapses, slow disease progression, manage symptoms, and improve quality of life. Here's a detailed overview of drugs used in the management of multiple sclerosis:

Disease-Modifying Therapies (DMTs):

1. Disease-modifying therapies are the cornerstone of treatment for relapsing forms of multiple sclerosis, including relapsing-remitting MS (RRMS) and secondary progressive MS (SPMS) with relapses. These medications work

by modulating the immune system to reduce inflammation and prevent further damage to the CNS. DMTs can be categorized into several classes:

a. **Interferon Beta (IFN-β):** Interferon beta medications, including interferon beta-1a (Avonex, Rebif) and interferon beta-1b (Betaseron, Extavia), are injectable therapies that help reduce the frequency and severity of relapses in RRMS. They have immunomodulatory effects and may also slow disease progression.

b. **Glatiramer Acetate (Copaxone):** Glatiramer acetate is a synthetic protein that mimics myelin basic protein, a component of the myelin sheath that is targeted by the immune system in MS. It is administered by subcutaneous injection and helps reduce the frequency of relapses in RRMS.

c. **Dimethyl Fumarate (Tecfidera):** Dimethyl fumarate is an oral medication that modulates the immune system and reduces inflammation in MS. It is taken twice daily and has been shown to reduce relapse rates and slow disability progression in RRMS.

d. **Fingolimod (Gilenya):** Fingolimod is an oral medication that acts as a sphingosine-1-phosphate receptor modulator, preventing lymphocytes from leaving lymph nodes and entering the CNS. It reduces relapse rates and slows disability progression in RRMS.

e. **Natalizumab (Tysabri):** Natalizumab is a monoclonal antibody that blocks the adhesion and migration of immune cells into the CNS. It is administered by intravenous infusion and is highly effective in reducing relapse rates in RRMS. However, it is associated with an increased risk of progressive multifocal leukoencephalopathy (PML), a rare but serious brain infection.

f. **Alemtuzumab (Lemtrada):** Alemtuzumab is a monoclonal antibody that targets CD52, a protein found on the surface of immune cells. It is administered by intravenous infusion and is used to treat RRMS.

Alemtuzumab can cause serious autoimmune side effects and requires close monitoring.

g. **Ocrelizumab (Ocrevus):** Ocrelizumab is a monoclonal antibody that targets CD20-positive B cells, which are believed to play a role in the pathogenesis of MS. It is administered by intravenous infusion and is approved for both RRMS and primary progressive MS (PPMS). Ocrelizumab reduces relapse rates, slows disability progression, and reduces the risk of disease activity in MS.

Symptomatic Treatments:

1. Symptomatic treatments are used to manage specific symptoms of multiple sclerosis, such as spasticity, fatigue, pain, and bladder dysfunction. These may include:

    a. **Muscle Relaxants**: Medications such as baclofen (Lioresal), tizanidine (Zanaflex), and dantrolene (Dantrium) may be prescribed to manage spasticity and muscle stiffness.

    b. **Modafinil (Provigil) and Amantadine**: These medications may be used to alleviate fatigue and improve wakefulness in individuals with MS.

    c. **Antidepressants:** Selective serotonin reuptake inhibitors (SSRIs) or tricyclic antidepressants may be prescribed to manage depression, which is common in individuals with MS.

    d. **Pain Medications:** Analgesics such as acetaminophen, nonsteroidal anti-inflammatory drugs (NSAIDs), or gabapentin (Neurontin) may be used to alleviate pain associated with MS, including neuropathic pain and musculoskeletal pain.

    e. **Bladder Medications**: Medications such as oxybutynin (Ditropan), tolterodine (Detrol), or mirabegron (Myrbetriq) may be prescribed to manage overactive bladder or urinary incontinence in individuals with MS.

Rehabilitation Therapies:

1. Rehabilitation therapies, including physical therapy, occupational therapy, and speech therapy, play a crucial role in managing MS symptoms and improving quality of life. These therapies help individuals with MS maintain mobility, independence, and functional abilities.

It's important for individuals with multiple sclerosis to work closely with a healthcare provider to develop a comprehensive treatment plan tailored to their specific needs and preferences. Treatment decisions may be influenced by factors such as disease severity, disease course, comorbidities, medication tolerability, and patient goals. Regular monitoring and adjustments to treatment may be necessary to optimize outcomes and manage disease progression over time.

DRUGS ACTING ON AUTONOMIC NERVOUS SYSTEM

The autonomic nervous system (ANS) regulates involuntary physiological processes in the body, including heart rate, blood pressure, digestion, and respiratory rate. Drugs acting on the autonomic nervous system can either stimulate (agonists) or inhibit (antagonists) the activity of autonomic receptors. Here's a detailed overview of drugs acting on the autonomic nervous system:

Sympathomimetic Drugs:

Sympathomimetic drugs, also known as adrenergic agonists, mimic the effects of the sympathetic nervous system by activating adrenergic receptors. These drugs exert their effects by binding to and activating alpha and beta adrenergic receptors located throughout the body. They can be used to treat a variety of medical conditions by modulating autonomic nervous system activity. Here's a detailed overview of sympathomimetic drugs:

1. Alpha-1 Agonists:

a. **Phenylephrine**: Phenylephrine is a selective alpha-1 adrenergic agonist used primarily as a nasal decongestant to relieve congestion associated with conditions such as the common cold, allergies, and sinusitis. It acts by causing vasoconstriction of blood vessels in the nasal mucosa, thereby reducing swelling and congestion.

b. **Midodrine:** Midodrine is an alpha-1 adrenergic agonist used to treat orthostatic hypotension, a condition characterized by a drop in blood pressure upon standing. It works by causing vasoconstriction of peripheral blood vessels, thereby increasing blood pressure and improving symptoms of orthostatic hypotension.

2. **Alpha-2 Agonists:**

a. **Clonidine:** Clonidine is an alpha-2 adrenergic agonist used to treat hypertension, attention deficit hyperactivity disorder (ADHD), and opioid withdrawal symptoms. It acts by stimulating alpha-2 adrenergic receptors in the brainstem, leading to decreased sympathetic outflow from the central nervous system and reduced peripheral vascular resistance.

b. **Methyldopa**: Methyldopa is a centrally acting alpha-2 adrenergic agonist used to treat hypertension, particularly during pregnancy. It is converted to alpha-methyl norepinephrine in the brain, where it stimulates alpha-2 adrenergic receptors to reduce sympathetic outflow and lower blood pressure.

3. **Beta Agonists:**

a. **Albuterol:** Albuterol is a selective beta-2 adrenergic agonist used as a bronchodilator to treat asthma and chronic obstructive pulmonary disease (COPD). It acts by relaxing smooth muscle in the airways, thereby relieving bronchoconstriction and improving airflow.

b. **Salmeterol:** Salmeterol is a long-acting beta-2 adrenergic agonist used as a maintenance treatment for asthma and COPD. It has a slower onset of action but a longer duration of effect compared to short-acting beta agonists like albuterol.

4. **Mixed Alpha/Beta Agonists:**

   a. **Epinephrine:** Epinephrine is a non-selective alpha and beta adrenergic agonist used in emergency situations to treat anaphylaxis, cardiac arrest, and severe asthma exacerbations. It acts by stimulating both alpha and beta adrenergic receptors, leading to vasoconstriction, bronchodilation, and increased heart rate and contractility.

Sympathomimetic drugs can have systemic effects beyond their intended therapeutic targets, leading to potential side effects such as hypertension, tachycardia, palpitations, anxiety, and tremor. Therefore, their use should be carefully monitored, and they should be prescribed at appropriate doses for the specific medical condition being treated. Additionally, caution should be exercised when using sympathomimetic drugs in patients with cardiovascular disease, as they can exacerbate underlying conditions such as hypertension and arrhythmias.

Sympatholytic Drugs:

Sympatholytic drugs, also known as adrenergic antagonists or adrenergic blockers, inhibit the effects of the sympathetic nervous system by blocking adrenergic receptors. These drugs act by competitively binding to adrenergic receptors, thereby preventing the binding of endogenous catecholamines such as norepinephrine and epinephrine. Sympatholytic drugs can be further classified based on their selectivity for alpha or beta adrenergic receptors. Here's a detailed overview of sympatholytic drugs:

1. **Alpha Blockers:**

   a. **Prazosin:** Prazosin is a selective alpha-1 adrenergic antagonist used to treat hypertension and symptoms of benign prostatic hyperplasia (BPH). By blocking alpha-1 adrenergic receptors on vascular smooth muscle cells, prazosin causes vasodilation and decreases peripheral vascular resistance, leading to lower blood pressure. It can also improve urinary flow in patients with BPH by relaxing smooth muscle in the prostate and bladder neck.

b. **Tamsulosin:** Tamsulosin is a selective alpha-1a adrenergic antagonist used primarily to treat symptoms of BPH. It selectively blocks alpha-1a adrenergic receptors in the prostate gland, bladder neck, and urethra, leading to relaxation of smooth muscle and improved urinary flow without affecting blood pressure significantly.

2. Beta Blockers:

a. **Propranolol:** Propranolol is a non-selective beta-adrenergic antagonist used to treat hypertension, angina, arrhythmias, migraines, and tremors. By blocking beta-1 adrenergic receptors in the heart, propranolol reduces heart rate and contractility, thereby decreasing cardiac output and blood pressure. It also blocks beta-2 adrenergic receptors in the lungs, leading to bronchoconstriction, which can exacerbate asthma symptoms in some patients.

b. **Metoprolol:** Metoprolol is a selective beta-1 adrenergic antagonist used to treat hypertension, angina, heart failure, and myocardial infarction. It selectively blocks beta-1 adrenergic receptors in the heart, leading to decreased heart rate and contractility without significantly affecting bronchial smooth muscle tone. This makes metoprolol a preferred beta blocker in patients with coexisting asthma or chronic obstructive pulmonary disease (COPD).

c. **Carvedilol:** Carvedilol is a non-selective beta-adrenergic antagonist with additional alpha-1 adrenergic blocking activity. It is used to treat heart failure, hypertension, and post-myocardial infarction. Carvedilol reduces heart rate, contractility, and peripheral vascular resistance, thereby improving cardiac function and reducing blood pressure. Its alpha-blocking activity further contributes to vasodilation and blood pressure reduction.

3. **Alpha/Beta Blockers:**

    a. **Labetalol:** Labetalol is a non-selective beta-adrenergic antagonist with additional alpha-1 adrenergic blocking activity. It is used primarily to treat hypertension, particularly in hypertensive emergencies such as preeclampsia and hypertensive crisis. Labetalol reduces blood pressure by blocking both beta and alpha adrenergic receptors, leading to decreased cardiac output and peripheral vascular resistance.

4. **Central Alpha-2 Agonists:**

    a. **Clonidine:** Although clonidine is classified as an alpha-2 adrenergic agonist, it acts centrally to inhibit sympathetic outflow from the brainstem. It is used to treat hypertension, ADHD, and opioid withdrawal symptoms. By stimulating alpha-2 adrenergic receptors in the brainstem, clonidine reduces sympathetic tone, leading to decreased peripheral vascular resistance and blood pressure.

Sympatholytic drugs are effective in treating conditions characterized by excessive sympathetic activity, such as hypertension, BPH, and certain cardiovascular disorders. However, they can also cause adverse effects such as orthostatic hypotension, bradycardia, fatigue, dizziness, and sexual dysfunction. Therefore, their use should be carefully monitored, and they should be prescribed at appropriate doses for the specific medical condition being treated. Additionally, gradual dose titration and patient education are important to minimize the risk of adverse effects and optimize therapeutic outcomes.

Parasympathomimetic Drugs:

Parasympathomimetic drugs, also known as cholinergic agonists, mimic the effects of the parasympathetic nervous system by activating cholinergic receptors. These drugs act by binding to and stimulating muscarinic or nicotinic cholinergic receptors, which are found throughout the body and mediate various physiological responses. Parasympathomimetic drugs can be used to treat a variety of medical conditions by enhancing parasympathetic nervous system activity. Here's a detailed overview of parasympathomimetic drugs:

Muscarinic Agonists:

1. Muscarinic agonists selectively stimulate muscarinic cholinergic receptors, which are found in various organs and tissues throughout the body. These receptors mediate responses such as smooth muscle contraction, glandular secretion, and slowing of heart rate. Muscarinic agonists can be further classified based on their selectivity for specific muscarinic receptor subtypes:

    a. **Pilocarpine:** Pilocarpine is a non-selective muscarinic agonist used primarily to treat glaucoma by reducing intraocular pressure. It stimulates muscarinic receptors in the eye, leading to increased aqueous humor outflow and decreased intraocular pressure. Pilocarpine can also be used to induce miosis (pupillary constriction) during ophthalmic procedures.

    b. **Bethanechol:** Bethanechol is a selective muscarinic agonist used to treat urinary retention and gastrointestinal motility disorders. It stimulates muscarinic receptors in the bladder and gastrointestinal tract, leading to smooth muscle contraction and increased peristalsis. Bethanechol is particularly useful in postoperative patients with urinary retention or ileus.

2. **Nicotinic Agonists:**

    Nicotinic agonists selectively stimulate nicotinic cholinergic receptors, which are found in autonomic ganglia and at the neuromuscular junction. Activation of nicotinic receptors leads to depolarization and subsequent excitation of postsynaptic neurons or muscle cells. Nicotinic agonists are less commonly used clinically compared to muscarinic agonists, but they can be useful in certain situations:

a. **Nicotine:** Nicotine is a natural alkaloid found in tobacco products and acts as a non-selective nicotinic agonist. It stimulates nicotinic receptors in autonomic ganglia and at the neuromuscular junction, leading to sympathetic and parasympathetic effects, as well as skeletal muscle contraction. While nicotine is highly addictive and associated with numerous adverse health effects, it has historically been used for its stimulant and cognitive-enhancing properties.

Parasympathomimetic drugs can produce a range of systemic effects beyond their intended therapeutic targets, leading to potential side effects such as bradycardia, hypotension, excessive salivation, lacrimation, bronchoconstriction, gastrointestinal cramping, and diarrhea. Therefore, their use should be carefully monitored, and they should be prescribed at appropriate doses for the specific medical condition being treated. Additionally, caution should be exercised when using parasympathomimetic drugs in patients with certain cardiovascular, respiratory, gastrointestinal, or urinary conditions, as they can exacerbate underlying symptoms or conditions.

Parasympatholytic Drugs:

Parasympatholytic drugs, also known as anticholinergic agents or cholinergic antagonists, inhibit the effects of the parasympathetic nervous system by blocking cholinergic receptors. These drugs act by competitively binding to muscarinic or nicotinic cholinergic receptors, thereby preventing the binding of endogenous acetylcholine and inhibiting parasympathetic neurotransmission. Parasympatholytic drugs can be used to treat a variety of medical conditions by reducing parasympathetic nervous system activity. Here's a detailed overview of parasympatholytic drugs:

Muscarinic Antagonists:

1. Muscarinic antagonists selectively block muscarinic cholinergic receptors, which are found in various organs and tissues throughout the body. These receptors mediate responses such as smooth muscle relaxation, decreased glandular secretion, and increased heart rate. Muscarinic antagonists can be further classified based on their selectivity for specific muscarinic receptor subtypes:

    a. **Atropine:** Atropine is a non-selective muscarinic antagonist used in a variety of clinical settings. It is used to treat bradycardia and heart block by blocking muscarinic receptors in the heart, leading to increased heart rate and conduction velocity. Atropine is also used to dilate the pupil (mydriasis) during ophthalmic procedures, to reduce gastrointestinal motility and secretions during surgery, and to reverse cholinergic toxicity from insecticide or nerve agent exposure.

    b. **Scopolamine:** Scopolamine is a non-selective muscarinic antagonist used primarily to prevent motion sickness and to treat nausea and vomiting associated with anesthesia or chemotherapy. It acts centrally to inhibit vestibular and gastrointestinal inputs to the vomiting center in the brainstem, thereby reducing the sensation of motion sickness and nausea.

Neuromuscular Blocking Agents:

1. Neuromuscular blocking agents selectively block nicotinic cholinergic receptors at the neuromuscular junction, leading to skeletal muscle paralysis. These drugs are used as adjuncts to anesthesia during surgery to facilitate endotracheal intubation and to provide muscle relaxation for surgical procedures. Neuromuscular blocking agents can be further classified based on their mechanism of action:

a. **Non-depolarizing Agents**: Non-depolarizing neuromuscular blockers such as rocuronium, vecuronium, and atracurium competitively block nicotinic receptors at the neuromuscular junction, preventing acetylcholine from binding and producing muscle contraction. These drugs induce skeletal muscle relaxation and paralysis, allowing for surgical manipulation and mechanical ventilation during anesthesia.

b. **Depolarizing Agents**: Depolarizing neuromuscular blockers such as succinylcholine produce initial depolarization of the motor endplate, followed by persistent depolarization and desensitization of nicotinic receptors, leading to muscle paralysis. Succinylcholine is used for rapid sequence induction of anesthesia and for endotracheal intubation due to its rapid onset and short duration of action.

Parasympatholytic drugs can produce a range of systemic effects beyond their intended therapeutic targets, leading to potential side effects such as tachycardia, dry mouth, urinary retention, constipation, blurred vision, and cognitive impairment. Therefore, their use should be carefully monitored, and they should be prescribed at appropriate doses for the specific medical condition being treated. Additionally, caution should be exercised when using parasympatholytic drugs in patients with certain cardiovascular, respiratory, gastrointestinal, or urinary conditions, as they can exacerbate underlying symptoms or conditions.

These drugs play crucial roles in the management of various medical conditions by modulating autonomic nervous system activity. However, their use requires careful consideration of indications, contraindications, and potential side effects. It's important for healthcare providers to assess individual patient characteristics and tailor treatment regimens accordingly to achieve optimal therapeutic outcomes while minimizing adverse effects.

Multiple-Choice Questions:

1. What is the primary action of Levodopa/Carbidopa in the treatment of Parkinsonism?

    A) It acts as a dopamine receptor agonist

    B) It increases dopamine levels by converting Levodopa to dopamine in the brain

    C) It inhibits monoamine oxidase B to increase dopamine levels\

    D) It inhibits catechol-O-methyltransferase

2. Which drug is a Non-Ergot Dopamine Agonist used in the treatment of Parkinson's disease?

    A) Pergolide

    B) Bromocriptine

    C) Ropinirole

    D) Selegiline

3. What is the main therapeutic effect of Cholinesterase inhibitors in Alzheimer's disease?

    A) They inhibit the breakdown of acetylcholine

    B) They block glutamate receptors

    C) They act as dopamine receptor agonists

    D) They stimulate nicotinic receptors

4. Which medication is an NMDA receptor antagonist used to manage moderate to severe Alzheimer's disease?

    A) Donepezil

    B) Galantamine

    C) Memantine

    D) Rivastigmine

5. Glatiramer Acetate, used in the treatment of Multiple Sclerosis, mimics which component?

    A) Myelin basic protein

B) Acetylcholine

C) Dopamine

D) GABA

6. Which drug is a selective beta-1 adrenergic antagonist primarily used to treat hypertension?

    A) Carvedilol

    B) Propranolol

    C) Metoprolol

    D) Tamsulosin

7. What is the primary use of Atropine?

    A) To prevent motion sickness

    B) To treat urinary retention

    C) To treat bradycardia and heart block

    D) To induce miosis

8. Which of the following is a depolarizing neuromuscular blocker?

    A) Rocuronium

    B) Vecuronium

    C) Atracurium

    D) Succinylcholine

9. Clonidine acts as an alpha-2 agonist to treat which condition?

    A) Asthma

    B) Hypertension

    C) Gastrointestinal motility disorders

    D) Glaucoma

10. Bethanechol is a muscarinic agonist used to treat:

    A) Motion sickness

    B) Urinary retention

    C) Myasthenia Gravis

    D) Glaucoma

11. What is the primary role of pharmacokinetic assessment in preclinical screening?

    A) To evaluate the psychological effects of drugs

    B) To measure the rate and extent of a drug's absorption, distribution, metabolism, and excretion

    C) To assess the financial cost of drug development

    D) To determine the drug's flavor and appearance

12. Which of the following tests is used to evaluate a compound's genotoxic potential?

    A) The Ames test

    B) Blood pressure measurement

    C) Electrocardiogram

    D) Reflex test

13. Which drug class is primarily used to treat anxiety disorders by enhancing the effects of GABA?

    A) SSRIs

    B) CNS stimulants

    C) Benzodiazepines

    D) Nootropics

14. What is the mechanism of action for first-generation antipsychotics?

    A) Blocking serotonin receptors

    B) Enhancing GABA transmission

    C) Blocking dopamine D2 receptors

    D) Inhibiting norepinephrine uptake

15. Which is an example of a disease-modifying therapy for multiple sclerosis?

    A) Ibuprofen

    B) Glatiramer acetate

    C) Aspirin

    D) Acetaminophen

16. What is the primary effect of CNS stimulants?

   A) They decrease heart rate and induce sleep.

   B) They increase neuronal activity and arousal.

   C) They reduce inflammation.

   D) They block neurotransmitter reuptake.

17. Which method is used to study the pharmacodynamics of a drug?

   A) Cost analysis

   B) Biomarker analysis

   C) Surveying patient satisfaction

   D) Packaging efficiency tests

18. What is the purpose of carcinogenicity studies in preclinical screening?

   A) To determine if the compound can cure cancer

   B) To identify if the compound causes metabolic issues

   C) To investigate if the compound has potential to cause cancer

   D) To check the compound's color and solubility

19. Which medication is used as a cognitive enhancer to improve alertness and cognitive function, and is also a treatment for narcolepsy?

   A) Paracetamol

   B) Modafinil

   C) Ciprofloxacin

   D) Vitamin C

20. What are the clinical uses of CNS depressants?

   A) To increase alertness and energy levels

   B) To treat anxiety disorders, insomnia, and seizures

   C) To enhance physical strength

   D) To stimulate appetite

Short Answer Type Questions (Subjective)

1. Describe the main function of Levodopa/Carbidopa in the treatment of Parkinson's disease.

2. What role do dopamine agonists play in managing Parkinsonism?

3. Explain how Cholinesterase inhibitors work in the treatment of Alzheimer's disease.

4. What is the mechanism of action of Memantine in Alzheimer's disease?

5. Describe the benefits and risks associated with the use of Interferon Beta in the treatment of Multiple Sclerosis.

6. How does Glatiramer Acetate contribute to the management of Multiple Sclerosis?

7. What are the primary uses of sympathomimetic drugs in treating conditions related to the autonomic nervous system?

8. Explain the function and therapeutic applications of Alpha Blockers like Prazosin.

9. What is the significance of Parasympathomimetic drugs, and how are they used in medical treatment?

10. Discuss the therapeutic uses and side effects of Parasympatholytic drugs like Atropine.

11. What are the primary objectives of preclinical screening in drug development?

12. Describe the types of studies involved in the toxicology assessment during preclinical screening.

13. What is the purpose of genotoxicity studies in preclinical screening?

14. How do efficacy evaluations in preclinical screening utilize disease models?

15. Explain the significance of dose-response relationships in preclinical screening.

16. What are the key components assessed in pharmacokinetic studies during preclinical screening?

17. How is the mechanism of action studied in pharmacodynamic assessments?

18. What role does formulation development play in preclinical screening?

19. Discuss the importance of adhering to Good Laboratory Practice (GLP) in preclinical studies.

20. What factors are considered in making a Go/No-Go decision at the end of preclinical screening?

Long Answer Type Questions (Subjective)

1. Provide a detailed discussion on the pharmacological management of Parkinsonism, highlighting the various classes of drugs used, including their mechanisms of action and potential side effects.

2. Describe the role of Disease-Modifying Therapies (DMTs) in the treatment of Multiple Sclerosis. Discuss at least three different DMTs, their mechanisms, and implications for patient management.

3. Explore the use of Cholinesterase inhibitors and NMDA receptor antagonists in the management of Alzheimer's disease, discussing their effectiveness, mechanisms of action, and the rationale behind combination therapy.

4. Analyze the use of drugs acting on the autonomic nervous system, including sympathomimetic and sympatholytic drugs. Discuss the clinical scenarios where these drugs are indicated and potential complications that may arise.

5. Provide an in-depth analysis of the impact and management strategies of the parasympathetic system's modulation through drugs, focusing on Parasympathomimetic and Parasympatholytic drugs, including their therapeutic applications and risks.

6. Provide a comprehensive overview of the safety assessments required in preclinical screening, including the types of studies conducted and their relevance to human safety.

7. Discuss the role and methodologies of pharmacokinetic and pharmacodynamic studies in preclinical screening, highlighting how they contribute to understanding a drug's behavior in the body.

8. Explain the process and importance of formulation development in the context of preclinical screening, including how different formulations can affect the bioavailability and stability of a drug.

9. Analyze the ethical considerations and regulatory compliance required in preclinical screening, detailing how these factors influence the drug development process.

10. Describe the challenges and considerations involved in translating preclinical findings to clinical trials, focusing on how data from animal models and in vitro studies are used to predict human responses.

Answer Key:

1. (A) They inhibit the breakdown of acetylcholine

2. (C) Ropinirole

3. (B) It increases dopamine levels by converting Levodopa to dopamine in the brain

4. (C) Memantine

5. (A) Myelin basic protein

6. (C) Metoprolol

7. (C) To treat bradycardia and heart block

8. (D) Succinylcholine

9. (B) Hypertension

10. (B) Urinary retention

11. B) To measure the rate and extent of a drug's absorption, distribution, metabolism, and excretion

12. A) The Ames test

13. C) Benzodiazepines

14. C) Blocking dopamine D2 receptors

15. B) Glatiramer acetate

16. B) They increase neuronal activity and arousal.

17. B) Biomarker analysis

18. C) To investigate if the compound has potential to cause cancer

19. B) Modafinil

20. B) To treat anxiety disorders, insomnia, and seizures

CHAPTER - 3

RESPIRATORY PHARMACOLOGY:

Preclinical screening in respiratory pharmacology involves a series of tests and evaluations conducted on potential drug candidates before they are tested on humans in clinical trials. This phase is crucial for assessing the safety, efficacy, and pharmacokinetic properties of the drugs. Here's an overview of the key aspects of preclinical screening in respiratory pharmacology:

1. **In Vitro Studies**: Before testing drugs in animals, researchers often begin with in vitro studies using cell cultures or isolated tissues. In respiratory pharmacology, these studies may involve lung epithelial cells, smooth muscle cells, or immune cells relevant to respiratory diseases. Researchers assess various parameters such as cell viability, inflammatory responses, and mucociliary clearance to evaluate the potential effects of drugs.

2. **In Vivo Animal Studies:**
   a. **Animal Models**: Various animal models are used to simulate respiratory conditions such as asthma, chronic obstructive pulmonary disease (COPD), and pulmonary fibrosis. For example, mice, rats, guinea pigs, and non-human primates may be used to study different aspects of respiratory diseases.

   b. **Efficacy Studies**: Animal models are used to assess the efficacy of drug candidates in treating respiratory conditions. Researchers measure parameters such as airway inflammation, bronchoconstriction, mucus production, and lung function to evaluate the effectiveness of drugs.

   c. **Safety Assessments**: Preclinical studies also evaluate the safety of drug candidates. Researchers assess potential adverse effects such as systemic toxicity, respiratory depression, cardiac effects, and immunotoxicity in animal models.

3. **Pharmacokinetic Studies:**

   a. **Absorption, Distribution, Metabolism, and Excretion (ADME):** Pharmacokinetic studies assess how drugs are absorbed, distributed, metabolized, and eliminated in the body. Researchers use techniques such as blood sampling, tissue distribution studies, and metabolic profiling to understand the pharmacokinetic properties of drug candidates.

   b. Drug Interactions: Preclinical studies may also investigate potential drug-drug interactions that could affect the pharmacokinetics of respiratory drugs.

4. **Toxicology Studies:**

   a. **Acute Toxicity**: Researchers evaluate the acute toxicity of drug candidates to determine the safe starting doses for subsequent studies.

   b. **Chronic Toxicity**: Long-term toxicology studies assess the potential adverse effects of prolonged drug exposure, including organ toxicity and carcinogenicity.

   c. **Reproductive and Developmental Toxicity**: These studies examine the effects of drugs on reproduction and fetal development, which are crucial for assessing the safety of drugs in pregnant women.

5. **Formulation Development:**

   a. Preclinical studies may involve optimizing the formulation of respiratory drugs to enhance their efficacy, stability, and safety. This includes selecting appropriate dosage forms (e.g., inhalers, nebulizers) and excipients to improve drug delivery to the lungs.

6. **Regulatory Requirements:**

   a. Preclinical data generated during these studies are submitted to regulatory authorities such as the FDA (in the United States) or the

EMA (in Europe) as part of the Investigational New Drug (IND) application. These agencies review the preclinical data to determine whether the drug can proceed to clinical trials.

Overall, preclinical screening in respiratory pharmacology plays a crucial role in identifying promising drug candidates while ensuring their safety and efficacy before advancing to clinical trials in humans.

ANTI-ASTHMATICS:

In preclinical screening for anti-asthmatic drugs, researchers aim to identify compounds that can effectively treat asthma by targeting various underlying mechanisms such as airway inflammation, bronchoconstriction, and airway hyperresponsiveness. Here's a detailed overview of the preclinical screening process for anti-asthmatic drugs:

1. **In Vitro Studies:**
   a. **Cell-Based Assays**: Researchers use cultured human or animal cells relevant to asthma, such as bronchial epithelial cells, mast cells, eosinophils, and T lymphocytes. These assays help assess the anti-inflammatory effects of drugs by measuring cytokine production, cell migration, and cell activation.
   b. **Contractility Assays**: Smooth muscle cells from airways are used to evaluate the bronchodilator effects of drugs. Researchers measure changes in cell contractility in response to drug treatment using techniques such as isometric tension recordings.

2. **In Vivo Animal Studies:**
   a. **Animal Models of Asthma**: Commonly used animal models include ovalbumin-induced asthma in mice and rats, allergen-induced asthma in guinea pigs, and house dust mite-induced asthma in non-human primates. These models mimic key features of human asthma,

including airway inflammation, bronchoconstriction, and airway hyperresponsiveness.

b. **Efficacy Studies**: Researchers assess the effectiveness of anti-asthmatic drugs in reducing airway inflammation, bronchoconstriction, and airway hyperresponsiveness in animal models. They measure parameters such as lung function, airway resistance, inflammatory cell infiltration, and cytokine levels in bronchoalveolar lavage fluid or lung tissue.

c. **Safety Assessments**: Preclinical studies also evaluate the safety of anti-asthmatic drugs in animal models. Researchers monitor potential adverse effects such as systemic toxicity, cardiovascular effects, and immunotoxicity.

3. **Pharmacokinetic Studies:**

a. **Drug Absorption and Distribution**: Pharmacokinetic studies assess how anti-asthmatic drugs are absorbed and distributed in the body after administration via different routes, such as oral, inhalation, or intravenous.

b. **Metabolism and Elimination**: Researchers investigate the metabolism and elimination of anti-asthmatic drugs to understand their pharmacokinetic properties and potential interactions with other drugs.

4. **Toxicology Studies:**

a. **Acute and Chronic Toxicity**: Toxicology studies evaluate the acute and chronic toxicity of anti-asthmatic drugs to determine safe dosing regimens. Researchers assess organ toxicity, including effects on the respiratory system, liver, kidneys, and cardiovascular system.

b. **Reproductive and Developmental Toxicity**: These studies examine the effects of anti-asthmatic drugs on reproduction and fetal development to ensure the safety of these drugs in pregnant women.

5. **Formulation Development:**

   a. Researchers optimize the formulation of anti-asthmatic drugs to improve their delivery to the lungs and enhance their efficacy. Inhalation formulations such as metered-dose inhalers, dry powder inhalers, and nebulizers are commonly used for asthma treatment.

6. **Regulatory Requirements:**

   a. Preclinical data generated during these studies are submitted to regulatory authorities as part of the drug approval process. Regulatory agencies review the preclinical data to assess the safety and efficacy of anti-asthmatic drugs before approving them for clinical trials.

Overall, preclinical screening plays a crucial role in identifying promising anti-asthmatic drug candidates and ensuring their safety and efficacy before advancing to clinical development. These studies provide valuable insights into the potential therapeutic benefits and risks associated with new asthma treatments.

DRUGS FOR COPD:

In preclinical screening for drugs targeting Chronic Obstructive Pulmonary Disease (COPD), researchers focus on identifying compounds that can effectively alleviate symptoms, reduce exacerbations, and potentially modify the progression of the disease. Here's a detailed overview of the preclinical screening process for drugs targeting COPD:

1. **In Vitro Studies:**

   a. **Cell-Based Assays:** Researchers use cultured human or animal cells relevant to COPD, such as bronchial epithelial cells, macrophages, neutrophils, and fibroblasts. These assays help assess the anti-inflammatory effects of drugs by measuring cytokine production, oxidative stress, and inflammatory cell activation.

b. **Mucus Production Assays**: Mucus hypersecretion is a characteristic feature of COPD. In vitro assays are used to evaluate the effects of drugs on mucus production by airway epithelial cells.

c. **Protease Inhibition Assays:** COPD is associated with increased protease activity, leading to tissue damage. Researchers assess the ability of drugs to inhibit protease activity using enzyme assays.

2. **In Vivo Animal Studies:**

   a. **Animal Models of COPD**: Commonly used animal models include cigarette smoke-induced COPD in mice, rats, and guinea pigs, as well as elastase-induced COPD models. These models mimic key features of human COPD, including chronic airway inflammation, emphysema, mucus hypersecretion, and airflow limitation.

   b. **Efficacy Studies**: Researchers assess the effectiveness of COPD drugs in reducing airway inflammation, mucus production, and lung damage in animal models. They measure parameters such as lung function, airway resistance, inflammatory cell infiltration, and lung histology.

   c. **Exacerbation Models**: Some preclinical studies involve exacerbation models to evaluate the effects of drugs on COPD exacerbations triggered by respiratory infections or environmental insults.

   d. **Safety Assessments**: Preclinical studies also evaluate the safety of COPD drugs in animal models. Researchers monitor potential adverse effects such as systemic toxicity, cardiovascular effects, and immunotoxicity.

3. **Pharmacokinetic Studies:**

   a. **Drug Absorption and Distribution**: Pharmacokinetic studies assess how COPD drugs are absorbed and distributed in the body after administration via different routes, such as oral, inhalation, or intravenous.

b. **Metabolism and Elimination**: Researchers investigate the metabolism and elimination of COPD drugs to understand their pharmacokinetic properties and potential interactions with other drugs.

4. **Toxicology Studies:**

   a. **Acute and Chronic Toxicity**: Toxicology studies evaluate the acute and chronic toxicity of COPD drugs to determine safe dosing regimens. Researchers assess organ toxicity, including effects on the respiratory system, liver, kidneys, and cardiovascular system.

   b. **Reproductive and Developmental Toxicity**: These studies examine the effects of COPD drugs on reproduction and fetal development to ensure their safety in pregnant women.

5. **Formulation Development:**

   a. Researchers optimize the formulation of COPD drugs to improve their delivery to the lungs and enhance their efficacy. Inhalation formulations such as metered-dose inhalers, dry powder inhalers, and nebulizers are commonly used for COPD treatment.

6. **Regulatory Requirements:**

   a. Preclinical data generated during these studies are submitted to regulatory authorities as part of the drug approval process. Regulatory agencies review the preclinical data to assess the safety and efficacy of COPD drugs before approving them for clinical trials.

Overall, preclinical screening plays a crucial role in identifying promising drug candidates for COPD and ensuring their safety and efficacy before advancing to clinical development. These studies provide valuable insights into the potential therapeutic benefits and risks associated with new COPD treatments.

ANTI-ALLERGIC:

Preclinical screening for anti-allergic drugs in respiratory pharmacology aims to identify compounds that can effectively alleviate allergic reactions in the respiratory system. Allergic respiratory conditions such as allergic rhinitis and allergic asthma are characterized by immune-mediated inflammation triggered by allergens. Here's a detailed overview of the preclinical screening process for anti-allergic drugs:

1. **In Vitro Studies:**

    a. **Cell-Based Assays**: Researchers use cultured human or animal cells relevant to allergic respiratory conditions, such as mast cells, basophils, eosinophils, and T lymphocytes. These assays help assess the anti-inflammatory effects of drugs by measuring cytokine production, histamine release, and cell activation.

    b. **IgE-Mediated Responses**: Allergic reactions are often mediated by immunoglobulin E (IgE) antibodies. In vitro assays are used to evaluate the ability of drugs to inhibit IgE-mediated responses, such as mast cell degranulation and histamine release.

    c. **Inflammatory Mediator Production**: Researchers assess the effects of drugs on the production of inflammatory mediators such as leukotrienes, prostaglandins, and cytokines involved in allergic inflammation.

2. **In Vivo Animal Studies:**

    a. **Animal Models of Allergic Respiratory Conditions**: Commonly used animal models include ovalbumin-induced allergic rhinitis and asthma in mice, rats, and guinea pigs, as well as allergen-induced models using specific allergens relevant to human allergies. These models mimic key features of human allergic respiratory conditions, including airway inflammation, mucus production, bronchoconstriction, and allergic sensitization.

    b. **Efficacy Studies**: Researchers assess the effectiveness of anti-allergic drugs in reducing allergic inflammation, airway hyperresponsiveness, and allergic symptoms in animal models. They measure parameters such as sneezing, nasal rubbing, airway resistance, inflammatory cell infiltration, and cytokine levels in bronchoalveolar lavage fluid or nasal lavage fluid.

c. **Allergic Sensitization Models**: Some preclinical studies involve models of allergic sensitization to evaluate the effects of drugs on the development of allergic responses to specific allergens.

d. **Safety Assessments**: Preclinical studies also evaluate the safety of anti-allergic drugs in animal models. Researchers monitor potential adverse effects such as systemic toxicity, cardiovascular effects, and immunotoxicity.

3. **Pharmacokinetic Studies:**

a. **Drug Absorption and Distribution**: Pharmacokinetic studies assess how anti-allergic drugs are absorbed and distributed in the body after administration via different routes, such as oral, intranasal, or intravenous.

b. **Metabolism and Elimination**: Researchers investigate the metabolism and elimination of anti-allergic drugs to understand their pharmacokinetic properties and potential interactions with other drugs.

4. **Toxicology Studies:**

a. **Acute and Chronic Toxicity**: Toxicology studies evaluate the acute and chronic toxicity of anti-allergic drugs to determine safe dosing regimens. Researchers assess organ toxicity, including effects on the respiratory system, liver, kidneys, and cardiovascular system.

b. **Reproductive and Developmental Toxicity**: These studies examine the effects of anti-allergic drugs on reproduction and fetal development to ensure their safety in pregnant women.

5. **Formulation Development:**

a. Researchers optimize the formulation of anti-allergic drugs to improve their delivery to the respiratory tract and enhance their efficacy.

Formulation options may include nasal sprays, inhalers, or oral formulations.

6. Regulatory Requirements:

a. Preclinical data generated during these studies are submitted to regulatory authorities as part of the drug approval process. Regulatory agencies review the preclinical data to assess the safety and efficacy of anti-allergic drugs before approving them for clinical trials.

Overall, preclinical screening plays a crucial role in identifying promising anti-allergic drug candidates and ensuring their safety and efficacy before advancing to clinical development. These studies provide valuable insights into the potential therapeutic benefits and risks associated with new treatments for allergic respiratory conditions.

REPRODUCTIVE PHARMACOLOGY

Preclinical screening in reproductive pharmacology involves evaluating the potential effects of drugs on reproductive processes and fetal development before they are tested in human clinical trials. This area of research is critical for ensuring the safety of medications for pregnant individuals and their offspring. Here's a detailed overview of the preclinical screening process in reproductive pharmacology:

1. In Vitro Studies:

a. **Cell Culture Assays**: Researchers use cultured cells relevant to reproductive tissues such as ovarian cells, testicular cells, placental cells, and embryonic stem cells. These assays help assess the direct effects of drugs on cellular processes such as cell proliferation, hormone production, and gene expression.

b. **Embryo Culture**: In vitro fertilization (IVF) techniques are used to culture embryos in the presence of drugs to evaluate their effects on early embryonic development, including blastocyst formation and implantation.

2. **In Vivo Animal Studies:**

   a. **Animal Models**: Various animal models are used to study reproductive processes and fetal development. Commonly used species include mice, rats, rabbits, and non-human primates.

   b. **Fertility Studies**: Researchers assess the effects of drugs on fertility by evaluating parameters such as mating behavior, estrous cycle length, sperm quality, ovulation, and fertilization rates.

   c. **Embryonic Development**: Drugs are administered to pregnant animals during different stages of gestation to evaluate their effects on embryonic and fetal development. Researchers examine parameters such as embryo viability, fetal growth, organ development, and the incidence of congenital malformations.

   d. **Reproductive Hormones**: The effects of drugs on reproductive hormone levels (e.g., estrogen, progesterone, testosterone) are evaluated to assess their potential impact on reproductive function.

3. **Pharmacokinetic Studies:**

   a. **Maternal Pharmacokinetics**: Pharmacokinetic studies assess how drugs are absorbed, distributed, metabolized, and eliminated in pregnant animals. Researchers investigate changes in drug exposure during pregnancy and their potential impact on maternal and fetal health.

   b. **Placental Transfer**: Studies evaluate the transfer of drugs across the placenta and their distribution in fetal tissues to understand the potential for fetal exposure.

4. **Toxicology Studies:**

a. **Maternal Toxicity**: Toxicology studies assess the potential adverse effects of drugs on pregnant animals, including maternal health, organ toxicity, and pregnancy outcomes.

b. **Developmental Toxicity**: Researchers evaluate the effects of drugs on embryonic and fetal development, including fetal viability, growth, structural abnormalities, and functional deficits.

c. **Perinatal and Postnatal Effects**: Some studies assess the effects of drug exposure during pregnancy on neonatal health, postnatal growth, behavior, and reproductive function in offspring.

5. **Reproductive Endocrinology:**

a. **Endocrine Disruption**: Drugs are evaluated for their potential to disrupt endocrine function, including effects on hormone synthesis, secretion, and receptor signaling pathways involved in reproductive processes.

b. **Gonadal Function**: Researchers assess the effects of drugs on gonadal function, gametogenesis, and sex hormone production in both males and females.

6. **Regulatory Requirements:**

a. Preclinical data generated from reproductive pharmacology studies are submitted to regulatory agencies as part of the drug approval process. Regulatory authorities review these data to assess the potential risks to reproductive health and ensure appropriate labeling and safety precautions for use during pregnancy.

Overall, preclinical screening in reproductive pharmacology plays a crucial role in identifying potential reproductive and developmental risks associated with drug exposure and informing clinical decisions regarding the use of medications during pregnancy and lactation.

APHRODISIACS:

Preclinical screening for aphrodisiacs in reproductive pharmacology involves evaluating compounds or substances for their potential to enhance sexual desire, arousal, and performance. These studies are conducted in animal models to assess the effects of aphrodisiacs on reproductive physiology, behavior, and hormone levels. Here's a detailed overview of the preclinical screening process:

1. **Animal Models:**
   a. Various animal models are used to study sexual behavior and reproductive function, including rodents (rats and mice), rabbits, and non-human primates (such as monkeys).
   b. Researchers select appropriate animal models based on their similarities to humans in terms of reproductive physiology and sexual behavior.

2. **Behavioral Studies:**
   a. **Mating Behavior**: Researchers assess the effects of aphrodisiacs on mating behavior, including measures such as mounting frequency, intromission latency, and ejaculation latency in male animals, as well as lordosis behavior and proceptive behavior in female animals.
   b. **Sexual Motivation**: Tests such as the female preference test and the male sexual incentive motivation test are used to evaluate the willingness of animals to engage in sexual activity in the presence of a potential mate.
   c. **Libido**: Researchers measure changes in sexual desire or libido by assessing the frequency and intensity of sexual behaviors in response to aphrodisiac treatment.

3. **Reproductive Physiology:**
   a. **Hormone Levels**: Aphrodisiacs may affect reproductive hormone levels, including testosterone, estrogen, progesterone, and luteinizing

hormone (LH). Researchers measure hormone levels in blood samples collected from animals before and after treatment with aphrodisiacs.

   b. **Sperm Parameters**: In male animals, researchers assess changes in sperm count, motility, morphology, and viability following treatment with aphrodisiacs.

4. **Neurochemical Studies:**

   a. Researchers investigate the effects of aphrodisiacs on neurotransmitter systems involved in sexual behavior, such as dopamine, serotonin, and noradrenaline.

   b. Neurochemical studies may involve analyzing neurotransmitter levels and receptor expression in specific brain regions implicated in sexual arousal and motivation.

5. **Pharmacokinetic Studies:**

   a. Researchers assess the absorption, distribution, metabolism, and excretion (ADME) of aphrodisiacs in animal models to understand their pharmacokinetic properties.

   b. Pharmacokinetic studies help determine the bioavailability and duration of action of aphrodisiac compounds after administration.

6. **Toxicology Studies:**

   a. Preclinical studies evaluate the safety of aphrodisiacs by assessing potential adverse effects on reproductive organs, cardiovascular function, liver function, and other physiological systems.

   b. Toxicology studies also examine the potential for reproductive toxicity, including effects on fertility, pregnancy outcomes, and offspring development.

7. **Regulatory Considerations:**

   a. Preclinical data on the safety and efficacy of aphrodisiacs are submitted to regulatory authorities as part of the drug approval process.

b. Regulatory agencies review preclinical data to assess the potential risks and benefits of aphrodisiacs and determine whether they can proceed to clinical trials in humans.

Overall, preclinical screening in reproductive pharmacology provides valuable insights into the potential effects of aphrodisiacs on sexual behavior, reproductive physiology, and overall health. These studies help identify promising compounds for further development as treatments for sexual dysfunction and enhancement.

ANTIFERTILITY AGENTS:

Preclinical screening for antifertility agents in reproductive pharmacology involves evaluating compounds or substances for their potential to prevent or reduce fertility in animal models. These studies aim to identify potential contraceptive methods or agents for both males and females. Here's a detailed overview of the preclinical screening process:

1. **Animal Models:**
   a. Researchers use various animal models to study reproductive physiology and fertility control, including rodents (mice and rats), rabbits, non-human primates, and occasionally larger mammals like dogs or pigs.
   b. Animal models are chosen based on their reproductive similarities to humans and their suitability for studying fertility control mechanisms.

2. **Female Reproductive Studies:**
   a. **Ovulation Inhibition**: Researchers evaluate the effects of potential antifertility agents on ovulation in female animals. Methods such as vaginal cytology, serum hormone analysis, or histological examination of ovarian tissue are used to assess ovulation.

b. **Implantation Prevention**: Drugs or compounds are tested for their ability to inhibit implantation of fertilized ova into the uterine lining. This is often assessed using methods such as examining uterine histology or measuring levels of implantation-related proteins.

c. **Embryo Toxicity**: Researchers assess whether antifertility agents cause toxicity to embryos or impair embryonic development, which could lead to miscarriage or fetal abnormalities.

3. **Male Reproductive Studies:**

a. **Spermatogenesis Inhibition**: Researchers evaluate the effects of potential antifertility agents on spermatogenesis (sperm production) in male animals. Methods such as sperm counts, motility analysis, and histological examination of testicular tissue are used to assess spermatogenesis.

b. **Sperm Function Inhibition**: Antifertility agents may target sperm function, such as sperm motility or ability to fertilize an egg. Researchers conduct tests such as sperm penetration assays to assess these parameters.

c. **Spermatogenic Cell Toxicity**: Researchers evaluate whether antifertility agents cause toxicity to spermatogenic cells or impair their function, which could lead to temporary or permanent infertility.

4. **Hormonal Studies:**

a. Researchers analyze changes in reproductive hormone levels, including gonadotropins (e.g., follicle-stimulating hormone, luteinizing hormone) and sex steroids (e.g., estrogen, progesterone, testosterone), in both male and female animals treated with potential antifertility agents.

b. Changes in hormone levels provide insights into the mechanisms of action of antifertility agents and their effects on the hypothalamic-pituitary-gonadal (HPG) axis.

5. **Mechanism of Action Studies:**
   a. Researchers investigate the mechanisms of action of potential antifertility agents, including their effects on reproductive hormone receptors, enzyme inhibition (e.g., aromatase inhibitors, 5-alpha-reductase inhibitors), and other molecular targets involved in reproductive physiology.
   b. Mechanistic studies provide insights into how antifertility agents exert their contraceptive effects and help identify potential targets for drug development.

6. **Toxicology Studies:**
   a. Researchers conduct toxicology studies to assess the safety of potential antifertility agents, including their effects on reproductive organs, hormonal balance, and overall health.
   b. Toxicity studies evaluate potential adverse effects such as organ toxicity, carcinogenicity, genotoxicity, and teratogenicity.

7. **Regulatory Considerations:**
   a. Preclinical data on the safety and efficacy of antifertility agents are submitted to regulatory agencies as part of the drug approval process.
   b. Regulatory authorities review preclinical data to assess the potential risks and benefits of antifertility agents and determine whether they can proceed to clinical trials in humans.

Overall, preclinical screening in reproductive pharmacology provides valuable insights into the potential contraceptive effects and safety profiles of antifertility agents. These studies are essential for identifying promising candidates for further development as contraceptive methods for humans.

ANALGESICS

Preclinical screening for analgesics involves evaluating potential compounds or substances for their ability to relieve pain in animal models before testing them in human clinical trials. The goal is to identify safe and effective pain-relieving drugs with minimal side effects. Here's a detailed overview of the preclinical screening process for analgesics:

Animal Models of Pain:

1. **Chemical Models:**

   a. **Formalin Test:** Injection of formalin into the paw induces biphasic pain responses characterized by licking, biting, and lifting of the injected paw. The first phase (0-5 minutes) reflects acute pain, while the second phase (15-60 minutes) represents inflammatory pain.

   b. **Acetic Acid Writhing Test**: Intraperitoneal injection of acetic acid induces abdominal writhing responses in rodents, reflecting visceral pain.

   c. **Carrageenan-Induced Hyperalgesia**: Injection of carrageenan into the paw produces localized inflammation and hyperalgesia, mimicking inflammatory pain states.

2. **Mechanical Models:**

   a. **Von Frey Filament Test**: Application of calibrated von Frey filaments to the plantar surface of the paw assesses mechanical allodynia. Withdrawal responses to filament application indicate reduced mechanical threshold.

   b. **Randall-Selitto Test**: Increasing pressure is applied to the tail or paw using a mechanical device until the animal exhibits a withdrawal response. This test measures mechanical nociceptive threshold and is commonly used for assessing analgesic effects.

3. **Thermal Models:**

a. **Hot Plate Test**: Animals are placed on a heated surface, and latency to respond (licking, jumping) is measured. This test assesses sensitivity to thermal pain and is commonly used for evaluating centrally acting analgesics.

b. **Tail Flick Test:** The tail is exposed to a radiant heat source, and the latency to flick the tail away is measured. This test evaluates spinal reflexive responses to noxious heat stimuli.

4. **Neuropathic Pain Models:**

a. **Chronic Constriction Injury (CCI):** Chronic constriction of peripheral nerves induces neuropathic pain behaviors, such as mechanical allodynia and thermal hyperalgesia.

b. **Spinal Nerve Ligation (SNL):** Ligation of spinal nerves produces neuropathic pain-like behaviors in animals, including mechanical allodynia and thermal hyperalgesia.

Behavioral Tests in Analgesics:

1. **Pain-Related Behavior Assessment:**

a. **Licking/Biting Responses**: Observing licking, biting, or paw guarding behaviors in response to noxious stimuli.

b. **Paw Withdrawal Threshold**: Assessing the force or intensity of mechanical stimuli required to elicit withdrawal responses.

2. **Locomotor Activity:**

a. Monitoring spontaneous locomotor activity using activity meters or video tracking systems to assess the impact of analgesics on overall motor function and activity levels.

3. **Cognitive Function:**

a. Evaluating cognitive function using tests such as the Morris water maze or novel object recognition test to assess potential cognitive side effects of analgesic agents.

4. **Side Effects:**

a. Assessing side effects such as sedation, motor impairment, or gastrointestinal disturbances using appropriate behavioral assays.

5. Dose-Response Relationship:

a. Investigating the dose-response relationship of analgesic agents by administering different doses and measuring pain-related behaviors or analgesic effects.

6. Comparative Efficacy:

a. Comparing the efficacy of different analgesic agents using behavioral tests to identify the most effective treatments for specific types of pain.

Mechanism of Action Studies:

1. Receptor Binding and Activation:

a. Mechanistic studies aim to elucidate the specific receptors or targets through which analgesic agents exert their effects. For example:

    i. Opioid analgesics act primarily by binding to and activating opioid receptors (mu, delta, kappa) in the central nervous system, leading to inhibition of pain signaling pathways.

    ii. Nonsteroidal anti-inflammatory drugs (NSAIDs) inhibit the enzyme cyclooxygenase (COX), thereby reducing the synthesis of prostaglandins and other inflammatory mediators.

    iii. Antidepressants such as tricyclic antidepressants (TCAs) and selective serotonin reuptake inhibitors (SSRIs) modulate neurotransmitter levels (e.g., serotonin, norepinephrine) in the brain to alleviate pain.

2. Neurotransmitter Modulation:

a. Analgesic agents may modulate the release or activity of neurotransmitters involved in pain transmission and modulation. For example:

i. Gabapentinoids such as gabapentin and pregabalin bind to voltage-gated calcium channels, reducing the release of excitatory neurotransmitters (e.g., glutamate) and inhibiting neuronal hyperexcitability.

ii. Cannabinoid receptor agonists such as tetrahydrocannabinol (THC) act on cannabinoid receptors in the central nervous system to modulate pain perception and inflammation.

3. **Peripheral vs. Central Effects:**

a. Some analgesic agents exert their effects primarily at the site of injury or inflammation (peripheral analgesia), while others act within the central nervous system (central analgesia). Mechanistic studies aim to delineate the site and mechanism of action of analgesic agents.

4. **Inflammatory Pathways:**

a. Inflammatory mediators play a crucial role in pain sensitization and chronic pain conditions. Mechanistic studies investigate the effects of analgesic agents on inflammatory pathways, including cytokine production, prostaglandin synthesis, and leukocyte activation.

5. **Plasticity and Neuroplastic Changes:**

a. Chronic pain conditions are associated with neuroplastic changes in the central nervous system, including sensitization of pain pathways and alterations in synaptic transmission. Mechanistic studies explore the effects of analgesic agents on neuroplasticity and synaptic plasticity mechanisms involved in chronic pain.

Pharmacokinetic Studies:

1. **Absorption:**

a. Pharmacokinetic studies assess the absorption of analgesic agents following administration via different routes (e.g., oral, intravenous, transdermal). This includes measuring plasma concentrations of the drug over time to determine absorption kinetics and bioavailability.

2. **Distribution:**

   a. Pharmacokinetic studies investigate the distribution of analgesic agents within the body, including their penetration into various tissues and compartments. Techniques such as tissue homogenization and liquid chromatography-mass spectrometry (LC-MS) are used to quantify drug concentrations in tissues.

3. **Metabolism:**

   a. Analgesic agents undergo metabolism in the liver and other tissues, leading to the formation of metabolites that may contribute to their pharmacological effects or toxicity. Metabolic studies involve identifying and quantifying metabolites using techniques such as high-performance liquid chromatography (HPLC) and mass spectrometry.

4. **Elimination:**

   a. Understanding the elimination kinetics of analgesic agents is essential for determining dosing regimens and potential drug interactions. Pharmacokinetic studies assess the clearance of drugs from the body via renal excretion, hepatic metabolism, or other routes.

5. **Drug Interactions:**

   a. Pharmacokinetic studies also evaluate potential drug-drug interactions that may affect the absorption, distribution, metabolism, or elimination of analgesic agents. This includes studying the effects of co-administered drugs on the pharmacokinetics of analgesic agents and vice versa.

Toxicology Studies:

1. **Acute Toxicity Studies:**

   a. These studies assess the potential adverse effects of analgesic agents following a single administration at high doses. They aim to identify acute toxic effects and determine the maximum tolerated dose.

b. Parameters evaluated may include changes in behavior, clinical signs of toxicity, organ weight, histopathological examination of tissues, and mortality rates.

2. **Subacute and Chronic Toxicity Studies:**
   a. Subacute and chronic toxicity studies involve repeated administration of analgesic agents over several weeks to months to assess potential adverse effects that may develop with prolonged exposure.
   b. These studies evaluate systemic toxicity, organ-specific effects, and reversibility of toxic effects upon cessation of treatment.

3. **Genotoxicity Studies:**
   a. Genotoxicity studies evaluate the potential of analgesic agents to induce genetic damage, including mutations, chromosomal aberrations, and DNA damage.
   b. These studies help assess the risk of long-term adverse effects, such as carcinogenesis, associated with the use of analgesic agents.

4. **Reproductive and Developmental Toxicity Studies:**
   a. These studies assess the effects of analgesic agents on reproductive function and fetal development.
   b. Parameters evaluated may include fertility, embryo-fetal development, postnatal development, and reproductive organ histopathology.

5. **Cardiovascular and Renal Safety Studies:**
   a. Specialized studies evaluate the cardiovascular and renal safety profiles of analgesic agents, including effects on blood pressure, cardiac function, renal function, and electrolyte balance.
   b. These studies help identify potential cardiovascular events (e.g., myocardial infarction, stroke) and renal toxicity associated with the use of analgesic agents.

Drug Interactions:

1. **Pharmacokinetic Interactions:**

a. Analgesic agents may interact with other drugs through alterations in pharmacokinetic parameters, such as absorption, distribution, metabolism, and elimination.

b. Studies assess the effects of co-administered drugs on the pharmacokinetics of analgesic agents and vice versa.

c. Drug-drug interaction studies may involve in vitro studies using liver microsomes or recombinant enzymes to evaluate metabolic pathways, as well as in vivo studies in animal models or human subjects to assess changes in drug concentrations and pharmacokinetic parameters.

2. Pharmacodynamic Interactions:

a. Pharmacodynamic interactions occur when drugs exert additive, synergistic, or antagonistic effects on the same physiological or biochemical pathway.

b. Analgesic agents may interact with other drugs that affect pain perception, central nervous system function, or cardiovascular and respiratory function.

c. Preclinical studies may involve behavioral assays or physiological measurements to assess the effects of drug combinations on pain sensitivity, motor function, respiratory rate, and cardiovascular parameters.

3. Clinical Studies:

a. Clinical trials assess the potential for drug interactions in human subjects receiving analgesic therapy in combination with other medications.

b. Pharmacokinetic studies measure drug concentrations in plasma or urine to evaluate changes in exposure and clearance.

c. Pharmacodynamic studies assess changes in pain scores, analgesic efficacy, adverse events, and other clinical parameters associated with drug interactions.

Overall, preclinical screening in analgesic research provides valuable insights into the potential efficacy, safety, and mechanism of action of potential pain-relieving drugs. These studies are essential for identifying promising candidates for further development as treatments for pain in humans.

ANTI-INFLAMMATORY

Preclinical screening for anti-inflammatory drugs involves evaluating compounds or substances for their ability to reduce inflammation in animal models before testing them in human clinical trials. The goal is to identify safe and effective anti-inflammatory agents with minimal side effects. Here's a detailed overview of the preclinical screening process for anti-inflammatory drugs:

Animal Models of Inflammation:

1. **Carrageenan-Induced Paw Edema**: Carrageenan, a polysaccharide extracted from seaweed, is commonly used to induce acute inflammation in animal models. Injection of carrageenan into the paw results in localized edema, accompanied by infiltration of inflammatory cells and release of pro-inflammatory mediators.

2. **Freund's Adjuvant-Induced Arthritis**: Freund's adjuvant, typically Complete Freund's Adjuvant (CFA) or Incomplete Freund's Adjuvant (IFA), is used to induce chronic inflammation and arthritis in animal models. Injection of adjuvant into the joints or subcutaneous tissue leads to joint swelling, erythema, and cartilage destruction resembling rheumatoid arthritis.

3. **LPS-Induced Systemic Inflammation**: Lipopolysaccharide (LPS), a component of the outer membrane of Gram-negative bacteria, is used to induce systemic inflammation in animal models. Injection of LPS results in a

systemic inflammatory response characterized by fever, cytokine release, and activation of immune cells.

4. **Cytokine-Induced Inflammation**: Administration of pro-inflammatory cytokines such as tumor necrosis factor-alpha (TNF-alpha), interleukin-1 (IL-1), or interleukin-6 (IL-6) can induce inflammation in animal models. This approach allows for the study of specific inflammatory pathways and the evaluation of anti-cytokine therapies.

5. **Autoimmune Disease Models**: Animal models of autoimmune diseases, such as experimental autoimmune encephalomyelitis (EAE) for multiple sclerosis or collagen-induced arthritis (CIA) for rheumatoid arthritis, mimic the immunological and inflammatory aspects of human autoimmune conditions.

Inflammatory Biomarkers:

1. **Cytokines and Chemokines**: Pro-inflammatory cytokines such as TNF-alpha, IL-1β, and IL-6 are key mediators of inflammation. Measurement of cytokine levels in serum or tissue samples provides quantitative assessment of inflammation and response to treatment.

2. **Acute Phase Proteins**: Acute phase proteins, including C-reactive protein (CRP) and serum amyloid A (SAA), are produced by the liver in response to inflammation. Elevated levels of acute phase proteins indicate systemic inflammation and can be used as biomarkers of disease activity.

3. **Cellular Infiltrates**: Inflammatory cell infiltrates, such as neutrophils, macrophages, and lymphocytes, are commonly observed in inflamed tissues. Quantification of inflammatory cell populations by histological analysis or flow cytometry provides insight into the extent and nature of inflammation.

4. **Eicosanoids**: Eicosanoids, including prostaglandins and leukotrienes, are lipid mediators of inflammation derived from arachidonic acid metabolism. Measurement of eicosanoid levels in tissues or body fluids reflects the

activation of inflammatory pathways and can be targeted by anti-inflammatory drugs.

5. **Matrix Metalloproteinases (MMPs)**: MMPs are enzymes involved in tissue remodeling and degradation of extracellular matrix components. Elevated levels of MMPs are associated with tissue damage and inflammation and can serve as biomarkers of disease severity.

Evaluation of Anti-inflammatory Agents:

1. **Inhibition of Inflammatory Mediators**: Anti-inflammatory agents are evaluated for their ability to inhibit the production or activity of pro-inflammatory mediators such as cytokines, eicosanoids, and acute phase proteins.

2. **Reduction of Inflammatory Cell Infiltration**: Effective anti-inflammatory agents should reduce the infiltration of inflammatory cells into inflamed tissues, as evidenced by histological analysis or flow cytometry.

3. **Attenuation of Inflammatory Biomarkers**: Treatment with anti-inflammatory agents should lead to a decrease in the levels of inflammatory biomarkers such as cytokines, acute phase proteins, and eicosanoids in serum or tissue samples.

4. **Improvement in Clinical Symptoms**: In addition to biochemical and histological endpoints, anti-inflammatory agents are assessed for their ability to improve clinical symptoms such as joint swelling, pain, and functional impairment in animal models of inflammation.

Behavioral Tests:

1. **Pain Sensitivity Tests**: Inflammatory conditions often result in hyperalgesia (increased pain sensitivity) and allodynia (pain in response to non-painful stimuli). Behavioral assays such as the von Frey filament test (to assess mechanical allodynia) or the hot plate test (to assess thermal hyperalgesia) can measure changes in pain sensitivity in response to inflammation and the effects of anti-inflammatory treatment.

2. **Locomotor Activity**: Inflammatory pain can also impact locomotor activity. Monitoring spontaneous activity using open field tests or activity chambers can provide insights into the effects of inflammation and anti-inflammatory treatment on overall mobility and exploration behavior.

3. **Anxiety-Like Behavior**: Inflammatory conditions may induce anxiety-like behaviors in animals. Tests such as the elevated plus maze or the light-dark box test can assess changes in anxiety-related behaviors and the anxiolytic effects of anti-inflammatory agents.

4. **Cognitive Function**: Inflammatory conditions can impair cognitive function, particularly in conditions like neuroinflammation. Behavioral assays such as the Morris water maze or novel object recognition test can evaluate changes in learning and memory following inflammation and treatment with anti-inflammatory agents.

5. **Social Interaction**: Inflammatory pain may also affect social behavior. Tests such as the social interaction test or the three-chamber social approach test can assess changes in social interaction and the effects of anti-inflammatory treatment on social behavior.

Histopathological Examination:

1. **Tissue Analysis**: Histopathological examination involves the microscopic examination of tissue samples to assess the extent and nature of inflammation. Tissues affected by inflammation, such as joints in arthritis models or organs in systemic inflammation models, are collected and stained to visualize inflammatory cell infiltration, tissue damage, and other pathological changes.

2. **Inflammatory Cell Infiltration**: Inflammatory infiltrates, including neutrophils, macrophages, and lymphocytes, can be quantified and characterized using histological staining techniques such as hematoxylin and eosin (H&E) staining or immunohistochemistry. The presence of

inflammatory cells within tissues is indicative of ongoing inflammation and can be used to assess the efficacy of anti-inflammatory treatment.

3. **Tissue Damage and Repair**: Inflammatory conditions often result in tissue damage, such as cartilage erosion in arthritis or neuronal loss in neuroinflammation. Histopathological examination allows for the assessment of tissue damage and the extent of tissue repair following treatment with anti-inflammatory agents.

4. **Fibrosis and Scarring**: Chronic inflammation may lead to fibrosis and scarring in affected tissues. Histological staining techniques such as Masson's trichrome or Sirius red staining can visualize collagen deposition and fibrotic changes, providing insights into the long-term consequences of inflammation and the efficacy of anti-inflammatory treatment in preventing tissue fibrosis.

5. **Resolution of Inflammation**: Effective anti-inflammatory agents should promote the resolution of inflammation and tissue healing. Histopathological examination allows for the assessment of inflammatory resolution, including the clearance of inflammatory infiltrates and the restoration of tissue architecture following treatment.

Mechanism of Action Studies:

1. **Inhibition of Inflammatory Mediators**: Anti-inflammatory agents exert their effects by targeting various mediators and pathways involved in the inflammatory response. Mechanistic studies aim to elucidate the specific targets and mechanisms of action of these agents. For example:

   - Nonsteroidal anti-inflammatory drugs (NSAIDs) inhibit the enzyme cyclooxygenase (COX), thereby reducing the production of prostaglandins, which are key mediators of inflammation and pain.
   - Corticosteroids exert anti-inflammatory effects by inhibiting the transcription of pro-inflammatory genes and suppressing the activity of immune cells, such as macrophages and lymphocytes.

o Biologic agents, such as monoclonal antibodies or soluble receptors, target specific cytokines or cell surface receptors involved in inflammatory signaling pathways.

2. **Modulation of Inflammatory Signaling Pathways**: Anti-inflammatory agents may modulate intracellular signaling pathways involved in the regulation of inflammation. Mechanistic studies investigate the impact of these agents on signaling molecules such as transcription factors, protein kinases, and inflammatory mediators.

3. **Cellular and Molecular Effects**: Mechanistic studies also explore the cellular and molecular effects of anti-inflammatory agents on immune cells, endothelial cells, and other cell types involved in the inflammatory response. This includes assessing changes in cell activation, cytokine production, and inflammatory gene expression.

4. **Resolution of Inflammation:** Some anti-inflammatory agents promote the resolution of inflammation by enhancing the clearance of inflammatory mediators and apoptotic cells, stimulating tissue repair processes, and modulating the activity of pro-resolving lipid mediators such as lipoxins and resolvins.

5. **Comparative Studies**: Mechanistic studies may involve comparative analyses of different anti-inflammatory agents to identify differences in their mechanisms of action, potency, and selectivity for specific targets. This information helps guide the selection and development of therapeutic agents with optimal efficacy and safety profiles.

Pharmacokinetic Studies:

1. **Absorption:** Pharmacokinetic studies assess the absorption of anti-inflammatory agents following administration via different routes (e.g., oral, intravenous, topical). This includes measuring plasma concentrations of the drug over time to determine absorption kinetics and bioavailability.

2. **Distribution**: Pharmacokinetic studies investigate the distribution of anti-inflammatory agents within the body, including their penetration into various tissues and compartments. Techniques such as tissue homogenization and liquid chromatography-mass spectrometry (LC-MS) are used to quantify drug concentrations in tissues.

3. **Metabolism**: Anti-inflammatory agents undergo metabolism in the liver and other tissues, leading to the formation of metabolites that may contribute to their pharmacological effects or toxicity. Metabolic studies involve identifying and quantifying metabolites using techniques such as high-performance liquid chromatography (HPLC) and mass spectrometry.

4. **Elimination:** Understanding the elimination kinetics of anti-inflammatory agents is essential for determining dosing regimens and potential drug interactions. Pharmacokinetic studies assess the clearance of drugs from the body via renal excretion, hepatic metabolism, or other routes.

5. **Drug Interactions**: Pharmacokinetic studies also evaluate potential drug-drug interactions that may affect the absorption, distribution, metabolism, or elimination of anti-inflammatory agents. This includes studying the effects of co-administered drugs on the pharmacokinetics of anti-inflammatory agents and vice versa.

Toxicology Studies:

1. **Acute Toxicity Studies**: These studies assess the potential adverse effects of anti-inflammatory agents following a single administration at high doses. They aim to identify acute toxic effects and determine the maximum tolerated dose.

2. **Subacute Toxicity Studies**: Subacute toxicity studies involve repeated administration of anti-inflammatory agents over several weeks to assess potential adverse effects that may develop with prolonged exposure. These studies evaluate systemic toxicity, organ-specific effects, and reversibility of toxic effects upon cessation of treatment.

3. **Chronic Toxicity Studies**: Chronic toxicity studies are conducted over a more extended period, typically several months to years, to evaluate the long-term effects of anti-inflammatory agents. These studies assess cumulative toxicity, carcinogenic potential, and effects on reproductive and developmental outcomes.

4. **Genotoxicity Studies**: Genotoxicity studies evaluate the potential of anti-inflammatory agents to induce genetic damage, including mutations, chromosomal aberrations, and DNA damage. These studies help assess the risk of long-term adverse effects, such as carcinogenesis.

5. **Reproductive and Developmental Toxicity Studies**: These studies assess the effects of anti-inflammatory agents on reproductive function and fetal development. They evaluate parameters such as fertility, embryo-fetal development, and postnatal development to identify potential risks to pregnant women and their offspring.

6. **Cardiovascular and Renal Safety Studies:** Anti-inflammatory agents, particularly nonsteroidal anti-inflammatory drugs (NSAIDs), may pose risks of cardiovascular events and renal toxicity. Specialized studies evaluate the cardiovascular and renal safety profiles of these agents, including effects on blood pressure, renal function, and cardiovascular endpoints.

7. **Immunotoxicity Studies**: Immunotoxicity studies assess the impact of anti-inflammatory agents on the immune system, including effects on immune cell function, cytokine production, and antibody responses. These studies help identify potential immunosuppressive or immunostimulatory effects of anti-inflammatory agents.

Regulatory Considerations:

1. **Regulatory Agencies**: Anti-inflammatory agents must undergo regulatory review and approval by government agencies, such as the U.S. Food and Drug Administration (FDA) in the United States or the European Medicines Agency (EMA) in the European Union. These agencies require

comprehensive data on safety, efficacy, and quality before granting marketing authorization.

2. **Preclinical Studies**: Regulatory agencies require preclinical data from toxicology studies to assess the safety profile of anti-inflammatory agents. These studies must be conducted in accordance with regulatory guidelines and Good Laboratory Practice (GLP) standards to ensure data integrity and reliability.

3. **Clinical Trials**: Clinical development of anti-inflammatory agents involves conducting well-controlled clinical trials to evaluate safety and efficacy in human subjects. Regulatory agencies review clinical trial data to assess the benefit-risk profile of anti-inflammatory agents and make regulatory decisions regarding approval for marketing and use.

4. **Risk Management Plans**: Regulatory agencies may require the development of risk management plans (RMPs) to mitigate identified risks associated with anti-inflammatory agents. RMPs include strategies for monitoring and managing known and potential risks, as well as communication plans to inform healthcare professionals and patients about safety concerns.

5. **Post-Marketing Surveillance**: After approval, regulatory agencies require ongoing post-marketing surveillance to monitor the safety of anti-inflammatory agents in real-world clinical practice. This includes adverse event reporting, pharmacovigilance activities, and periodic safety updates to assess and communicate emerging safety concerns.

Overall, preclinical screening in anti-inflammatory research provides valuable insights into the potential efficacy, safety, and mechanism of action of potential anti-inflammatory drugs. These studies are essential for identifying promising candidates for further development as treatments for inflammatory diseases in humans.

ANTIPYRETIC AGENTS

Preclinical screening for antipyretic agents involves evaluating compounds or substances for their ability to reduce fever in animal models before testing them in human clinical trials. Fever is often caused by inflammation or infection, and antipyretic drugs aim to lower body temperature by acting on the thermoregulatory centers in the brain. Here's a detailed overview of the preclinical screening process for antipyretic agents:

Animal Models of Fever:

1. **Endotoxin-Induced Fever**: Lipopolysaccharide (LPS), a component of the outer membrane of Gram-negative bacteria, is commonly used to induce fever in animals. LPS stimulates the release of pro-inflammatory cytokines such as interleukin-1 (IL-1), interleukin-6 (IL-6), and tumor necrosis factor-alpha (TNF-alpha), leading to fever.

2. **Cytokine-Induced Fever**: Certain cytokines, such as IL-1β, IL-6, and TNF-alpha, are potent pyrogens that can induce fever when administered to animals. These cytokines can be injected directly or induced through other means such as viral or bacterial infections.

3. **Viral and Bacterial Infections**: Infectious agents like influenza virus or certain bacteria can cause fever in animals. These models mimic natural infections and are valuable for studying the fever response and testing antipyretic agents.

4. **Pyrogenic Cytokine Injection**: Administration of purified pyrogenic cytokines like IL-1β, IL-6, or TNF-alpha can induce fever in animals. This approach allows for precise control over the fever-inducing stimulus.

Body Temperature Measurement Techniques:

1. **Rectal Temperature Measurement**: This is one of the most common methods used to measure body temperature in animals. A lubricated

thermometer is inserted into the animal's rectum for a short period to obtain a temperature reading.

2. **Implantable Temperature Transponders**: These are small electronic devices implanted subcutaneously in animals to continuously monitor body temperature. This method provides real-time temperature data without causing stress to the animals.

3. **Infrared Thermography**: Infrared thermography involves capturing thermal images of the animal's body surface using an infrared camera. Changes in body temperature can be detected and quantified from these images.

4. **Telemetry Systems**: Telemetry systems involve implanting temperature-sensing devices (telemeters) into animals. These devices transmit temperature data wirelessly to a receiver, allowing for continuous, remote monitoring of body temperature.

5. **Subcutaneous Temperature Probes**: Small temperature probes can be implanted subcutaneously in animals to measure body temperature. This method provides continuous temperature monitoring without causing discomfort to the animals.

Evaluation of Antipyretic Agents:

1. **Temperature Reduction**: The primary endpoint in evaluating antipyretic agents is their ability to reduce elevated body temperature induced by fever-inducing stimuli. This is typically assessed by comparing pre- and post-treatment body temperature measurements.

2. **Time Course of Action**: Antipyretic agents may exhibit different onset and duration of action profiles. Monitoring body temperature over time allows for assessment of the time course of antipyretic effects.

3. **Dose-Response Relationship**: Studying the effect of different doses of antipyretic agents on fever response helps determine the dose-response relationship and optimal dosing regimens.

4. **Mechanism of Action**: Animal models are valuable for elucidating the mechanisms underlying the antipyretic effects of drugs. This may involve studying the impact of antipyretic agents on cytokine release, inflammatory pathways, or thermoregulatory mechanisms.

Behavioral Tests:

1. **Lethargy and Activity Monitoring**: Fever in animals is often associated with lethargy and reduced activity. Monitoring spontaneous locomotor activity using activity meters or video tracking systems can provide quantitative measures of changes in activity level associated with fever.

2. **Feeding Behavior**: Fever can affect feeding behavior in animals, leading to reduced food intake. Evaluating food consumption before and after induction of fever can provide insights into the impact of fever on appetite and feeding behavior.

3. **Social Interaction Tests:** Fever may alter social behavior in animals. Social interaction tests, such as the social preference test or social novelty preference test, assess changes in social behavior following induction of fever and treatment with antipyretic agents.

4. **Exploratory Behavior**: Fever can influence exploratory behavior in animals. Tests such as the open field test or elevated plus maze assess changes in exploratory activity and anxiety-like behavior associated with fever.

5. **Nociception Tests**: Fever can modulate pain sensitivity in animals. Nociception tests, such as the hot plate test or tail flick test, measure pain response thresholds and can be used to assess the analgesic effects of antipyretic agents.

6. **Sleep-Wake Cycle**: Fever may disrupt the sleep-wake cycle in animals. Monitoring sleep patterns using EEG or activity monitoring can provide insights into the effects of fever and antipyretic treatment on sleep architecture.

Antipyretic Efficacy Studies:

1. **Behavioral Responses to Fever**: Behavioral tests are used to assess the impact of fever on various behavioral parameters, providing baseline measurements before antipyretic treatment. Changes in behavior following induction of fever serve as indicators of fever severity.

2. **Effects of Antipyretic Agents on Behavior**: Antipyretic agents are administered to animals following induction of fever, and behavioral tests are used to evaluate their efficacy in reversing fever-induced changes in behavior. Reduction in lethargy, improvement in activity levels, and normalization of feeding and social behavior indicate the effectiveness of antipyretic treatment.

3. **Dose-Response Relationships**: Behavioral tests can be used to assess the dose-response relationship of antipyretic agents. Administering different doses of the antipyretic agent and measuring behavioral responses can help determine the optimal dose for fever reduction.

4. **Comparative Efficacy Studies**: Behavioral tests allow for the comparison of the efficacy of different antipyretic agents. Assessing behavioral responses to fever and antipyretic treatment across different agents helps identify the most effective treatments for fever management.

5. **Mechanistic Insights**: Behavioral tests can provide insights into the mechanisms underlying the antipyretic effects of agents. Changes in behavior following treatment may reflect alterations in central nervous system function, inflammation, or thermoregulatory mechanisms.

Mechanism of Action Studies:

1. **Prostaglandin Inhibition**: Many antipyretic agents, such as nonsteroidal anti-inflammatory drugs (NSAIDs) like aspirin, ibuprofen, and naproxen, exert their antipyretic effects by inhibiting the enzyme cyclooxygenase (COX). COX inhibition reduces the production of prostaglandins,

particularly prostaglandin E2 (PGE2), which play a key role in fever induction in response to pyrogenic stimuli.

2. **Central Nervous System Effects**: Some antipyretic agents, such as acetaminophen (paracetamol), are thought to exert their antipyretic effects primarily in the central nervous system. The exact mechanism of acetaminophen's antipyretic action is not fully understood but may involve inhibition of prostaglandin synthesis in the hypothalamus, which is the primary thermoregulatory center in the brain.

3. **Neurotransmitter Modulation**: Fever is regulated by a complex interplay of neurotransmitters and neuropeptides in the central nervous system. Some antipyretic agents may modulate the activity of these neurotransmitter systems, such as serotonin, dopamine, and gamma-aminobutyric acid (GABA), to influence thermoregulatory pathways and reduce fever.

4. **Cytokine Modulation**: Antipyretic agents may also exert their effects by modulating the production or activity of pro-inflammatory cytokines involved in fever induction. This can include inhibition of cytokine synthesis, such as interleukin-1 (IL-1) and interleukin-6 (IL-6), or modulation of cytokine signaling pathways.

5. **Peripheral Actions**: In addition to central mechanisms, some antipyretic agents may exert peripheral effects, such as reducing inflammation and cytokine release at the site of infection or tissue injury, which can contribute to fever reduction.

Pharmacokinetic Studies:

1. **Absorption**: Pharmacokinetic studies assess the absorption of antipyretic agents following administration via different routes (e.g., oral, intravenous, rectal). This includes measuring plasma concentrations of the drug over time to determine absorption kinetics and bioavailability.

2. **Distribution**: Pharmacokinetic studies also investigate the distribution of antipyretic agents within the body, including their penetration into various

tissues and compartments. Techniques such as tissue homogenization and liquid chromatography-mass spectrometry (LC-MS) are used to quantify drug concentrations in tissues.

3. **Metabolism**: Antipyretic agents undergo metabolism in the liver and other tissues, leading to the formation of metabolites that may contribute to their pharmacological effects or toxicity. Metabolic studies involve identifying and quantifying metabolites using techniques such as high-performance liquid chromatography (HPLC) and mass spectrometry.

4. **Elimination**: Understanding the elimination kinetics of antipyretic agents is essential for determining dosing regimens and potential drug interactions. Pharmacokinetic studies assess the clearance of drugs from the body via renal excretion, hepatic metabolism, or other routes.

5. **Drug Interactions**: Pharmacokinetic studies also evaluate potential drug-drug interactions that may affect the absorption, distribution, metabolism, or elimination of antipyretic agents. This includes studying the effects of co-administered drugs on the pharmacokinetics of antipyretic agents and vice versa.

Toxicology Studies:

1. **Acute Toxicity Studies**: These studies assess the potential adverse effects of antipyretic agents following a single administration at high doses. They aim to identify acute toxic effects and determine the maximum tolerated dose.

2. **Subacute Toxicity Studies**: Subacute toxicity studies involve repeated administration of antipyretic agents over several weeks to assess potential adverse effects that may develop with prolonged exposure. These studies evaluate systemic toxicity, organ-specific effects, and reversibility of toxic effects upon cessation of treatment.

3. **Chronic Toxicity Studies**: Chronic toxicity studies are conducted over a more extended period, typically several months to years, to evaluate the long-term effects of antipyretic agents. These studies assess cumulative

toxicity, carcinogenic potential, and effects on reproductive and developmental outcomes.

4. **Genotoxicity Studies**: Genotoxicity studies evaluate the potential of antipyretic agents to induce genetic damage, including mutations, chromosomal aberrations, and DNA damage. These studies help assess the risk of long-term adverse effects, such as carcinogenesis.

5. **Reproductive and Developmental Toxicity Studies**: These studies assess the effects of antipyretic agents on reproductive function and fetal development. They evaluate parameters such as fertility, embryo-fetal development, and postnatal development to identify potential risks to pregnant women and their offspring.

6. **Cardiovascular and Renal Safety Studies**: Antipyretic agents, particularly NSAIDs, may pose risks of cardiovascular events and renal toxicity. Specialized studies evaluate the cardiovascular and renal safety profiles of these agents, including effects on blood pressure, renal function, and cardiovascular endpoints.

7. **Immunotoxicity Studies**: Immunotoxicity studies assess the impact of antipyretic agents on the immune system, including effects on immune cell function, cytokine production, and antibody responses. These studies help identify potential immunosuppressive or immunostimulatory effects of antipyretic agents.

Regulatory Considerations:

1. **Regulatory Agencies**: Antipyretic agents must undergo regulatory review and approval by government agencies, such as the U.S. Food and Drug Administration (FDA) in the United States or the European Medicines Agency (EMA) in the European Union. These agencies require comprehensive data on safety, efficacy, and quality before granting marketing authorization.

2. **Preclinical Studies**: Regulatory agencies require preclinical data from toxicology studies to assess the safety profile of antipyretic agents. These studies must be conducted in accordance with regulatory guidelines and Good Laboratory Practice (GLP) standards to ensure data integrity and reliability.

3. **Clinical Trials**: Clinical development of antipyretic agents involves conducting well-controlled clinical trials to evaluate safety and efficacy in human subjects. Regulatory agencies review clinical trial data to assess the benefit-risk profile of antipyretic agents and make regulatory decisions regarding approval for marketing and use.

4. **Risk Management Plans**: Regulatory agencies may require the development of risk management plans (RMPs) to mitigate identified risks associated with antipyretic agents. RMPs include strategies for monitoring and managing known and potential risks, as well as communication plans to inform healthcare professionals and patients about safety concerns.

5. **Post-Marketing Surveillance**: After approval, regulatory agencies require ongoing post-marketing surveillance to monitor the safety of antipyretic agents in real-world clinical practice. This includes adverse event reporting, pharmacovigilance activities, and periodic safety updates to assess and communicate emerging safety concerns.

Overall, preclinical screening in antipyretic research provides valuable insights into the potential efficacy, safety, and mechanism of action of potential antipyretic drugs. These studies are essential for identifying promising candidates for further development as treatments for fever in humans.

GASTROINTESTINAL DRUGS

Preclinical screening for gastrointestinal drugs involves evaluating compounds or substances for their effects on gastrointestinal function, including digestion, absorption, motility, and secretion. These studies aim to identify safe and effective drugs for the treatment of gastrointestinal disorders such as acid reflux, peptic ulcers, inflammatory bowel disease, and irritable bowel syndrome. Here's a detailed overview of the preclinical screening process for gastrointestinal drugs:

- **In Vitro Studies:**
  - **Cell Culture Assays**: Researchers use cultured cells derived from gastrointestinal tissues (e.g., epithelial cells, smooth muscle cells, enterocytes) to assess the effects of potential drugs on cellular processes such as ion transport, mucin secretion, and inflammatory mediator release.
  - **Permeability Studies**: In vitro models such as Caco-2 cell monolayers are used to evaluate the permeability of drugs across the intestinal epithelium and assess their potential for oral absorption.
  - **Gastrointestinal Motility Assays**: Researchers use isolated tissue preparations (e.g., intestinal segments, stomach strips) to study the effects of drugs on gastrointestinal motility, including contraction and relaxation of smooth muscle.
- **In Vivo Animal Studies:**
  - **Animal Models of Gastrointestinal Disorders**: Researchers use various animal models to mimic gastrointestinal conditions, including acid-induced ulcers, colitis models, and models of gastric motility disorders.
  - **Efficacy Studies**: Animals are treated with potential gastrointestinal drugs, and parameters such as gastric acid secretion, gastric emptying rate, intestinal transit time, and colonic motility are measured to assess drug efficacy.

- **Safety Assessments**: Preclinical studies evaluate the safety of gastrointestinal drugs in animals, including acute and chronic toxicity assessments, as well as examination of potential adverse effects on gastrointestinal tissues and other organs.

- **Mechanism of Action Studies:**
    - Researchers investigate the mechanisms of action underlying the effects of potential gastrointestinal drugs. These may include modulation of neurotransmitter systems (e.g., cholinergic, adrenergic), inhibition of inflammatory pathways (e.g., NF-kB, cytokines), or enhancement of mucosal protection mechanisms.
    - Mechanistic studies help elucidate how gastrointestinal drugs exert their effects and identify potential targets for drug development.

- **Pharmacokinetic Studies:**
    - Researchers assess the pharmacokinetic properties of potential gastrointestinal drugs, including absorption, distribution, metabolism, and excretion (ADME).
    - Pharmacokinetic studies help determine the bioavailability, half-life, and tissue distribution of gastrointestinal drugs after administration via different routes (such as oral, intravenous, or rectal).

- **Toxicology Studies:**
    - Preclinical toxicology studies evaluate the safety of potential gastrointestinal drugs, including acute and chronic toxicity assessments.
    - Researchers assess potential adverse effects on vital organs, including the liver, kidneys, gastrointestinal tract, and cardiovascular system.
    - Toxicology studies also evaluate potential risks such as genotoxicity, carcinogenicity, and reproductive toxicity.

- **Regulatory Considerations:**
  - Preclinical data on the safety and efficacy of gastrointestinal drugs are submitted to regulatory agencies as part of the drug approval process.
  - Regulatory authorities review preclinical data to assess the potential risks and benefits of gastrointestinal drugs and determine whether they can proceed to clinical trials in humans.

Overall, preclinical screening in gastrointestinal drug research provides valuable insights into the potential efficacy, safety, and mechanism of action of potential drugs for gastrointestinal disorders. These studies are essential for identifying promising candidates for further development as treatments for gastrointestinal diseases in humans.

ANTI-ULCER:

Preclinical screening for anti-ulcer drugs involves evaluating compounds or substances for their ability to prevent or treat ulcers in animal models before testing them in human clinical trials. Ulcers can occur in various parts of the gastrointestinal tract, including the stomach (gastric ulcers) and the duodenum (duodenal ulcers), and they can be caused by factors such as excessive gastric acid secretion, Helicobacter pylori infection, or nonsteroidal anti-inflammatory drugs (NSAIDs). Here's a detailed overview of the preclinical screening process for anti-ulcer drugs:

1. **Animal Models of Ulcers:**
   a. Researchers use various animal models to induce ulcers and mimic different ulcerogenic conditions, such as NSAID-induced ulcers, ethanol-induced gastric lesions, or Helicobacter pylori infection models.

b. Commonly used animals include rats, mice, rabbits, and occasionally larger animals like dogs or pigs.

2. Assessment of Ulcer Parameters:

a. Researchers assess various parameters related to ulcer formation and healing, including ulcer index (size and number of ulcers), gastric acidity, mucosal blood flow, and histopathological changes in the gastric or duodenal mucosa.

b. Scoring systems are often used to quantify ulcer severity and evaluate the efficacy of anti-ulcer treatments.

3. Evaluation of Gastric Secretion:

a. Researchers measure gastric acid secretion and mucosal protective factors such as mucin and bicarbonate secretion in response to potential anti-ulcer drugs.

b. Techniques such as gastric perfusion studies or measurement of gastric pH are used to assess changes in gastric acid secretion and mucosal defense mechanisms.

4. Healing Studies:

a. Researchers evaluate the effects of potential anti-ulcer drugs on ulcer healing and mucosal repair using models of chronic ulcers or delayed ulcer healing.

b. Parameters such as ulcer area reduction, epithelial cell proliferation, collagen deposition, and angiogenesis are assessed to monitor the progression of ulcer healing.

5. Mechanism of Action Studies:

a. Researchers investigate the mechanisms underlying the anti-ulcer effects of potential drugs. These may include inhibition of gastric acid secretion (e.g., proton pump inhibitors), enhancement of mucosal defense mechanisms (e.g., prostaglandin analogs), or anti-inflammatory effects (e.g., corticosteroids).

b. Mechanistic studies help elucidate how anti-ulcer drugs exert their effects and identify potential targets for drug development.

6. Pharmacokinetic Studies:

a. Researchers assess the pharmacokinetic properties of potential anti-ulcer drugs, including absorption, distribution, metabolism, and excretion (ADME).

b. Pharmacokinetic studies help determine the bioavailability, half-life, and tissue distribution of anti-ulcer compounds after administration via different routes (such as oral, intravenous, or topical).

7. Toxicology Studies:

a. Preclinical toxicology studies evaluate the safety of potential anti-ulcer drugs, including acute and chronic toxicity assessments.

b. Researchers assess potential adverse effects on vital organs, including the liver, kidneys, gastrointestinal tract, and cardiovascular system.

c. Toxicology studies also evaluate potential risks such as genotoxicity, carcinogenicity, and reproductive toxicity.

8. Regulatory Considerations:

a. Preclinical data on the safety and efficacy of anti-ulcer drugs are submitted to regulatory agencies as part of the drug approval process.

b. Regulatory authorities review preclinical data to assess the potential risks and benefits of anti-ulcer drugs and determine whether they can proceed to clinical trials in humans.

Overall, preclinical screening in anti-ulcer research provides valuable insights into the potential efficacy, safety, and mechanism of action of potential drugs for the treatment of ulcers. These studies are essential for identifying promising candidates for further development as treatments for gastrointestinal ulcers in humans.

ANTI -EMETIC:

Preclinical screening for anti-emetic drugs involves evaluating compounds or substances for their ability to prevent or alleviate nausea and vomiting in animal models before testing them in human clinical trials. Nausea and vomiting can be caused by various factors, including chemotherapy, radiation therapy, motion sickness, gastrointestinal disorders, or medications. Here's a detailed overview of the preclinical screening process for anti-emetic drugs:

1. **Animal Models of Nausea and Vomiting:**
   a. Researchers use various animal models to induce nausea and vomiting, including administration of emetogenic agents such as cisplatin, apomorphine, or motion stimuli (e.g., rotation or vertical oscillation).
   b. Commonly used animals include rats, mice, ferrets, and dogs, depending on the specific emetic challenge being studied.

2. **Assessment of Emetic Parameters:**
   a. Researchers assess various parameters related to nausea and vomiting, including the frequency, latency, and duration of emetic episodes, as well as the severity of nausea-related behaviors (e.g., gaping, retching).
   b. Scoring systems are often used to quantify emetic responses and evaluate the efficacy of anti-emetic treatments.

3. **Mechanism of Action Studies:**
   a. Researchers investigate the mechanisms underlying the anti-emetic effects of potential drugs. These may include modulation of neurotransmitter systems such as dopamine (D2), serotonin (5-HT3), or histamine (H1), as well as activation of receptors involved in the regulation of nausea and vomiting.
   b. Mechanistic studies help elucidate how anti-emetic drugs exert their effects and identify potential targets for drug development.

4. **Pharmacokinetic Studies:**

   a. Researchers assess the pharmacokinetic properties of potential anti-emetic drugs, including absorption, distribution, metabolism, and excretion (ADME).

   b. Pharmacokinetic studies help determine the bioavailability, half-life, and tissue distribution of anti-emetic compounds after administration via different routes (such as oral, intravenous, or transdermal).

5. **Toxicology Studies:**

   a. Preclinical toxicology studies evaluate the safety of potential anti-emetic drugs, including acute and chronic toxicity assessments.

   b. Researchers assess potential adverse effects on vital organs, including the liver, kidneys, gastrointestinal tract, and cardiovascular system.

   c. Toxicology studies also evaluate potential risks such as genotoxicity, carcinogenicity, and reproductive toxicity.

6. **Drug Interactions:**

   a. Researchers investigate potential drug interactions between anti-emetic compounds and other medications commonly used in the management of nausea and vomiting.

   b. Studies assess the pharmacokinetic and pharmacodynamic interactions to ensure safe and effective co-administration of anti-emetic drugs with other treatments.

7. **Regulatory Considerations:**

   a. Preclinical data on the safety and efficacy of anti-emetic drugs are submitted to regulatory agencies as part of the drug approval process.

   b. Regulatory authorities review preclinical data to assess the potential risks and benefits of anti-emetic drugs and determine whether they can proceed to clinical trials in humans.

Overall, preclinical screening in anti-emetic research provides valuable insights into the potential efficacy, safety, and mechanism of action of potential drugs for the prevention and treatment of nausea and vomiting. These studies are essential for identifying promising candidates for further development as treatments for emetic symptoms in humans.

ANTI- DIARRHEAL:

Preclinical screening for anti-diarrheal drugs involves evaluating compounds or substances for their ability to prevent or alleviate diarrhea in animal models before testing them in human clinical trials. Diarrhea can result from various causes, including infections, dietary factors, medications, and gastrointestinal disorders. Here's a detailed overview of the preclinical screening process for anti-diarrheal drugs:

1. **Animal Models of Diarrhea:**
    a. Researchers use various animal models to induce diarrhea, including administration of diarrheagenic agents such as castor oil, magnesium sulfate, or bacterial toxins (e.g., cholera toxin).
    b. Commonly used animals include mice, rats, rabbits, and occasionally larger animals like pigs or non-human primates.

2. **Assessment of Diarrheal Parameters:**
    a. Researchers assess various parameters related to diarrhea, including stool consistency, frequency, and volume, as well as changes in gastrointestinal transit time and fecal water content.
    b. Scoring systems are often used to quantify diarrhea severity and evaluate the efficacy of anti-diarrheal treatments.

3. **Mechanism of Action Studies:**
    a. Researchers investigate the mechanisms underlying the anti-diarrheal effects of potential drugs. These may include modulation of intestinal motility (e.g., through inhibition of smooth muscle contraction or stimulation of fluid absorption), blockade of intestinal ion channels or

transporters involved in fluid secretion, or targeting of inflammatory pathways.

b. Mechanistic studies help elucidate how anti-diarrheal drugs exert their effects and identify potential targets for drug development.

4. **Pharmacokinetic Studies:**

a. Researchers assess the pharmacokinetic properties of potential anti-diarrheal drugs, including absorption, distribution, metabolism, and excretion (ADME).

b. Pharmacokinetic studies help determine the bioavailability, half-life, and tissue distribution of anti-diarrheal compounds after administration via different routes (such as oral, intravenous, or rectal).

5. **Toxicology Studies:**

a. Preclinical toxicology studies evaluate the safety of potential anti-diarrheal drugs, including acute and chronic toxicity assessments.

b. Researchers assess potential adverse effects on vital organs, including the liver, kidneys, gastrointestinal tract, and cardiovascular system.

c. Toxicology studies also evaluate potential risks such as genotoxicity, carcinogenicity, and reproductive toxicity.

6. **Drug Interactions:**

a. Researchers investigate potential drug interactions between anti-diarrheal compounds and other medications commonly used in the management of diarrhea or other co-existing conditions.

b. Studies assess the pharmacokinetic and pharmacodynamic interactions to ensure safe and effective co-administration of anti-diarrheal drugs with other treatments.

7. **Regulatory Considerations:**

a. Preclinical data on the safety and efficacy of anti-diarrheal drugs are submitted to regulatory agencies as part of the drug approval process.

b. Regulatory authorities review preclinical data to assess the potential risks and benefits of anti-diarrheal drugs and determine whether they can proceed to clinical trials in humans.

Overall, preclinical screening in anti-diarrheal research provides valuable insights into the potential efficacy, safety, and mechanism of action of potential drugs for the prevention and treatment of diarrhea. These studies are essential for identifying promising candidates for further development as treatments for diarrheal diseases in humans.

LAXATIVES:

Preclinical screening for laxatives involves evaluating compounds or substances for their ability to promote bowel movements and relieve constipation in animal models before testing them in human clinical trials. Constipation can occur due to various factors, including dietary habits, medication side effects, neurological disorders, or gastrointestinal motility disorders. Here's a detailed overview of the preclinical screening process for laxatives:

1. **Animal Models of Constipation:**
   a. Researchers use various animal models to mimic constipation, including models of slow colonic transit, opioid-induced constipation, or dietary-induced constipation.
   b. Commonly used animals include mice, rats, guinea pigs, and rabbits, depending on the specific constipation model being studied.

2. **Assessment of Laxative Effects:**
   a. Researchers assess various parameters related to laxative effects, including fecal output, stool frequency, consistency, and transit time.

b. Methods such as fecal pellet counts, fecal water content measurements, and gastrointestinal transit assays are used to quantify laxative effects and evaluate the efficacy of potential treatments.

3. **Mechanism of Action Studies:**

   a. Researchers investigate the mechanisms underlying the laxative effects of potential drugs. These may include stimulation of gastrointestinal motility (e.g., through activation of enteric nerves or smooth muscle contraction), inhibition of water and electrolyte absorption in the colon, or lubrication of fecal material to facilitate passage.

   b. Mechanistic studies help elucidate how laxatives exert their effects and identify potential targets for drug development.

4. **Pharmacokinetic Studies:**

   a. Researchers assess the pharmacokinetic properties of potential laxatives, including absorption, distribution, metabolism, and excretion (ADME).

   b. Pharmacokinetic studies help determine the bioavailability, half-life, and tissue distribution of laxative compounds after administration via different routes (such as oral, rectal, or subcutaneous).

5. **Toxicology Studies:**

   a. Preclinical toxicology studies evaluate the safety of potential laxatives, including acute and chronic toxicity assessments.

   b. Researchers assess potential adverse effects on vital organs, including the liver, kidneys, gastrointestinal tract, and cardiovascular system.

   c. Toxicology studies also evaluate potential risks such as genotoxicity, carcinogenicity, and reproductive toxicity.

6. **Drug Interactions:**

a. Researchers investigate potential drug interactions between laxative compounds and other medications commonly used in the management of constipation or other co-existing conditions.

b. Studies assess the pharmacokinetic and pharmacodynamic interactions to ensure safe and effective co-administration of laxatives with other treatments.

7. Regulatory Considerations:

a. Preclinical data on the safety and efficacy of laxatives are submitted to regulatory agencies as part of the drug approval process.

b. Regulatory authorities review preclinical data to assess the potential risks and benefits of laxatives and determine whether they can proceed to clinical trials in humans.

Overall, preclinical screening in laxative research provides valuable insights into the potential efficacy, safety, and mechanism of action of potential drugs for the treatment of constipation. These studies are essential for identifying promising candidates for further development as treatments for constipation in humans.

MCQs

1. What is commonly used to induce acute inflammation in animal models for anti-inflammatory drug testing?

    A) Carrageenan

    B) Lipopolysaccharide (LPS)

    C) Freund's Adjuvant

    D) Tumor Necrosis Factor-alpha (TNF-alpha)

2. Which animal model is used for studying chronic inflammation and mimics conditions similar to rheumatoid arthritis?

A) Carrageenan-Induced Paw Edema

B) Freund's Adjuvant-Induced Arthritis

C) LPS-Induced Systemic Inflammation

D) Cytokine-Induced Inflammation

3. Which method is NOT commonly used to measure body temperature in animal studies for antipyretic drugs?

A) Rectal Temperature Measurement

B) Subcutaneous Temperature Probes

C) Optical Scanning

D) Infrared Thermography

4. What is the primary endpoint in evaluating antipyretic agents in preclinical studies?

A) Cytokine release

B) Inhibition of prostaglandin synthesis

C) Temperature reduction

D) Increase in activity levels

5. Which method is typically used to induce diarrhea in animal models for anti-diarrheal drug testing?

A) Castor oil administration

B) Carrageenan injection

C) Freund's Adjuvant

D) LPS injection

6. What is the main mechanism by which NSAIDs exert their antipyretic effects?

A) Inhibition of COX enzyme

B) Stimulation of serotonin receptors

C) Activation of GABA receptors

D) Modulation of dopamine pathways

7. Which technique is used to assess drug absorption in preclinical screening for gastrointestinal drugs?

    A) Caco-2 cell monolayers

    B) Infrared thermography

    C) Telemetry systems

    D) Optical density measurement

8. What is the purpose of using animal models like experimental autoimmune encephalomyelitis (EAE) in preclinical screening for anti-inflammatory drugs?

    A) To study bacterial infections

    B) To mimic human autoimmune conditions

    C) To evaluate fever reduction

    D) To measure neurotransmitter levels

9. In preclinical studies, what is a critical assessment for anti-ulcer drugs?

    A) Plasma cytokine levels

    B) Ulcer index

    C) Neuronal firing rates

    D) Skin temperature

10. Which of the following is NOT a primary focus of laxative preclinical studies?

    A) Enhancing mucosal protection

    B) Facilitating fecal passage

    C) Increasing stool frequency

    D) Reducing fever

11. What type of cell cultures are typically used in preclinical studies of respiratory pharmacology?

    A) Hepatocytes

    B) Lung epithelial cells

    C) Neurons

D) Keratinocytes

12. Which animal model is often used to mimic COPD in preclinical studies?

    A) Ovalbumin-induced asthma

    B) Cigarette smoke-induced COPD

    C) Collagen-induced arthritis

    D) LPS-induced inflammation

13. What is the primary focus of pharmacokinetic studies in respiratory pharmacology?

    A) Absorption, Distribution, Metabolism, and Excretion (ADME)

    B) DNA mutagenicity

    C) Protein binding capacity

    D) Allergic reaction potential

14. Which method assesses bronchodilator effects of drugs in vitro for anti-asthmatic drugs?

    A) Cell viability tests

    B) Contractility assays on smooth muscle cells

    C) Inflammation marker assays

    D) Cytokine profiling

15. What parameter is NOT commonly measured in safety assessments for respiratory drugs?

    A) Cardiac effects

    B) Respiratory depression

    C) Renal function

    D) Immunotoxicity

16. What type of toxicity studies might be conducted to evaluate chronic exposure to a respiratory drug candidate?

    A) Acute toxicity

    B) Chronic toxicity

    C) Sensitization studies

D) Genotoxicity

17. In preclinical testing for anti-allergic drugs, what is a typical in vitro assay used?

   A) IgE-mediated response assays

   B) Glucose tolerance tests

   C) Coagulation factor analysis

   D) Bone density tests

18. Which formulation is commonly developed for administering anti-asthmatic drugs?

   A) Oral tablets

   B) Transdermal patches

   C) Inhalers

   D) Subcutaneous injections

19. What is assessed in reproductive pharmacology studies focusing on antifertility agents?

   A) Ovulation inhibition

   B) Cardiac function

   C) Neurological function

   D) Renal clearance

20. What behavioral test is used to assess pain-related behavior in analgesic preclinical studies?

   A) Cognitive function tests

   B) Licking/biting responses

   C) Cardiovascular monitoring

   D) Weight tracking

Short Answer Type Questions

1. What induces acute inflammation in the Carrageenan-Induced Paw Edema model?

2. Describe a key characteristic of Freund's Adjuvant-Induced Arthritis in animal models.

3. How is systemic inflammation induced in preclinical studies for anti-inflammatory drugs?

4. What role do cytokines play in inflammation, as measured in anti-inflammatory drug testing?

5. Explain the importance of pharmacokinetic studies in the development of antipyretic agents.

6. How do NSAIDs typically reduce fever according to preclinical studies?

7. What is the significance of Caco-2 cell monolayers in gastrointestinal drug testing?

8. Why are experimental autoimmune models like EAE used in anti-inflammatory drug research?

9. What parameters are assessed in the evaluation of anti-ulcer drugs in preclinical studies?

10. What is a common method to induce diarrhea in preclinical studies for anti-diarrheal drugs?

11. What type of cells are commonly used in respiratory pharmacology in vitro studies?

12. Describe a common animal model used for studying COPD in preclinical trials.

13. What are the four main focuses of pharmacokinetic studies in drug development?

14. How do researchers assess the efficacy of anti-asthmatic drugs in preclinical studies?

15. What safety parameters are typically evaluated in the preclinical testing of respiratory drugs?

16. Why are chronic toxicity studies important in the development of respiratory drugs?

17. What role do IgE-mediated response assays play in the preclinical testing of anti-allergic drugs?

18. Which drug formulation is predominantly used for anti-asthmatic treatments and why?

19. What is the significance of evaluating ovulation inhibition in the development of antifertility agents?

20. What is measured in the formalin test used in analgesic drug testing?

Long Answer Type Questions

1. Discuss the various methods used to measure body temperature in animal studies during the evaluation of antipyretic drugs and their significance.

2. Describe the role of cytokine modulation in the mechanism of action for antipyretic agents, focusing on their impact on fever pathways.

3. Explain the process and importance of toxicology studies in the preclinical screening of gastrointestinal drugs.

4. Outline the steps involved in the pharmacokinetic assessment of anti-emetic drugs and how these studies contribute to drug development.

5. Discuss the use of animal models in the preclinical testing of anti-diarrheal drugs, focusing on how these models help determine the efficacy and safety of the drugs.

6. Explain the importance and methodologies of in vitro studies in the development of drugs for respiratory diseases.

7. Discuss the role and impact of pharmacokinetic studies in the formulation and development of respiratory pharmacology drugs.

8. Describe the process and significance of chronic toxicity studies in evaluating the long-term safety of respiratory drugs.

9. Outline the procedures and importance of IgE-mediated response assays in the development of anti-allergic medications.

10. Explain the various behavioral tests used in preclinical screening for analgesics and how they contribute to the understanding of drug efficacy and safety.

Answer Key for MCQs

1. (A) Carrageenan
2. (B) Freund's Adjuvant-Induced Arthritis
3. (C) Optical Scanning
4. (C) Temperature reduction
5. (A) Castor oil administration
6. (A) Inhibition of COX enzyme
7. (A) Caco-2 cell monolayers
8. (B) To mimic human autoimmune conditions
9. (B) Ulcer index
10. (B) Lung epithelial cells
11. (B) Cigarette smoke-induced COPD
12. (A) Absorption, Distribution, Metabolism, and Excretion (ADME)
13. (B) Contractility assays on smooth muscle cells
14. (C) Renal function
15. (B) Chronic toxicity
16. (A) IgE-mediated response assays
17. (C) Inhalers
18. (A) Ovulation inhibition
19. (B) Licking/biting responses

CHAPTER - 4

CARDIOVASCULAR PHARMACOLOGY:

In preclinical screening of new substances for cardiovascular pharmacological activity, researchers typically employ a variety of methods to assess efficacy, safety, and mechanisms of action. These methods include in vivo studies, in vitro experiments, and sometimes alternative animal models to mimic human cardiovascular physiology. Here's a breakdown of each approach:

1. **In Vivo Studies:**
   a. **Animal Models**: Commonly used animals include mice, rats, rabbits, dogs, and non-human primates. These animals can be subjected to various cardiovascular tests, such as electrocardiography (ECG), blood pressure measurement, echocardiography, and assessment of cardiac function under different conditions.
   b. **Endpoints**: Researchers measure parameters like heart rate, blood pressure, cardiac output, electrocardiographic changes, and histological changes in heart tissue.
   c. **Pharmacological Interventions**: Animals are administered the test substance, and their cardiovascular parameters are monitored to evaluate the drug's effects.

2. **In Vitro Experiments:**
   a. **Cell Culture Studies**: Cardiomyocytes, endothelial cells, smooth muscle cells, and fibroblasts can be cultured in vitro to study the direct effects of the test substance on these cells.
   b. **Isolated Tissue Preparations**: Researchers can use isolated heart muscle preparations (e.g., Langendorff-perfused heart) or blood vessel segments to assess the substance's effects on cardiac contractility, vascular tone, and endothelial function.

c. **Receptor Binding Assays**: These assays help understand the substance's interaction with specific cardiovascular receptors, providing insights into its mechanism of action.

3. **Alternative Models:**

    a. **Organ-on-a-Chip Technology**: Microfluidic devices can mimic the structure and function of human organs, including the heart and blood vessels, allowing for more physiologically relevant testing.

    b. **Computer Modeling and Simulation**: Computational models can simulate cardiovascular physiology and predict the effects of the test substance based on its pharmacological properties and interactions with biological targets.

    c. **Human-Derived Cells and Tissues**: Researchers sometimes use human-derived cells or tissues (such as induced pluripotent stem cell-derived cardiomyocytes) to study drug effects in a more human-relevant context.

Throughout these studies, researchers assess not only the pharmacological efficacy of the test substance but also its safety profile, including potential adverse effects on cardiovascular function. Data from preclinical screening inform decisions about the substance's advancement to clinical trials and provide valuable insights into its therapeutic potential and limitations.

ANTIHYPERTENSIVES:

In preclinical screening for antihypertensive drugs, researchers aim to identify compounds that effectively lower blood pressure while minimizing adverse effects. Here's a detailed overview of the methods and considerations involved:

1. In Vivo Studies:

a. **Animal Models**: Various animal models of hypertension are used, including spontaneously hypertensive rats (SHR), renovascular hypertensive models (e.g., renal artery ligation or constriction), deoxycorticosterone acetate (DOCA)-salt induced hypertension, and angiotensin II-induced hypertension models. These models mimic different aspects of human hypertension and allow researchers to study the effects of potential antihypertensive drugs.

b. **Endpoints**: Key endpoints in in vivo studies include blood pressure measurements via invasive (catheterization) or non-invasive (tail-cuff) methods. Other relevant endpoints include heart rate, cardiac output, renal function (e.g., glomerular filtration rate), and histological examination of target organs (e.g., heart, kidney, blood vessels).

c. **Pharmacological Interventions**: Animals are treated with the test substances, either acutely or chronically, and their blood pressure and other relevant parameters are monitored to assess efficacy and safety. This may involve single-dose studies to evaluate acute effects or chronic administration to assess long-term efficacy and potential adverse effects.

2. **In Vitro Experiments:**

a. **Cell Culture Studies**: Endothelial cells, vascular smooth muscle cells, and renal cells can be cultured to study the effects of potential antihypertensive drugs on cellular processes relevant to blood pressure regulation. This includes assessing vasodilation, vascular remodeling, and renin-angiotensin-aldosterone system (RAAS) activity.

b. **Vascular Reactivity Assays**: Isolated blood vessel segments are used to assess the vasodilatory or vasoconstrictive effects of test substances. This helps determine their potential to affect vascular tone and blood pressure regulation. Techniques such as wire myography allow precise measurement of vascular responses to various stimuli.

c. **Renal Perfusion Studies**: Isolated kidney preparations can be perfused to evaluate the effects of test substances on renal function and blood pressure regulation via the renin-angiotensin-aldosterone system (RAAS). This allows researchers to study the effects of potential drugs on renal blood flow, sodium excretion, and renin release.

d. **Mechanistic Studies**: Receptor binding assays and enzyme inhibition assays are used to elucidate the mechanisms of action of potential antihypertensive drugs. This includes studying their interactions with relevant receptors (e.g., angiotensin II receptors) or enzymes (e.g., ACE inhibitors) involved in blood pressure regulation.

3. Mechanistic Studies:

a. **Receptor Binding Assays**: Many antihypertensive drugs exert their effects by binding to specific receptors involved in blood pressure regulation. For example, angiotensin II receptor antagonists selectively block the angiotensin II type 1 (AT1) receptor. Receptor binding assays, such as radioligand binding assays or fluorescence polarization assays, are used to assess the affinity and selectivity of potential drugs for their target receptors.

b. **Enzyme Inhibition Assays**: Some antihypertensive drugs function by inhibiting enzymes involved in blood pressure regulation. For instance, angiotensin-converting enzyme (ACE) inhibitors block the conversion of angiotensin I to angiotensin II. Enzyme inhibition assays, such as fluorogenic substrate assays or colorimetric assays, are used to measure the potency and selectivity of potential inhibitors.

c. **Ion Channel Modulation**: Certain antihypertensive drugs act by modulating ion channels involved in vascular smooth muscle contraction and relaxation. For example, calcium channel blockers inhibit calcium influx into vascular smooth muscle cells, leading to vasodilation. Patch-clamp electrophysiology techniques are used to study the effects of potential drugs on ion channel currents and membrane potential.

d. **Second Messenger Pathways**: Many signaling pathways are involved in blood pressure regulation, including cyclic adenosine monophosphate (cAMP), cyclic guanosine monophosphate (cGMP), and intracellular calcium signaling. Mechanistic studies assess how potential antihypertensive drugs modulate these pathways and downstream cellular responses using techniques such as Western blotting, ELISA, and immunohistochemistry.

4. **Safety Pharmacology:**

a. **Cardiovascular Safety**: Antihypertensive drugs can affect cardiovascular parameters beyond blood pressure regulation, including heart rate, cardiac contractility, and electrocardiographic parameters. Safety pharmacology studies assess the effects of potential drugs on these cardiovascular parameters using telemetry systems, electrocardiography (ECG), echocardiography, and hemodynamic monitoring.

b. **Renal Function**: Antihypertensive drugs often impact renal function, including glomerular filtration rate (GFR), renal blood flow, and electrolyte excretion. Safety pharmacology studies evaluate the effects of potential drugs on renal function using techniques such as renal clearance studies, urine output measurements, and assessment of electrolyte balance.

c. **Central Nervous System Effects**: Some antihypertensive drugs can cross the blood-brain barrier and affect central nervous system function, leading to potential CNS-related adverse effects such as dizziness, sedation, or cognitive impairment. Safety pharmacology studies assess the potential CNS effects of drugs using behavioral assays, neuroimaging techniques, and neurological examinations.

d. **Metabolic Effects**: Antihypertensive drugs may impact metabolic parameters such as glucose and lipid metabolism, potentially leading to adverse metabolic effects such as hyperglycemia or dyslipidemia. Safety pharmacology studies evaluate the metabolic effects of drugs using biochemical assays, metabolic profiling techniques, and glucose tolerance tests.

Throughout preclinical screening, researchers aim to identify compounds with potent antihypertensive effects, favorable pharmacokinetic properties, and an acceptable safety profile. Data from these studies inform the selection of lead compounds for further development and provide insights into their potential clinical utility in treating hypertension.

ANTIARRYTHMICS:

In preclinical screening for antiarrhythmic drugs, researchers focus on identifying compounds that can prevent or terminate cardiac arrhythmias effectively while minimizing proarrhythmic risks and adverse effects. Here's a detailed overview of the methods and considerations involved:

1. **In Vivo Studies:**

a. **Animal Models**: Various animal models of arrhythmias are used, including drug-induced arrhythmias, electrical stimulation-induced arrhythmias, and genetically modified models of arrhythmogenic diseases (e.g., long QT syndrome, Brugada syndrome). These models mimic different aspects of human arrhythmias and allow researchers to study the effects of potential antiarrhythmic drugs.

b. **Endpoints**: Key endpoints in in vivo studies include electrocardiographic (ECG) parameters such as heart rate, QT interval, QRS duration, and arrhythmia incidence (e.g., ventricular tachycardia, ventricular fibrillation). Hemodynamic parameters such as blood pressure and cardiac contractility may also be assessed.

c. **Pharmacological Interventions**: Animals are treated with the test substances, either acutely or chronically, and their ECG parameters and arrhythmia incidence are monitored to assess efficacy and safety. This may involve single-dose studies to evaluate acute effects or chronic administration to assess long-term efficacy and potential adverse effects.

2. **In Vitro Experiments:**

   a. **Cardiomyocyte Culture Studies**: Primary cardiomyocytes or cardiomyocyte cell lines are cultured to study the effects of potential antiarrhythmic drugs on cellular electrophysiology. Patch-clamp electrophysiology techniques are used to measure action potentials and ion channel currents, providing insights into the drug's effects on cardiac ion channels and membrane excitability.

   b. **Isolated Heart Preparations**: Isolated heart preparations, such as Langendorff-perfused hearts or working heart preparations, are used to study the effects of potential antiarrhythmic drugs on cardiac electrophysiology and contractility in a controlled environment. These studies allow researchers to assess drug effects on arrhythmia susceptibility and cardiac function.

   c. **Arrhythmia Models**: In vitro models of arrhythmias, such as reentrant circuits in cardiac tissue slices or induced arrhythmias in engineered cardiac constructs, can be used to study the mechanisms of arrhythmia initiation and termination and evaluate the efficacy of potential antiarrhythmic drugs in preventing or terminating arrhythmias.

d. **Mechanistic Studies**: In vitro studies help elucidate the mechanisms of action of potential antiarrhythmic drugs, including their effects on cardiac ion channels (e.g., sodium channels, potassium channels, calcium channels), intracellular signaling pathways (e.g., cyclic nucleotide signaling), and cardiac tissue excitability.

3. Mechanistic Studies:

a. **Ion Channel Effects**: Antiarrhythmic drugs often exert their effects by modulating cardiac ion channels. Mechanistic studies aim to elucidate these effects, such as blocking sodium channels (class I agents), prolonging action potential duration by blocking potassium channels (class III agents), or inhibiting calcium channels (class IV agents). Techniques like patch-clamp electrophysiology are used to measure ion channel currents and action potentials in isolated cardiomyocytes or cell lines.

b. **Action Potential Duration (APD) Prolongation**: Some antiarrhythmic drugs target repolarization mechanisms, prolonging the action potential duration and refractory period. Studies evaluate APD changes induced by drugs using voltage-sensitive dyes, patch-clamp recordings, or microelectrode techniques in cardiac tissues or isolated cells.

c. **Reentry Inhibition**: Antiarrhythmic drugs may prevent reentrant arrhythmias by slowing conduction velocity or increasing refractoriness. Mechanistic studies assess drug effects on reentry using tissue preparations (e.g., Langendorff-perfused hearts) or computer simulations to model arrhythmia mechanisms and predict drug efficacy.

d. **Arrhythmia Models:** Various in vitro and in vivo models are used to study arrhythmia mechanisms and drug effects. These include induced arrhythmia models (e.g., pacing-induced arrhythmias, ischemia-reperfusion models) and genetically modified animal models of arrhythmogenic diseases (e.g., long QT syndrome, catecholaminergic polymorphic ventricular tachycardia).

4. Safety Pharmacology:

a. **Proarrhythmic Risk Assessment**: Antiarrhythmic drugs may have proarrhythmic potential, increasing the risk of arrhythmias or exacerbating existing arrhythmias. Safety pharmacology studies evaluate the proarrhythmic risk of drugs using in vitro assays (e.g., hERG channel assays, action potential duration assays) and in vivo models (e.g., QT prolongation studies, arrhythmia induction assays).

b. **Cardiovascular Safety**: Safety pharmacology studies assess the cardiovascular safety profile of antiarrhythmic drugs, including effects on cardiac contractility, hemodynamics, and conduction parameters. Techniques such as telemetry, echocardiography, and ECG monitoring are used to evaluate these parameters in animal models.

c. **Off-Target Effects**: Antiarrhythmic drugs may have off-target effects on non-cardiac tissues or organ systems, leading to adverse effects. Safety pharmacology studies assess potential off-target effects on respiratory, central nervous, and gastrointestinal systems, as well as hepatic and renal function.

d. **Metabolic Effects**: Some antiarrhythmic drugs may impact metabolic parameters such as glucose and lipid metabolism. Safety pharmacology studies evaluate drug effects on metabolic parameters using biochemical assays, metabolic profiling, and glucose tolerance tests.

Throughout preclinical screening, researchers aim to identify compounds with potent antiarrhythmic effects, a favorable safety profile, and minimal proarrhythmic risks. Data from these studies inform the selection of lead compounds for further development and provide insights into their potential clinical utility in treating cardiac arrhythmias.

ANTIANGINAL:

In preclinical screening for antianginal drugs, researchers aim to identify compounds that can effectively relieve angina symptoms by improving myocardial oxygen supply or reducing myocardial oxygen demand. Here's a detailed overview of the methods and considerations involved:

1. **In Vivo Studies:**
   a. **Animal Models:** Various animal models of angina are used, including models of myocardial ischemia induced by coronary artery ligation, constriction, or occlusion, as well as models of microvascular dysfunction. These models replicate different aspects of human angina and allow researchers to study the effects of potential antianginal drugs.

   b. **Endpoints**: Key endpoints in in vivo studies include assessment of myocardial ischemia, such as electrocardiographic (ECG) changes indicative of myocardial infarction or ischemia (ST-segment elevation or depression), changes in hemodynamic parameters (blood pressure, heart rate), and evaluation of exercise tolerance using treadmill or exercise wheel tests.

   c. **Pharmacological Interventions**: Animals are treated with the test substances, either acutely or chronically, and their myocardial ischemia and exercise tolerance are monitored to assess efficacy and safety. This may involve single-dose studies to evaluate acute effects or chronic administration to assess long-term efficacy and potential adverse effects.

2. **In Vitro Experiments:**

   a. **Cardiomyocyte Culture Studies**: Primary cardiomyocytes or cardiomyocyte cell lines are cultured to study the effects of potential antianginal drugs on cellular processes such as contractility, oxygen consumption, and metabolism. High-throughput assays, such as Seahorse XF Analyzer, are used to measure cellular respiration and mitochondrial function.

   b. **Coronary Artery Vasoreactivity Assays**: Isolated coronary artery segments are used to assess the vasodilatory effects of potential antianginal drugs on coronary circulation. Wire myography techniques allow precise measurement of vascular responses to various stimuli, including endothelium-dependent and -independent vasodilators.

   c. **Ischemia-Reperfusion Models**: In vitro models of ischemia-reperfusion injury, using isolated perfused hearts or cardiac tissue slices, can be used to study the effects of potential antianginal drugs on myocardial injury, arrhythmias, and recovery of cardiac function following ischemic insult.

   d. **Mechanistic Studies**: In vitro studies help elucidate the mechanisms of action of potential antianginal drugs, including their effects on cardiac ion channels (e.g., calcium channels, potassium channels), endothelial function, oxidative stress, and myocardial metabolism.

3. **Mechanistic Studies:**

   a. **Effects on Coronary Circulation**: Antianginal drugs primarily aim to improve myocardial perfusion by dilating coronary arteries or increasing coronary blood flow. Mechanistic studies investigate the effects of these drugs on coronary vascular tone, endothelial function, and microvascular circulation using techniques such as isolated vessel studies, coronary angiography, and microcirculation imaging.

b. **Modulation of Cardiac Ion Channels**: Many antianginal drugs exert their effects by modulating cardiac ion channels, particularly calcium channels and potassium channels. Mechanistic studies use patch-clamp electrophysiology techniques to measure drug effects on ion channel currents and action potentials in isolated cardiomyocytes or recombinant cell lines expressing specific ion channels.

c. **Myocardial Oxygen Consumption**: Antianginal drugs aim to reduce myocardial oxygen demand by decreasing heart rate, contractility, or afterload. Mechanistic studies assess the effects of these drugs on myocardial oxygen consumption using techniques such as oxygen consumption measurements in isolated hearts or cardiomyocytes, and metabolic flux analysis.

d. **Myocardial Metabolism**: Some antianginal drugs exert their effects by altering myocardial metabolism, such as increasing glucose utilization or shifting substrate preference from fatty acids to glucose. Mechanistic studies investigate the effects of these drugs on myocardial metabolism using techniques such as metabolomics, radiotracer imaging, and metabolic flux analysis.

4. Safety Pharmacology:

a. **Cardiovascular Safety**: Safety pharmacology studies evaluate the cardiovascular safety profile of antianginal drugs, including effects on heart rate, blood pressure, cardiac contractility, and conduction parameters. Techniques such as telemetry, echocardiography, and electrocardiography (ECG) are used to monitor cardiovascular parameters in animal models.

b. **Arrhythmogenic Potential**: Some antianginal drugs may have proarrhythmic effects, increasing the risk of arrhythmias. Safety pharmacology studies assess the proarrhythmic risk of drugs using in vitro assays (e.g., hERG channel assays, action potential duration assays) and in vivo models (e.g., QT prolongation studies, arrhythmia induction assays).

c. **Hemodynamic Effects**: Antianginal drugs may cause hemodynamic effects such as hypotension or fluid retention, particularly in patients with heart failure. Safety pharmacology studies evaluate the hemodynamic effects of drugs using techniques such as blood pressure monitoring, echocardiography, and invasive hemodynamic measurements.

d. **Off-Target Effects:** Safety pharmacology studies assess potential off-target effects of antianginal drugs on non-cardiovascular systems, including respiratory, central nervous, gastrointestinal, and renal systems. These studies aim to identify potential adverse effects and inform safety considerations in drug development.

Throughout preclinical screening, researchers aim to identify compounds with potent antianginal effects, a favorable safety profile, and minimal adverse effects. Data from these studies inform the selection of lead compounds for further development and provide insights into their potential clinical utility in treating angina pectoris.

ANTIATHEROSCLEROTIC AGENTS:

In preclinical screening for antiatherosclerotic agents, researchers focus on identifying compounds that can prevent or reverse the progression of atherosclerosis, a chronic inflammatory disease characterized by the accumulation of lipid-rich plaques in the arterial walls. Here's a detailed overview of the methods and considerations involved:

1. **In Vivo Studies:**

    a. **Animal Models**: Various animal models of atherosclerosis are used, including genetically modified models (e.g., ApoE-deficient mice, LDL receptor-deficient mice), dietary-induced models (e.g., high-fat diet-fed rabbits or pigs), and vascular injury models (e.g., wire injury or balloon injury). These models mimic different aspects of human atherosclerosis and allow researchers to study the effects of potential antiatherosclerotic agents.

    b. **Endpoints**: Key endpoints in in vivo studies include assessment of atherosclerotic lesion size and composition, lipid profiles (total cholesterol, LDL cholesterol, HDL cholesterol, triglycerides), inflammatory markers (e.g., cytokines, adhesion molecules), and endothelial function. Techniques such as histological staining, immunohistochemistry, and quantitative image analysis are used to evaluate atherosclerotic lesions.

    c. **Pharmacological Interventions**: Animals are treated with the test substances, either prophylactically or therapeutically, and their atherosclerotic lesion development, lipid profiles, and inflammatory markers are monitored to assess efficacy and safety. This may involve short-term studies to evaluate acute effects or long-term studies to assess chronic administration and potential adverse effects.

2. **In Vitro Experiments:**

    a. **Cell Culture Studies**: Endothelial cells, vascular smooth muscle cells, macrophages, and foam cells are cultured to study the effects of potential antiatherosclerotic agents on cellular processes such as endothelial function, vascular inflammation, foam cell formation, and cholesterol efflux. Techniques such as ELISA, qPCR, and immunocytochemistry are used to assess cellular responses.

b. **Foam Cell Formation Assays**: Macrophages are exposed to oxidized LDL or other atherogenic stimuli to induce foam cell formation, a key process in atherosclerosis. Potential antiatherosclerotic agents are added to assess their ability to inhibit foam cell formation and promote cholesterol efflux using techniques such as Oil Red O staining and cholesterol efflux assays.

c. **Endothelial Function Assays**: Endothelial cells are cultured or isolated endothelial function is assessed to study the effects of potential antiatherosclerotic agents on endothelial function, including vasodilation, nitric oxide production, and adhesion molecule expression. Techniques such as flow-mediated dilation assays and cell adhesion assays are used to evaluate endothelial function.

d. **Inflammatory Marker Assays**: Inflammatory markers such as cytokines, chemokines, and adhesion molecules play a key role in atherosclerosis. Potential antiatherosclerotic agents are assessed for their effects on inflammatory marker expression using techniques such as ELISA, multiplex cytokine assays, and flow cytometry.

3. **Mechanistic Studies:**

a. **Lipid Metabolism:** Antiatherosclerotic agents often target lipid metabolism to reduce the accumulation of atherogenic lipoproteins, such as low-density lipoprotein (LDL) cholesterol, within the arterial wall. Mechanistic studies investigate the effects of these agents on lipid metabolism, including inhibition of cholesterol synthesis, promotion of reverse cholesterol transport, and modulation of lipoprotein particle size and composition.

b. **Inflammation:** Chronic inflammation plays a critical role in the development and progression of atherosclerosis. Mechanistic studies assess the effects of antiatherosclerotic agents on inflammatory pathways, including inhibition of cytokine production, suppression of inflammatory cell recruitment and activation, and modulation of inflammatory signaling cascades (e.g., NF-κB, MAPK).

c. **Endothelial Function**: Endothelial dysfunction is an early event in atherosclerosis and contributes to plaque formation and progression. Mechanistic studies investigate the effects of antiatherosclerotic agents on endothelial function, including enhancement of nitric oxide bioavailability, reduction of oxidative stress, and inhibition of endothelial activation and dysfunction.

d. **Vascular Smooth Muscle Cell (VSMC) Proliferation and Migration**: Vascular smooth muscle cell proliferation and migration contribute to the development of atherosclerotic lesions and plaque instability. Mechanistic studies assess the effects of antiatherosclerotic agents on VSMC proliferation and migration, including inhibition of growth factor signaling pathways and modulation of extracellular matrix remodeling.

4. Safety Pharmacology:

a. **Cardiovascular Safety**: Safety pharmacology studies evaluate the cardiovascular safety profile of antiatherosclerotic agents, including effects on heart rate, blood pressure, cardiac contractility, and electrocardiographic parameters. Techniques such as telemetry, echocardiography, and electrocardiography (ECG) are used to monitor cardiovascular parameters in animal models.

b. **Hepatotoxicity:** Many antiatherosclerotic agents target lipid metabolism and may affect hepatic function. Safety pharmacology studies assess the potential for hepatotoxicity, including effects on liver enzymes, histopathological changes in liver tissue, and markers of liver injury (e.g., bilirubin, alkaline phosphatase).

c. **Renal Function**: Some antiatherosclerotic agents may affect renal function, particularly those that target the renin-angiotensin-aldosterone system (RAAS). Safety pharmacology studies evaluate the effects of drugs on renal function, including glomerular filtration rate, renal blood flow, and markers of renal injury (e.g., creatinine, blood urea nitrogen).

d. **Off-Target Effects**: Safety pharmacology studies assess potential off-target effects of antiatherosclerotic agents on non-cardiovascular systems, including respiratory, central nervous, gastrointestinal, and endocrine systems. These studies aim to identify potential adverse effects and inform safety considerations in drug development.

Throughout preclinical screening, researchers aim to identify compounds with potent antiatherosclerotic effects, favorable safety profiles, and minimal adverse effects. Data from these studies inform the selection of lead compounds for further development and provide insights into their potential clinical utility in preventing or treating atherosclerosis and its complications.

DIURETICS:

In preclinical screening for diuretics, researchers focus on identifying compounds that can effectively increase urine production and reduce fluid retention, thereby lowering blood pressure and relieving symptoms associated with conditions like hypertension, heart failure, and edema. Here's a detailed overview of the methods and considerations involved:

1. **In Vivo Studies:**

    a. **Animal Models**: Various animal models are used to evaluate the efficacy and safety of diuretics, including rodents (rats and mice) and larger animals (e.g., dogs, pigs). These models may involve inducing volume overload through methods such as salt loading or infusion of hypertonic solutions to mimic conditions like heart failure or hypertension.

b. **Endpoints**: Key endpoints in in vivo studies include changes in urine output, electrolyte balance (sodium, potassium, chloride), blood pressure, cardiac function, and body weight. These endpoints help assess the diuretic effect, hemodynamic effects, and potential adverse effects of diuretic treatment.

c. **Pharmacological Interventions**: Animals are treated with the test diuretic agents, and their urine output, electrolyte excretion, and hemodynamic parameters are monitored over time. Chronic studies may involve prolonged treatment to assess long-term efficacy and potential adverse effects such as electrolyte imbalances or renal dysfunction.

2. **In Vitro Experiments:**
   a. **Cell Culture Studies**: Renal epithelial cell lines (e.g., MDCK, HEK293) or primary cultures of renal tubular cells can be used to study the mechanisms of action of diuretics at the cellular level. These studies help elucidate the effects of diuretics on ion transporters (e.g., sodium channels, sodium-potassium ATPase) and water permeability in renal tubular cells.

   b. **Isolated Kidney Preparations**: Isolated kidney perfusion studies allow researchers to directly assess the effects of diuretics on renal function in a controlled environment. Techniques such as isolated perfused kidney or isolated tubule preparations can be used to measure changes in urine flow rate, electrolyte excretion, and renal blood flow in response to diuretic treatment.

c. **Ion Transport Assays**: Diuretics exert their effects by interfering with ion transport processes in the kidney, such as sodium reabsorption in the renal tubules. In vitro assays using membrane vesicles or isolated membrane fractions can be used to assess the inhibitory effects of diuretics on specific ion transporters (e.g., sodium-hydrogen exchanger, sodium-chloride symporter).

d. **In Silico Modeling**: Computational modeling approaches, such as physiologically based pharmacokinetic (PBPK) modeling and systems pharmacology modeling, can be used to simulate the pharmacokinetics and pharmacodynamics of diuretics and predict their effects on renal function and fluid-electrolyte balance.

3. **Mechanistic Studies:**

a. **Ion Transport Mechanisms**: Diuretics exert their effects by modulating ion transport mechanisms in the kidney. Mechanistic studies aim to elucidate these mechanisms, including inhibition of sodium reabsorption in the renal tubules. For example, thiazide diuretics inhibit the sodium-chloride symporter (NCC) in the distal convoluted tubule, while loop diuretics inhibit the sodium-potassium-chloride cotransporter (NKCC2) in the thick ascending limb of the loop of Henle.

b. **Effects on Renal Hemodynamics**: Some diuretics, such as loop diuretics, may also affect renal hemodynamics by increasing renal blood flow and glomerular filtration rate. Mechanistic studies investigate the effects of diuretics on renal blood flow autoregulation, renal vascular resistance, and tubuloglomerular feedback mechanisms.

c. **Electrolyte Handling**: Diuretics can alter electrolyte balance by increasing urinary excretion of sodium, potassium, chloride, and water. Mechanistic studies assess the effects of diuretics on electrolyte transporters and channels in the kidney, such as the epithelial sodium channel (ENaC), potassium channels, and the aquaporin water channels.

d. **Renin-Angiotensin-Aldosterone System (RAAS) Modulation**: Some diuretics, such as thiazide diuretics, may also modulate the activity of the renin-angiotensin-aldosterone system. Mechanistic studies investigate the effects of diuretics on aldosterone secretion, angiotensin II levels, and RAAS-mediated sodium reabsorption in the kidney.

4. Safety Pharmacology:

a. **Electrolyte Imbalance:** Diuretics can lead to electrolyte imbalances, such as hypokalemia (with loop and thiazide diuretics), hyperkalemia (with potassium-sparing diuretics), hyponatremia, and hypomagnesemia. Safety pharmacology studies evaluate the effects of diuretics on electrolyte balance in animal models and assess strategies to mitigate electrolyte disturbances.

b. **Hemodynamic Effects**: Diuretics can cause changes in blood pressure, particularly in individuals with heart failure or hypertension. Safety pharmacology studies assess the hemodynamic effects of diuretics, including changes in blood pressure, heart rate, and cardiac contractility, using telemetry, echocardiography, and invasive hemodynamic measurements.

c. **Renal Function**: Diuretics can affect renal function, particularly in patients with impaired renal function or volume depletion. Safety pharmacology studies evaluate the effects of diuretics on renal function parameters such as glomerular filtration rate, renal blood flow, and markers of renal injury (e.g., serum creatinine, blood urea nitrogen).

d. **Drug Interactions**: Diuretics may interact with other medications, such as antihypertensive drugs, nonsteroidal anti-inflammatory drugs (NSAIDs), and certain antibiotics. Safety pharmacology studies assess potential drug interactions and their impact on efficacy and safety profiles of diuretics in combination therapy.

Throughout preclinical screening, researchers aim to identify compounds with potent diuretic effects, a favorable safety profile, and minimal adverse effects on electrolyte balance and renal function. Data from these studies inform the selection of lead compounds for further development and provide insights into their potential clinical utility in managing cardiovascular and renal conditions characterized by fluid retention.

DRUGS FOR METABOLIC DISORDERS

In preclinical screening for drugs targeting metabolic disorders, researchers focus on identifying compounds that can modulate key metabolic pathways involved in conditions such as diabetes, obesity, dyslipidemia, and metabolic syndrome. Here's a detailed overview of the methods and considerations involved:

1. **In Vivo Studies:**
   a. **Animal Models**: Various animal models of metabolic disorders, including genetically modified mice, diet-induced obesity models, and insulin-resistant models, are commonly used. These models mimic different aspects of human metabolic diseases and allow researchers to study the effects of potential therapeutic agents.
   b. **Endpoints**: Measurement of glucose metabolism parameters (e.g., fasting blood glucose, insulin sensitivity), lipid profiles (e.g., cholesterol, triglycerides), body weight, adiposity, and markers of inflammation and oxidative stress.

c. **Pharmacological Interventions**: Animals are treated with the test substances, and their metabolic parameters, including glucose and lipid metabolism, body composition, and insulin sensitivity, are monitored to assess efficacy and safety.

2. **In Vitro Experiments:**

   a. **Cell Culture Studies**: Adipocytes, hepatocytes, myocytes, and pancreatic beta cells can be cultured to study the effects of potential metabolic drugs on cellular processes such as glucose uptake, lipid metabolism, insulin signaling, and hormone secretion.

   b. **Mitochondrial Function Assays**: Mitochondrial dysfunction is implicated in various metabolic disorders. Assays measuring mitochondrial respiration, ATP production, and reactive oxygen species (ROS) generation help evaluate the effects of test substances on mitochondrial function.

   c. **Adipogenesis and Lipogenesis Assays**: Adipocyte differentiation and lipid accumulation assays are used to assess the effects of potential drugs on adipose tissue development and lipid storage.

3. **Mechanistic Studies:**

   a. **Insulin Sensitization**: Drugs targeting insulin signaling pathways, such as insulin sensitizers or insulin receptor agonists, are evaluated for their ability to improve insulin sensitivity and glucose uptake in insulin-resistant tissues.

   b. **Glucose Regulation**: Compounds that modulate glucose metabolism pathways, such as glucagon-like peptide-1 (GLP-1) receptor agonists or sodium-glucose cotransporter 2 (SGLT2) inhibitors, are assessed for their effects on glucose homeostasis and glycemic control.

   c. **Lipid Metabolism**: Agents targeting lipid metabolism, including lipase inhibitors, peroxisome proliferator-activated receptor (PPAR) agonists, or cholesterol absorption inhibitors, are evaluated for their effects on lipid levels and lipid-related parameters.

4. **Safety Pharmacology:**

   a. **Hepatic and Renal Function**: Potential adverse effects on liver and kidney function, especially for drugs targeting lipid metabolism, are evaluated to ensure the drug's safety profile.

   b. **Cardiovascular Effects**: Metabolic drugs can impact cardiovascular risk factors such as blood pressure, heart rate, and vascular function. Their effects on cardiovascular parameters and potential cardiovascular safety are assessed.

Throughout preclinical screening, researchers aim to identify compounds with potent metabolic effects, favorable safety profiles, and minimal adverse effects. Data from these studies inform the selection of lead compounds for further development and provide insights into their potential clinical utility in managing metabolic disorders.

ANTI-DIABETIC:

In preclinical screening for anti-diabetic drugs, researchers focus on identifying compounds that can effectively lower blood glucose levels, improve insulin sensitivity, and mitigate complications associated with diabetes mellitus. Here's a detailed overview of the methods and considerations involved:

1. **In Vivo Studies:**

   a. **Animal Models**: Various animal models of diabetes are used, including genetically modified models (e.g., db/db mice, ob/ob mice, Zucker diabetic fatty rats), chemically induced models (e.g., streptozotocin-induced diabetes), and diet-induced models (e.g., high-fat diet-induced insulin resistance). These models mimic different aspects of human diabetes and allow researchers to study the effects of potential anti-diabetic drugs.

b. **Endpoints:** Key endpoints in in vivo studies include blood glucose levels (fasting glucose, glucose tolerance tests), insulin sensitivity (insulin tolerance tests, hyperinsulinemic-euglycemic clamp), glycated hemoglobin (HbA1c), lipid profiles (total cholesterol, triglycerides), and body weight. These endpoints help assess the anti-diabetic effects, metabolic parameters, and potential adverse effects of drug treatment.

c. **Pharmacological Interventions**: Animals are treated with the test anti-diabetic agents, and their metabolic parameters, glucose homeostasis, and insulin sensitivity are monitored over time. Chronic studies may involve prolonged treatment to assess long-term efficacy and potential adverse effects such as hypoglycemia or weight gain.

2. **In Vitro Experiments:**

a. **Cell Culture Studies**: Pancreatic beta-cell lines (e.g., INS-1, MIN6) or primary cultures of pancreatic islets are used to study the effects of potential anti-diabetic drugs on insulin secretion, beta-cell proliferation, and beta-cell survival. These studies help elucidate the mechanisms of action of drugs on pancreatic function and glucose homeostasis.

b. **Adipocyte Culture Studies**: Adipocyte cell lines or primary cultures of adipocytes are used to study the effects of potential anti-diabetic drugs on adipocyte differentiation, adipokine secretion (e.g., adiponectin, leptin), and lipid metabolism. These studies help assess the effects of drugs on adipose tissue function and insulin sensitivity.

c. **Muscle Cell Culture Studies**: Skeletal muscle cell lines or primary cultures of myocytes are used to study the effects of potential anti-diabetic drugs on glucose uptake, glycogen synthesis, and mitochondrial function. These studies help assess the effects of drugs on skeletal muscle metabolism and insulin sensitivity.

d. **Hepatocyte Culture Studies**: Hepatocyte cell lines or primary cultures of hepatocytes are used to study the effects of potential anti-diabetic drugs on hepatic glucose production, lipid metabolism, and insulin signaling. These studies help assess the effects of drugs on hepatic glucose homeostasis and lipid accumulation.

3. Mechanistic Studies:

a. **Insulin Sensitization**: Many anti-diabetic drugs work by improving insulin sensitivity in target tissues, such as skeletal muscle, adipose tissue, and liver. Mechanistic studies aim to elucidate the molecular mechanisms underlying insulin sensitization, including activation of insulin signaling pathways (e.g., PI3K-Akt pathway), modulation of glucose transporter expression (e.g., GLUT4), and inhibition of pro-inflammatory pathways (e.g., JNK-IRS1 pathway).

b. **Pancreatic β-Cell Function**: Some anti-diabetic drugs enhance pancreatic β-cell function and insulin secretion. Mechanistic studies investigate the effects of these drugs on β-cell survival, proliferation, and insulin granule exocytosis. This may involve studying intracellular signaling pathways (e.g., cAMP-PKA pathway, calcium signaling) and transcription factors (e.g., PDX-1, MafA) involved in β-cell function.

c. **Glucose Homeostasis**: Anti-diabetic drugs target various processes involved in glucose homeostasis, including hepatic glucose production, intestinal glucose absorption, and renal glucose reabsorption. Mechanistic studies assess the effects of drugs on these processes using in vitro assays (e.g., hepatocyte cultures, intestinal epithelial cell cultures) and animal models.

d. **Inflammation and Metabolic Dysregulation**: Chronic low-grade inflammation and metabolic dysregulation play key roles in the pathogenesis of type 2 diabetes. Mechanistic studies investigate the effects of anti-diabetic drugs on inflammatory signaling pathways (e.g., NF-κB, JNK) and adipokine secretion (e.g., adiponectin, leptin) to improve metabolic health and insulin sensitivity.

4. **Safety Pharmacology:**

   a. **Hypoglycemia**: One of the most significant safety concerns with anti-diabetic drugs is hypoglycemia, especially in patients on intensive glycemic control regimens. Safety pharmacology studies assess the risk of hypoglycemia associated with anti-diabetic drugs using animal models and in vitro assays to evaluate drug effects on glucose sensing, counter-regulatory hormone secretion, and glycemic response to fasting or glucose challenge.

   b. **Cardiovascular Safety**: Given the high prevalence of cardiovascular disease in patients with diabetes, safety pharmacology studies evaluate the cardiovascular safety profile of anti-diabetic drugs. This includes assessing effects on blood pressure, heart rate, cardiac function, and arrhythmia risk using telemetry, echocardiography, and electrocardiography in animal models.

   c. **Renal Safety**: Some anti-diabetic drugs may have adverse effects on renal function, particularly in patients with pre-existing renal impairment. Safety pharmacology studies assess renal function parameters such as glomerular filtration rate, renal blood flow, and markers of renal injury (e.g., serum creatinine, blood urea nitrogen) to ensure renal safety of anti-diabetic drugs.

   d. **Hepatotoxicity**: Liver function may be affected by certain anti-diabetic drugs, especially those metabolized by the liver or associated with hepatic steatosis. Safety pharmacology studies evaluate markers of hepatotoxicity, liver enzymes, and histopathological changes in liver tissue to assess hepatic safety of anti-diabetic drugs.

Throughout preclinical screening, researchers aim to identify compounds with potent anti-diabetic effects, favorable safety profiles, and minimal adverse effects. Data from these studies inform the selection of lead compounds for further development and provide insights into their potential clinical utility in managing diabetes mellitus and its complications.

ANTIDYSLIPIDEMIC AGENTS:

In preclinical screening for antidyslipidemic agents, researchers aim to identify compounds that can effectively lower lipid levels in the blood, particularly cholesterol and triglycerides, and mitigate the risk of cardiovascular diseases associated with dyslipidemia. Here's a detailed overview of the methods and considerations involved:

1. **In Vivo Studies:**

   a. **Animal Models**: Various animal models of dyslipidemia are used, including genetically modified models (e.g., ApoE-deficient mice, LDL receptor-deficient mice), diet-induced models (e.g., high-fat diet-fed rabbits, pigs), and transgenic models (e.g., mice overexpressing human PCSK9). These models mimic different aspects of human dyslipidemia and allow researchers to study the effects of potential antidyslipidemic agents.

   b. **Endpoints**: Key endpoints in in vivo studies include changes in lipid profiles (total cholesterol, LDL cholesterol, HDL cholesterol, triglycerides), atherosclerotic lesion size and composition, inflammatory markers (e.g., cytokines, adhesion molecules), and cardiovascular outcomes (e.g., atherosclerosis progression, plaque stability). These endpoints help assess the lipid-lowering effects, anti-inflammatory effects, and cardiovascular benefits of antidyslipidemic agents.

c. **Pharmacological Interventions**: Animals are treated with the test antidyslipidemic agents, and their lipid profiles, atherosclerotic burden, and cardiovascular outcomes are monitored over time. Chronic studies may involve prolonged treatment to assess long-term efficacy and potential adverse effects such as hepatotoxicity or myopathy.

2. In Vitro Experiments:

a. **Hepatocyte Culture Studies**: Hepatocyte cell lines or primary cultures of hepatocytes are used to study the effects of potential antidyslipidemic agents on hepatic lipid metabolism, including cholesterol synthesis, uptake, and secretion. These studies help assess the effects of drugs on hepatic cholesterol homeostasis and triglyceride metabolism.

b. **Macrophage Foam Cell Formation Assays**: Macrophages are exposed to oxidized LDL or other atherogenic stimuli to induce foam cell formation, a key process in atherosclerosis. Potential antidyslipidemic agents are added to assess their ability to inhibit foam cell formation and promote cholesterol efflux using techniques such as Oil Red O staining and cholesterol efflux assays.

c. **Endothelial Cell Culture Studies**: Endothelial cell lines or primary cultures of endothelial cells are used to study the effects of potential antidyslipidemic agents on endothelial function, including modulation of adhesion molecule expression, endothelial nitric oxide production, and endothelial barrier function. These studies help assess the effects of drugs on endothelial dysfunction and atherosclerosis progression.

d. **Inflammatory Marker Assays**: Inflammatory markers such as cytokines, chemokines, and adhesion molecules play a key role in atherosclerosis. Potential antidyslipidemic agents are assessed for their effects on inflammatory marker expression using techniques such as ELISA, multiplex cytokine assays, and flow cytometry.

3. **Mechanistic Studies:**

   a. **Cholesterol Synthesis Inhibition**: Some antidyslipidemic agents, such as statins, work by inhibiting the enzyme HMG-CoA reductase, which is involved in cholesterol synthesis in the liver. Mechanistic studies elucidate the effects of statins on cholesterol synthesis pathways, including downstream effects on intracellular cholesterol levels, LDL receptor expression, and cholesterol trafficking.

   b. **LDL Receptor Modulation**: Other antidyslipidemic agents, such as PCSK9 inhibitors, work by increasing the expression and activity of LDL receptors on hepatocytes, leading to enhanced clearance of LDL cholesterol from the bloodstream. Mechanistic studies investigate the effects of PCSK9 inhibitors on LDL receptor recycling, degradation, and intracellular trafficking pathways.

   c. **Triglyceride Metabolism Regulation**: Antidyslipidemic agents targeting triglyceride metabolism, such as fibrates and omega-3 fatty acids, modulate pathways involved in triglyceride synthesis, transport, and clearance. Mechanistic studies assess the effects of these agents on lipoprotein lipase activity, hepatic fatty acid oxidation, and peroxisome proliferator-activated receptor (PPAR) signaling pathways.

   d. **Bile Acid Sequestration**: Bile acid sequestrants bind bile acids in the intestine, preventing their reabsorption and promoting their fecal excretion, leading to increased hepatic conversion of cholesterol into bile acids and decreased plasma cholesterol levels. Mechanistic studies investigate the effects of bile acid sequestrants on bile acid synthesis pathways, cholesterol absorption, and enterohepatic circulation.

4. **Safety Pharmacology:**
   a. **Hepatotoxicity:** Some antidyslipidemic agents may cause hepatotoxicity, including statins, fibrates, and niacin. Safety pharmacology studies assess markers of hepatotoxicity, liver enzymes (e.g., ALT, AST), and histopathological changes in liver tissue to evaluate the hepatic safety profile of antidyslipidemic agents.
   b. **Muscle Toxicity**: Statins are associated with the risk of muscle toxicity, including myopathy and rhabdomyolysis. Safety pharmacology studies assess markers of muscle damage (e.g., creatine kinase) and histopathological changes in muscle tissue to evaluate the muscle safety profile of statins and other antidyslipidemic agents.
   c. **Renal Function**: Some antidyslipidemic agents may affect renal function, particularly fibrates and niacin. Safety pharmacology studies assess renal function parameters such as glomerular filtration rate, renal blood flow, and markers of renal injury (e.g., serum creatinine, blood urea nitrogen) to evaluate the renal safety profile of antidyslipidemic agents.
   d. **Drug Interactions**: Antidyslipidemic agents may interact with other medications, such as anticoagulants, immunosuppressants, and antidiabetic drugs. Safety pharmacology studies assess potential drug interactions and their impact on efficacy and safety profiles of antidyslipidemic agents in combination therapy.

Throughout preclinical screening, researchers aim to identify compounds with potent antidyslipidemic effects, favorable safety profiles, and minimal adverse effects. Data from these studies inform the selection of lead compounds for further development and provide insights into their potential clinical utility in managing dyslipidemia and preventing cardiovascular diseases.

ANTI-CANCER AGENTS:

While anti-cancer agents may not typically fall under the category of drugs for metabolic disorders, I can offer insight into how potential metabolic effects of anti-cancer agents may be assessed in preclinical screening. Some anti-cancer agents have been found to affect metabolic pathways, and understanding these effects is crucial for both optimizing cancer treatment and managing potential metabolic side effects. Here's a detailed overview:

1. **In Vivo Studies:**

    a. **Animal Models**: Animal models of cancer, such as xenograft models (where human cancer cells are injected into animals) or genetically engineered mouse models (GEMMs) of cancer, can be used to study the effects of drugs used for metabolic disorders on tumor growth, metastasis, and response to therapy. For example, mice with diet-induced obesity may be used to study the impact of anti-diabetic drugs on cancer development.

    b. **Endpoint**s: In vivo studies may measure tumor volume, tumor growth rate, metastatic spread, and overall survival in animals treated with both the drug of interest and cancer cells. These studies help determine the potential anti-cancer effects of drugs used for metabolic disorders and their impact on tumor biology.

2. **In Vitro Experiments:**

    a. **Cell Culture Studies:** Cancer cell lines cultured in vitro can be treated with drugs used for metabolic disorders to assess their effects on cell proliferation, apoptosis, migration, invasion, and metabolic pathways. These studies provide mechanistic insights into how these drugs may influence cancer cell behavior.

b. **Metabolic Assays**: Drugs used for metabolic disorders may modulate cellular metabolism, which can impact cancer cell growth and survival. In vitro metabolic assays, such as Seahorse XF assays or metabolomics profiling, can be used to measure changes in cellular metabolism in response to drug treatment.

c. **Molecular Mechanisms**: In vitro experiments can elucidate the molecular mechanisms underlying the potential anti-cancer effects of drugs used for metabolic disorders. Techniques such as Western blotting, qPCR, and immunofluorescence can be used to assess changes in signaling pathways, gene expression, and protein levels in cancer cells treated with these drugs.

3. Mechanistic Studies:

a. **Metabolic Pathways Interplay**: Drugs used for metabolic disorders often modulate cellular metabolism pathways. Mechanistic studies aim to understand how alterations in metabolic pathways induced by these drugs may impact cancer cell growth, survival, and response to treatment. For example, drugs targeting AMP-activated protein kinase (AMPK) or mTOR pathways may affect both metabolic disorders and cancer cell metabolism.

b. **Cellular Signaling**: Many drugs for metabolic disorders influence cellular signaling pathways involved in cell growth, proliferation, and survival. Mechanistic studies investigate how these drugs affect signaling pathways such as PI3K/Akt/mTOR, MAPK, and Wnt/β-catenin, which are commonly dysregulated in cancer. Understanding these mechanisms helps elucidate potential anti-cancer effects.

c. **Immune Modulation**: Some drugs used for metabolic disorders have immunomodulatory effects that may impact the tumor microenvironment and anti-tumor immune responses. Mechanistic studies explore how these drugs affect immune cell function, cytokine production, and immune checkpoint pathways, which are crucial in cancer progression and treatment response.

4. **Safety Pharmacology:**

   a. **Off-Target Effects**: Safety pharmacology studies assess potential off-target effects of drugs for metabolic disorders when used as anti-cancer agents. These studies investigate whether the drugs interact with unintended targets, leading to adverse effects or altered pharmacokinetics. Understanding off-target effects helps mitigate safety concerns.

   b. **Cardiotoxicity**: Some drugs for metabolic disorders may have cardiotoxic effects, such as QT interval prolongation or impaired cardiac function, which could be detrimental in cancer patients, especially those receiving cardiotoxic cancer therapies. Safety pharmacology studies evaluate cardiac electrophysiology, contractility, and structural integrity to assess cardiotoxic potential.

   c. **Hepatotoxicity**: Drugs used for metabolic disorders may affect liver function, leading to hepatotoxicity. Safety pharmacology studies monitor liver enzymes, histopathological changes, and bile flow to assess hepatic safety. Liver function is critical in cancer patients due to potential interactions with chemotherapy agents and the need for optimal drug metabolism.

   d. **Renal Function**: Safety pharmacology studies also evaluate renal function parameters, such as glomerular filtration rate and renal blood flow, to assess potential nephrotoxicity of drugs used for metabolic disorders as anti-cancer agents. Maintaining renal function is crucial for drug clearance and preventing drug-induced nephropathy.

While the primary focus of preclinical screening for anti-cancer agents is on their efficacy against cancer cells, understanding their metabolic effects is increasingly recognized as crucial for optimizing treatment outcomes and managing potential metabolic complications. Data from these studies inform the selection of lead compounds for further development and provide insights into their mechanisms of action and potential metabolic interactions.

HEPATOPROTECTIVE SCREENING METHODS

Hepatoprotective screening methods aim to identify compounds that can protect the liver from damage caused by various hepatotoxic agents, including drugs, toxins, and pathogens. Here's a detailed overview of the methods and considerations involved in preclinical screening for hepatoprotective agents:

In Vivo Studies:

Hepatoprotective screening methods involve a range of in vivo studies aimed at identifying compounds or interventions that can protect the liver from damage caused by various toxins, drugs, or diseases. These studies typically employ animal models to evaluate the hepatoprotective effects of test substances. Here's a detailed overview of in vivo studies commonly used in hepatoprotective screening:

1. **Animal Models:**

    a. **Carbon Tetrachloride (CCl4)-Induced Hepatotoxicity**: CCl4 is a well-established hepatotoxin that induces liver injury by generating free radicals and causing lipid peroxidation. Animal models exposed to CCl4 are widely used to mimic acute or chronic liver injury, making them valuable for evaluating hepatoprotective agents.

b. **Acetaminophen (APAP)-Induced Hepatotoxicity**: APAP overdose is a common cause of drug-induced liver injury. Animal models treated with toxic doses of APAP replicate acute hepatocellular necrosis and are employed to screen for hepatoprotective compounds that mitigate APAP-induced liver damage.

c. **Alcoholic Liver Disease (ALD) Models**: Chronic alcohol consumption leads to liver inflammation, steatosis, fibrosis, and cirrhosis. Animal models exposed to alcohol through liquid diets or intragastric administration are used to assess the hepatoprotective effects of compounds against ALD progression.

d. **Non-Alcoholic Fatty Liver Disease (NAFLD) Models**: NAFLD encompasses a spectrum of liver disorders characterized by hepatic steatosis in the absence of significant alcohol consumption. Animal models fed high-fat or high-cholesterol diets can develop features of NAFLD, providing a platform to study hepatoprotective interventions for metabolic liver diseases.

2. **Endpoints and Assessments**:

   a. **Liver Function Tests:** Serum biomarkers of liver injury, such as alanine aminotransferase (ALT), aspartate aminotransferase (AST), and alkaline phosphatase (ALP), are measured to assess hepatocellular damage and liver function following treatment with hepatoprotective agents.

   b. **Liver Histopathology**: Liver tissue samples are collected and subjected to histopathological analysis to evaluate the extent of liver injury, inflammation, necrosis, fibrosis, and steatosis. Histological scoring systems provide quantitative assessment of liver histology.

   c. **Oxidative Stress Markers**: Levels of oxidative stress markers, such as malondialdehyde (MDA), superoxide dismutase (SOD), catalase

(CAT), and glutathione (GSH), are measured to assess the antioxidant and free radical scavenging properties of hepatoprotective compounds.

    d. **Inflammatory Markers**: Inflammatory cytokines and chemokines, including tumor necrosis factor-alpha (TNF-α), interleukin-6 (IL-6), and interleukin-1 beta (IL-1β), are quantified to evaluate the anti-inflammatory effects of hepatoprotective agents.

3. Experimental Design:

    a. **Dose-Response Studies**: Different doses of test compounds are administered to animals to determine the dose-dependent hepatoprotective effects and identify the optimal therapeutic dose.

    b. **Pre-Treatment vs. Post-Treatment**: Animals may be pre-treated with hepatoprotective agents before exposure to hepatotoxic insults or treated post-injury to assess both preventive and therapeutic effects.

    c. **Duration of Treatment**: Short-term and long-term treatment regimens are evaluated to assess the duration-dependent effects of hepatoprotective agents on liver injury and recovery.

In summary, in vivo studies in hepatoprotective screening involve the use of animal models exposed to hepatotoxic insults to evaluate the protective effects of test compounds on liver injury. These studies employ a range of endpoints and experimental designs to assess liver function, histopathology, oxidative stress, and inflammation, providing valuable insights into the potential therapeutic utility of hepatoprotective agents.

IN VITRO EXPERIMENTS:

In vitro experiments in hepatoprotective screening methods involve using isolated liver cells or liver cell lines to assess the protective effects of compounds or interventions against liver injury. These experiments provide valuable insights into the mechanisms of hepatoprotection and complement in vivo studies. Here's a detailed overview of common in vitro experiments used in hepatoprotective screening:

1. **Cell Culture Models:**
   a. **Hepatocyte Cultures**: Primary hepatocytes isolated from animal models or human donors, as well as hepatocyte cell lines (e.g., HepG2, Huh7), are used to study hepatoprotective effects. Hepatocytes are exposed to hepatotoxic agents or conditions to induce liver injury, and the protective effects of test compounds are evaluated by assessing cell viability, enzyme release, and other markers of liver function.
   b. **Liver Slices**: Precision-cut liver slices (PCLS) are thin sections of liver tissue that maintain the structural and functional integrity of the liver. PCLS can be used to assess hepatotoxicity and evaluate the hepatoprotective effects of compounds by measuring tissue viability, enzyme release, and metabolic activity.

2. **Endpoints and Assessments:**
   a. **Cell Viability Assays**: Cell viability is assessed using assays such as MTT (3-(4,5-dimethylthiazol-2-yl)-2,5-diphenyltetrazolium bromide), MTS (3-(4,5-dimethylthiazol-2-yl)-5-(3-carboxymethoxyphenyl)-2-(4-sulfophenyl)-2H-tetrazolium), or ATP (adenosine triphosphate) assays to quantify viable cells following exposure to hepatotoxic insults and test compounds.
   b. **Liver Enzyme Release**: The release of liver enzymes such as alanine aminotransferase (ALT) and aspartate aminotransferase (AST) into the culture medium is measured to assess hepatocellular damage and evaluate the protective effects of compounds.
   c. **Oxidative Stress Markers**: Levels of oxidative stress markers, including reactive oxygen species (ROS), lipid peroxidation products (e.g., malondialdehyde, 4-hydroxynonenal), and antioxidant enzymes

(e.g., superoxide dismutase, catalase), are quantified to evaluate the antioxidant properties of hepatoprotective agents.

d. **Inflammatory Mediators**: The production of inflammatory mediators such as cytokines (e.g., interleukin-6, tumor necrosis factor-alpha) and chemokines (e.g., interleukin-8) is measured to assess the anti-inflammatory effects of compounds on liver cells.

3. **Experimental Design:**

a. **Pre-Treatment vs. Post-Treatment**: Cells may be pre-treated with hepatoprotective compounds before exposure to hepatotoxic insults or treated post-injury to assess both preventive and therapeutic effects.

b. **Dose-Response Studies**: Different concentrations of test compounds are evaluated to determine the dose-dependent effects on cell viability, enzyme release, and other endpoints.

c. **Mechanistic Studies**: Additional experiments, such as gene expression analysis, immunoblotting, and immunofluorescence, may be performed to elucidate the underlying mechanisms of hepatoprotection, including modulation of cell signaling pathways, apoptosis, and autophagy.

In summary, in vitro experiments in hepatoprotective screening methods involve using liver cell cultures to assess the protective effects of compounds against liver injury induced by hepatotoxic agents. These experiments provide mechanistic insights into hepatoprotection and complement in vivo studies by offering a controlled environment to study cellular responses to hepatotoxic insults and test the efficacy of potential hepatoprotective agents.

MECHANISTIC STUDIES:

Mechanistic studies in hepatoprotective screening methods aim to elucidate the underlying mechanisms by which potential hepatoprotective agents exert their effects. Understanding these mechanisms is crucial for identifying promising candidates for further development and therapeutic application. Here's a detailed overview of common mechanistic studies used in hepatoprotective screening:

1. **Antioxidant Activity:**
   a. **Scavenging of Reactive Oxygen Species (ROS)**: Hepatoprotective agents may exert antioxidant effects by scavenging ROS, such as superoxide radicals, hydrogen peroxide, and hydroxyl radicals. Mechanistic studies involve assessing the ability of compounds to directly neutralize ROS using chemical assays or fluorescence-based probes.

   b. **Induction of Antioxidant Enzymes**: Some hepatoprotective agents upregulate the expression and activity of endogenous antioxidant enzymes, such as superoxide dismutase (SOD), catalase (CAT), and glutathione peroxidase (GPx). Mechanistic studies investigate the transcriptional regulation and enzymatic activity of these antioxidant enzymes following treatment with test compounds.

2. **Anti-Inflammatory Effects**:
   a. **Inhibition of Inflammatory Mediators:** Hepatoprotective agents may attenuate liver inflammation by inhibiting the production or activity of pro-inflammatory cytokines (e.g., TNF-α, IL-6, IL-1β) and chemokines (e.g., MCP-1). Mechanistic studies measure changes in inflammatory mediator levels using ELISA, qPCR, or immunoblotting assays.

   b. **Modulation of NF-κB Pathway**: Nuclear factor-kappa B (NF-κB) signaling plays a central role in liver inflammation and injury. Hepatoprotective agents may suppress NF-κB activation and translocation to the nucleus, thereby reducing the expression of pro-inflammatory genes. Mechanistic studies assess NF-κB activity using reporter gene assays or immunoblotting.

3. **Anti-Apoptotic and Anti-Necrotic Effects:**

   a. **Inhibition of Caspase Activation**: Apoptosis and necrosis contribute to liver injury in various hepatotoxic conditions. Hepatoprotective agents may inhibit caspase activation and downstream apoptotic pathways. Mechanistic studies evaluate caspase activity and cleavage of caspase substrates following treatment with test compounds.

   b. **Maintenance of Mitochondrial Function**: Mitochondrial dysfunction is a hallmark of liver injury. Hepatoprotective agents may preserve mitochondrial integrity and function by regulating mitochondrial membrane potential, ATP production, and reactive oxygen species generation. Mechanistic studies employ mitochondrial assays, such as JC-1 staining and oxygen consumption rate measurements.

4. **Modulation of Cell Signaling Pathways:**

   a. **PI3K/Akt Pathway**: The phosphatidylinositol 3-kinase (PI3K)/Akt pathway regulates cell survival and apoptosis. Hepatoprotective agents may activate Akt signaling, leading to enhanced cell survival and protection against liver injury. Mechanistic studies assess Akt phosphorylation and downstream targets using immunoblotting.

   b. **Nrf2/ARE Pathway:** The nuclear factor erythroid 2-related factor 2 (Nrf2)/antioxidant response element (ARE) pathway regulates the expression of antioxidant and detoxifying enzymes. Hepatoprotective agents may activate Nrf2 and induce the expression of cytoprotective genes. Mechanistic studies measure Nrf2 nuclear translocation and ARE-driven gene expression.

5. **Metabolic Regulation:**

   a. **Lipid Metabolism**: Dysregulation of lipid metabolism contributes to liver steatosis and injury. Hepatoprotective agents may modulate lipid metabolism by regulating lipid synthesis, oxidation, and storage.

Mechanistic studies investigate changes in lipid droplet accumulation, fatty acid oxidation, and triglyceride synthesis.

b. **Glucose Homeostasis**: Hepatoprotective agents may improve glucose homeostasis by enhancing insulin sensitivity and glycogen storage. Mechanistic studies assess glucose uptake, glycogen content, and insulin signaling in hepatocytes following treatment with test compounds.

In summary, mechanistic studies in hepatoprotective screening methods involve investigating the antioxidant, anti-inflammatory, anti-apoptotic, and metabolic effects of potential hepatoprotective agents. These studies provide valuable insights into the underlying mechanisms of hepatoprotection and inform the development of novel therapeutic strategies for liver diseases.

SAFETY PHARMACOLOGY:

Safety pharmacology studies in hepatoprotective screening methods are crucial for assessing the potential adverse effects and ensuring the safety of candidate compounds intended for liver protection. These studies aim to identify any toxicological concerns associated with hepatoprotective agents and provide essential information for regulatory approval and clinical development. Here's a detailed overview of safety pharmacology assessments commonly employed in hepatoprotective screening:

1. **General Toxicity Studies:**

   a. **Acute Toxicity**: Acute toxicity studies evaluate the safety of hepatoprotective agents following single-dose administration. Animals are monitored for signs of toxicity, such as changes in behavior, clinical signs, and mortality, to determine the maximum tolerated dose (MTD) and acute toxic effects.

   b. **Subacute and Chronic Toxicity**: Subacute and chronic toxicity studies assess the safety of hepatoprotective agents following repeated dosing over an extended period. Animals undergo detailed clinical observations, hematological and biochemical analyses, and histopathological examination of major organs, including the liver, to identify potential adverse effects.

2. **Cardiovascular Safety:**
   a. **Electrocardiography (ECG):** ECG assessments monitor changes in cardiac rhythm, conduction intervals (e.g., QT interval), and cardiac repolarization associated with hepatoprotective agents. Prolongation of QT interval may indicate a risk of cardiac arrhythmias and torsades de pointes.
   b. **Blood Pressure Monitoring**: Continuous blood pressure monitoring using telemetry systems evaluates the effects of hepatoprotective agents on systemic blood pressure and cardiovascular hemodynamics. Significant alterations in blood pressure may indicate potential cardiovascular toxicity.

3. **Respiratory Safety:**
   a. **Respiratory Rate Monitoring**: Changes in respiratory rate and pattern are monitored to assess respiratory safety. Hepatoprotective agents may affect respiratory function directly or indirectly through systemic effects.

4. **Renal Safety:**
   a. **Renal Function Tests**: Hepatoprotective agents may exert renal effects, such as nephrotoxicity or alterations in renal function. Renal function tests, including measurement of serum creatinine, blood urea nitrogen (BUN), and urine output, evaluate renal safety profiles.

5. **Hepatic Safety:**
   a. **Liver Enzymes**: Serum levels of liver enzymes, such as alanine aminotransferase (ALT), aspartate aminotransferase (AST), and

alkaline phosphatase (ALP), are monitored to assess hepatotoxicity associated with hepatoprotective agents.

  b. **Liver Histopathology:** Histopathological examination of liver tissue provides detailed information on the structural and cellular changes induced by hepatoprotective agents. Evaluation of liver architecture, inflammation, necrosis, fibrosis, and steatosis helps identify hepatotoxic effects.

6. **Metabolic Safety:**

  a. **Glucose and Lipid Metabolism**: Hepatoprotective agents may influence glucose and lipid metabolism, potentially affecting glycemic control and lipid profiles. Monitoring of blood glucose levels, insulin sensitivity, and lipid parameters assesses metabolic safety.

7. **Immunotoxicity:**

  a. **Immune Function Tests**: Assessment of immune cell populations, cytokine levels, and immune responses helps identify potential immunotoxic effects associated with hepatoprotective agents.

In summary, safety pharmacology studies in hepatoprotective screening methods encompass a range of assessments to evaluate the safety profiles of candidate compounds, including cardiovascular, respiratory, renal, hepatic, metabolic, and immunotoxicity endpoints. These studies provide critical data for assessing the overall safety of hepatoprotective agents and guiding their further development for clinical use.

Throughout preclinical screening, researchers aim to identify compounds with potent hepatoprotective effects, favorable safety profiles, and minimal adverse effects. Data from these studies inform the selection of lead compounds for further development and provide insights into their potential clinical utility in preventing and treating liver diseases.

MCQs

1. Which animal model is commonly used to study hypertension in preclinical screening of antihypertensive drugs?

    A) Spontaneously hypertensive rats

    B) db/db mice

    C) Apolipoprotein E-deficient mice

    D) Zucker diabetic fatty rats

2. In the context of antiarrhythmic drug screening, which method is essential for detecting and analyzing arrhythmias?

    A) Electrocardiography (ECG)

    B) Positron emission tomography (PET)

    C) High-performance liquid chromatography (HPLC)

    D) Enzyme-linked immunosorbent assay (ELISA)

3. What is the primary focus of pharmacokinetic studies in the development of cardiovascular drugs?

    A) Enzyme inhibition

    B) Receptor binding affinity

    C) Absorption, Distribution, Metabolism, and Excretion (ADME)

    D) Antigen-antibody interactions

4. Which in vitro method is used to assess vasodilatory effects in antianginal drug development?

    A) Cell viability assays

    B) Vascular reactivity assays

    C) PCR amplification

    D) Western blot analysis

5. What type of toxicity is a key concern in the safety pharmacology of antihypertensive drugs?

    A) Neurotoxicity

    B) Cardiotoxicity

C) Hepatotoxicity

D) Ototoxicity

6. In antiatherosclerotic agent screening, which animal model is NOT typically used?

    A) LDL receptor-deficient (LDLR-/-) mice

    B) Spontaneously hypertensive rats (SHR)

    C) Apolipoprotein E-deficient (apoE-/-) mice

    D) C57BL/6 mice

7. Which assay is crucial for understanding drug interactions with specific cardiovascular receptors?

    A) Receptor binding assays

    B) Electrophoresis

    C) Northern blot analysis

    D) Tissue culture

8. What is a major endpoint in the in vivo studies of antiarrhythmic drugs?

    A) Increase in body temperature

    B) Reduction of arrhythmia severity

    C) Increase in muscle mass

    D) Reduction in cognitive function

9. In the development of antianginal drugs, which method is used to monitor myocardial ischemia?

    A) Monitoring of glycolysis

    B) Electrocardiographic changes

    C) Protein synthesis rates

    D) Antibody production levels

10. What type of model is primarily used in hepatoprotective drug screening?

    A) Neurodegenerative disease models

    B) Liver injury models

    C) Pancreatic disease models

D) Renal disease models

11. What is a primary method to evaluate renal function in the development of antihypertensive drugs?

    A) Renal perfusion studies

    B) Muscle contraction tests

    C) Skin irritation tests

    D) Lung function tests

12. Which parameter is not typically assessed in preclinical testing of cardiovascular drugs?

    A) Blood pressure

    B) Heart rate

    C) Blood glucose levels

    D) Cardiac output

13. What type of cells is typically used in in vitro experiments for cardiovascular pharmacology?

    A) Neurons

    B) Cardiomyocytes

    C) Osteoblasts

    D) Epidermal cells

14. Which technique is NOT commonly used in the study of antiarrhythmic drugs?

    A) Ion channel assays

    B) Patch-clamp techniques

    C) PET scans

    D) Electrophysiological studies

15. In the context of antiatherosclerotic screening, what does the foam cell formation assay evaluate?

    A) Neuronal plaque formation

    B) Lipid accumulation in macrophages

C) Bone density changes

D) Muscle fiber regeneration

16. Which is NOT a focus of diuretic drug screening?

A) Increase in urine output

B) Electrolyte balance

C) Bone marrow suppression

D) Blood pressure changes

17. What method is used to study drug effects on calcium channels in antianginal drug development?

A) Calcium imaging

B) Flow cytometry

C) Gas chromatography

D) Mass spectrometry

18. What is often measured in pharmacological interventions for antihypertensives?

A) Cognitive enhancement

B) Blood pressure

C) Hair growth

D) Skin elasticity

19. Which model is typically NOT used in hepatoprotective drug screening?

A) Carbon tetrachloride-induced liver injury

B) High-fat diet-induced obesity

C) Acetaminophen-induced hepatotoxicity

D) Renal ischemia models

20. Which approach is NOT used in the preclinical screening of cardiovascular drugs?

A) Computer modeling and simulation

B) Organ-on-a-chip technology

C) Large-scale clinical trials

D) Human-derived cells and tissues

Short Answer Type Questions

1. What are the primary animal models used in the preclinical study of antihypertensive drugs?

2. Describe how electrocardiography (ECG) is utilized in the preclinical study of antiarrhythmic drugs.

3. What is the purpose of using renal perfusion studies in the development of antihypertensive drugs?

4. How do receptor binding assays aid in understanding the mechanism of action of cardiovascular drugs?

5. What role do platelet aggregation assays play in the preclinical study of antianginal drugs?

6. Explain the significance of ion transport assays in the study of diuretic drugs.

7. How are endothelial cells used in the preclinical studies of antihypertensive drugs?

8. What are the typical endpoints measured in animal models during the preclinical testing of antiarrhythmic drugs?

9. Describe how isolated tissue preparations are used in cardiovascular pharmacology studies.

10. How does organ-on-a-chip technology benefit cardiovascular drug development?

11. What are the major adverse effects assessed in the safety pharmacology of antihypertensive drugs?

12. How is the vasodilatory effect of antianginal drugs evaluated in preclinical studies?

13. Explain the importance of metabolic modulation in the action of antianginal drugs.

14. What role do human-derived cells and tissues play in cardiovascular pharmacology?

15. How are computer modeling and simulation used in the preclinical phase of drug development?

16. Describe how a Langendorff-perfused heart model is used in cardiovascular drug research.

17. What are foam cell formation assays, and why are they important in antiatherosclerotic agent studies?

18. How do researchers assess the anti-inflammatory effects of potential antiatherosclerotic agents?

19. What is the significance of assessing myocardial blood flow in antianginal drug research?

20. Explain how mitochondrial function is assessed in the study of drugs for metabolic disorders.

Long Answer Type Questions

1. Discuss the methods and models used in the preclinical screening of antihypertensive drugs and how they simulate aspects of human hypertension.

2. Describe the comprehensive approach taken in preclinical screening to evaluate the efficacy and safety of antiarrhythmic drugs, including both in vivo and in vitro techniques.

3. Explain how animal models, specifically coronary artery ligation models, are employed to assess the efficacy of antianginal drugs and the endpoints that are typically evaluated.

4. Detail the various in vitro experiments conducted during the preclinical testing of diuretics and their significance in understanding the drug's mechanism of action on renal electrolyte handling.

5. Discuss the application of organ-on-a-chip technology and human-derived cells in cardiovascular drug development and how they contribute to more physiologically relevant testing compared to traditional methods.

6. Explain the role of mitochondrial function assays in the evaluation of drugs for metabolic disorders and their importance in understanding drug effects on cellular energy dynamics.

7. Describe the various in vivo and in vitro methods used in the preclinical study of antidyslipidemic agents, focusing on how these methods help assess the drug's effect on lipid metabolism and atherosclerosis prevention.

8. Provide an overview of the use of pharmacological interventions in animal models for studying anti-diabetic drugs, focusing on how these interventions mimic human diabetic conditions.

9. Discuss how safety pharmacology is integrated into the preclinical testing of cardiovascular drugs, specifically focusing on cardiotoxicity and renal function assessments.

10. Elaborate on the use of cell culture studies, specifically cardiomyocyte and endothelial cell assays, in the preclinical assessment of cardiovascular drugs and their relevance to human cardiovascular diseases.

Answer Key for MCQs

1. (A) Spontaneously hypertensive rats

2. (A) Electrocardiography (ECG)

3. (C) Absorption, Distribution, Metabolism, and Excretion (ADME)

4. (B) Vascular reactivity assays

5. (B) Cardiotoxicity

6. (D) C57BL/6 mice

7. (A) Receptor binding assays

8. (B) Reduction of arrhythmia severity

9. (B) Electrocardiographic changes

10. (B) Liver injury models

11. (A) Renal perfusion studies

12. (C) Blood glucose levels

13. (B) Cardiomyocytes

14. (C) PET scans

15. (B) Lipid accumulation in macrophages

16. (C) Bone marrow suppression

17. (A) Calcium imaging

18. (B) Blood pressure

19. (D) Renal ischemia models

20. (C) Large-scale clinical trials

CHAPTER - 5

IMMUNOMODULATORS:

Immunomodulators are substances that can either enhance or suppress the immune response, making them crucial in various areas of medicine, including preclinical screening of new substances for pharmacological activity. Here's an overview of how immunomodulators are assessed in preclinical screening using in vivo, in vitro, and other animal alternative models:

In Vivo Models:

In preclinical screening of new substances for pharmacological activity using in vivo models, immunomodulators play a crucial role in assessing their effects on the immune system and their potential therapeutic applications. Here's how immunomodulators are involved in the preclinical screening process using in vivo models:

1. Selection of Immunomodulators:

a. Researchers identify and select potential immunomodulatory compounds based on their ability to modulate immune responses, either by enhancing or suppressing immune function.

b. Compounds may be sourced from natural products, chemical libraries, or designed through synthetic chemistry approaches.

2. Disease Models and Therapeutic Efficacy:

a. Immunomodulators are evaluated in relevant in vivo disease models to assess their therapeutic efficacy in treating immune-related disorders such as autoimmune diseases, inflammatory conditions, or cancer.

b. Animal models recapitulate key aspects of human diseases, allowing researchers to assess the impact of immunomodulators on disease progression, symptoms, and overall health outcomes.

3. Immunophenotyping and Immune Response Assessment:

a. In vivo studies involve analyzing changes in immune cell populations, cytokine profiles, and inflammatory markers in response to immunomodulator treatment.

b. Techniques such as flow cytometry, ELISA, and immunohistochemistry are used to assess immune cell activation, proliferation, migration, and function.

4. Pharmacokinetic and Pharmacodynamic Analysis:

a. Researchers study the pharmacokinetics of immunomodulators in vivo, including absorption, distribution, metabolism, and excretion (ADME) properties.

b. Pharmacodynamic analysis involves evaluating the relationship between drug exposure and immune response, including dose-response relationships and time-course effects.

5. Safety and Toxicity Evaluation:

a. Preclinical studies assess the safety and toxicity of immunomodulators to determine their potential adverse effects on vital organs, immune function, and overall health.

b. Toxicological assessments include examining organ histopathology, serum biomarkers, and physiological parameters to identify potential risks and safety concerns.

6. Mechanistic Studies:

a. Researchers investigate the underlying mechanisms of action of immunomodulators in vivo, elucidating their effects on immune cell signaling pathways, cytokine production, and immune cell interactions.

b. Mechanistic insights provide a deeper understanding of how immunomodulators modulate immune responses and inform future therapeutic strategies.

7. Optimization of Dosing Regimens:

a. In vivo studies help optimize dosing regimens for immunomodulators, including determining the appropriate dose, frequency, and duration of treatment to achieve therapeutic efficacy while minimizing adverse effects.

b. Pharmacokinetic-pharmacodynamic modeling and simulation guide dose selection and regimen optimization based on preclinical data.

8. Data Analysis and Interpretation:

a. Researchers analyze and interpret preclinical data to assess the efficacy, safety, and pharmacological activity of immunomodulators in vivo.

b. Statistical analysis, data visualization, and comparison with control groups are used to evaluate treatment effects and draw conclusions from preclinical studies.

9. Validation and Reproducibility:

a. Findings from in vivo preclinical studies are validated through replication studies and independent verification to ensure the reproducibility and reliability of results.

b. Robust preclinical data support the translatability and predictive value of in vivo models for assessing the pharmacological activity of immunomodulators.

10. Reporting and Documentation:

a. Comprehensive study reports document experimental protocols, results, statistical analysis, and conclusions from in vivo preclinical studies.

b. Regulatory submissions summarize preclinical data for review by regulatory agencies and support the progression of immunomodulators to clinical trials.

In summary, immunomodulators are evaluated in preclinical screening using in vivo models to assess their therapeutic potential, safety profile, and mechanistic properties in the context of immune-related diseases. In vivo preclinical studies provide valuable insights into the pharmacological activity of immunomodulators and inform their clinical development pathway.

In Vitro Models:

In preclinical screening of new substances for pharmacological activity using in vitro models, immunomodulators play a critical role in assessing their effects on the immune system and their potential therapeutic applications. Here's how immunomodulators are involved in the preclinical screening process using in vitro models:

1. Selection of Immunomodulators:

   a. Researchers identify and select potential immunomodulatory compounds based on their ability to modulate immune responses, either by enhancing or suppressing immune function.

   b. Compounds may be sourced from natural products, chemical libraries, or designed through synthetic chemistry approaches.

2. Cell-Based Assays and Functional Studies:

   a. Immunomodulators are evaluated using various in vitro cell-based assays to assess their effects on immune cell function, proliferation, activation, and cytokine production.

   b. Functional studies may include assays such as T-cell proliferation assays, cytokine release assays, and phagocytosis assays to characterize the immunomodulatory properties of compounds.

3. Immunophenotyping and Biomarker Analysis:

   a. In vitro studies involve analyzing changes in immune cell populations, surface markers, and cytokine profiles in response to immunomodulator treatment.

   b. Flow cytometry, ELISA, and multiplex cytokine assays are used to quantify immune cell subsets, activation markers, and secreted cytokines.

4. Mechanistic Studies:

a. Researchers investigate the underlying mechanisms of action of immunomodulators in vitro, elucidating their effects on immune cell signaling pathways, gene expression profiles, and protein interactions.

b. Molecular biology techniques such as Western blotting, RT-qPCR, and immunoprecipitation are used to study molecular targets and pathways involved in immune modulation.

5. Dose-Response Relationships:

a. In vitro dose-response studies are conducted to determine the concentration-dependent effects of immunomodulators on immune cell function and viability.

b. Concentration-response curves and IC50 values are used to assess potency and efficacy of compounds in modulating immune responses.

6. Evaluation of Immunomodulatory Activity:

a. Immunomodulators are assessed for their ability to regulate immune responses under various conditions, including inflammation, infection, and autoimmune diseases.

b. In vitro models simulate specific aspects of immune dysfunction and disease pathology, allowing researchers to evaluate the therapeutic potential of immunomodulators in relevant contexts.

7. High-Throughput Screening:

a. High-throughput screening (HTS) assays are used to rapidly screen large compound libraries for immunomodulatory activity, identifying lead compounds for further evaluation.

b. Automated platforms and robotic systems facilitate the screening of thousands of compounds in parallel, accelerating the drug discovery process.

8. Safety and Toxicity Assessment:

a. In vitro studies assess the safety profile of immunomodulators by examining their cytotoxic effects on immune cells, potential for inducing apoptosis or cell death, and impact on cell viability and proliferation.

b. Toxicological endpoints such as cell morphology, membrane integrity, and metabolic activity are evaluated to identify potential adverse effects.

9. Optimization of Drug Candidates:

a. In vitro screening assays inform the optimization of lead compounds by guiding structure-activity relationship (SAR) studies and medicinal chemistry efforts.

b. Structure-activity relationships elucidated from in vitro data help refine compound design and enhance immunomodulatory potency, selectivity, and pharmacokinetic properties.

10. Data Analysis and Interpretation:

a. Researchers analyze and interpret in vitro data to assess the immunomodulatory activity, efficacy, and mechanism of action of compounds.

b. Statistical analysis, dose-response modeling, and comparison with control groups are used to quantify treatment effects and draw conclusions from preclinical screening studies.

In summary, immunomodulators are evaluated in preclinical screening using in vitro models to assess their effects on immune cell function, cytokine production, and molecular mechanisms of action. In vitro preclinical studies provide valuable insights into the immunomodulatory properties of compounds and inform their progression to in vivo efficacy and safety studies.

Other Animal Alternative Models:

In preclinical screening of new substances for pharmacological activity, including immunomodulators, researchers often utilize alternative animal models alongside traditional in vivo models to assess their effects on the immune system and their potential therapeutic applications. Here's how immunomodulators are involved in the preclinical screening process using alternative animal models:

1. Zebrafish Models:

a. Zebrafish embryos and larvae provide a transparent and genetically tractable model for studying immune responses and drug effects in vivo.

b. Immunomodulatory compounds can be administered to zebrafish embryos, and their effects on immune cell development, inflammation, and infection responses can be monitored using microscopy and fluorescent reporters.

2. Drosophila melanogaster (Fruit Fly) Models:

a. Drosophila models offer a cost-effective and genetically manipulable system for studying innate immune responses and host-pathogen interactions.

b. Immunomodulatory compounds can be tested in fruit flies to assess their effects on immune cell function, antimicrobial peptide production, and resistance to infections.

3. Caenorhabditis elegans (Roundworm) Models:

a. C. elegans provides a simple multicellular organism for studying innate immune responses, stress signaling, and host-microbe interactions.

b. Immunomodulators can be evaluated in nematodes to investigate their effects on immune cell activation, pathogen clearance, and longevity in response to infection or stress.

4. Galleria mellonella (Wax Moth) Larvae Models:

a. G. mellonella larvae serve as an alternative model for studying innate immune responses and evaluating drug efficacy in vivo.

b. Immunomodulatory compounds can be administered to wax moth larvae, and their effects on immune cell activation, microbial clearance, and survival can be assessed to screen for potential therapeutic agents.

5. Ex Vivo Organ Culture Models:

a. Ex vivo organ culture models, such as precision-cut tissue slices or explant cultures, provide a platform for studying immune responses in intact tissues outside the organism.

b. Immunomodulators can be tested in ex vivo tissue cultures to assess their effects on immune cell infiltration, cytokine production, and tissue inflammation in a controlled environment.

6. Patient-Derived Organoid Models:

a. Patient-derived organoids, generated from primary cells or induced pluripotent stem cells (iPSCs), recapitulate tissue architecture and function in vitro.

b. Immunomodulatory compounds can be screened in patient-derived organoids to evaluate their effects on tissue-specific immune responses, inflammation, and disease pathology in a personalized context.

7. Humanized Mouse Models:

a. Humanized mouse models, engrafted with human immune cells or tissues, provide a platform for studying human-specific immune responses and evaluating immunomodulatory compounds in vivo.

b. Immunomodulators can be administered to humanized mice to assess their effects on immune cell engraftment, function, and interactions with host tissues in a humanized immune environment.

8. Computational Models and In Silico Approaches:

a. Computational models, such as quantitative systems pharmacology (QSP) models and in silico simulations, complement experimental approaches by predicting drug effects on immune responses and host-pathogen interactions.

b. Immunomodulators can be screened in silico to prioritize lead compounds, optimize dosing regimens, and predict their efficacy and safety profiles before experimental validation.

In summary, alternative animal models and experimental approaches provide valuable tools for preclinical screening of immunomodulators, offering insights into their effects on immune function, inflammation, and disease pathology. By leveraging these alternative models alongside traditional in vivo and in vitro assays, researchers can accelerate the discovery and development of novel immunomodulatory agents for therapeutic applications.

Overall, preclinical screening of immunomodulators involves a combination of in vivo, in vitro, and alternative models to comprehensively evaluate their pharmacological activity and potential therapeutic applications. These approaches help researchers identify promising candidates for further development and clinical testing.

IMMUNOSUPPRESSANT:

In preclinical screening of new substances for pharmacological activity, including potential immunosuppressants, researchers utilize a variety of methods to assess their efficacy, safety, and mechanisms of action. Here's how these substances are evaluated using in vivo, in vitro, and other animal alternative models:

In Vivo Models:

In preclinical screening of new substances for pharmacological activity, particularly immunosuppressants, using in vivo models involves a comprehensive evaluation of their effects on the immune system and their potential therapeutic applications. Here's how immunosuppressants are involved in the preclinical screening process using in vivo models:

1. Selection of Immunosuppressants:

a. Researchers identify and select potential immunosuppressant compounds based on their ability to modulate immune responses and inhibit specific immune cell functions.

b. Compounds may be sourced from natural products, chemical libraries, or designed through synthetic chemistry approaches.

2. Disease Models and Therapeutic Efficacy:

a. Immunosuppressants are evaluated in relevant in vivo disease models to assess their therapeutic efficacy in immune-mediated disorders such as autoimmune diseases, organ transplantation, and inflammatory conditions.

b. Animal models recapitulate key aspects of human diseases, allowing researchers to assess the impact of immunosuppressants on disease progression, tissue damage, and clinical symptoms.

3. Immune Response Assessment:

a. In vivo studies involve analyzing changes in immune cell populations, cytokine profiles, and inflammatory markers in response to immunosuppressant treatment.

b. Techniques such as flow cytometry, ELISA, and immunohistochemistry are used to quantify immune cell subsets, activation markers, and secreted cytokines in tissues and blood samples.

4. Pharmacokinetic and Pharmacodynamic Analysis:

a. Researchers study the pharmacokinetics of immunosuppressants in vivo, including absorption, distribution, metabolism, and excretion (ADME) properties.

b. Pharmacodynamic analysis involves evaluating the relationship between drug exposure and immune response inhibition, including dose-response relationships and time-course effects.

5. Evaluation of Immunomodulatory Activity:

a. Immunomodulatory effects of immunosuppressants are assessed in vivo by monitoring changes in immune cell function, proliferation, activation, and cytokine production.

b. Animal models provide insights into the systemic effects of immunosuppressants on immune responses and their potential off-target effects on non-immune tissues.

6. Safety and Toxicity Evaluation:

a. Preclinical studies assess the safety and toxicity of immunosuppressants to determine their potential adverse effects on vital organs, immune function, and overall health.

b. Toxicological assessments include examining organ histopathology, serum biomarkers, and physiological parameters to identify potential risks and safety concerns associated with long-term treatment.

7. Mechanistic Studies:

a. Researchers investigate the underlying mechanisms of action of immunosuppressants in vivo, elucidating their effects on immune cell signaling pathways, cytokine production, and immune cell interactions.

b. Molecular biology techniques such as Western blotting, RT-qPCR, and immunoprecipitation are used to study molecular targets and pathways involved in immune suppression.

8. Optimization of Dosing Regimens:

a. In vivo studies help optimize dosing regimens for immunosuppressants, including determining the appropriate dose, frequency, and duration of treatment to achieve therapeutic efficacy while minimizing adverse effects.

b. Pharmacokinetic-pharmacodynamic modeling and simulation guide dose selection and regimen optimization based on preclinical data.

9. Data Analysis and Interpretation:

a. Researchers analyze and interpret preclinical data to assess the efficacy, safety, and pharmacological activity of immunosuppressants in vivo.

b. Statistical analysis, data visualization, and comparison with control groups are used to quantify treatment effects and draw conclusions from preclinical screening studies.

10. Reporting and Documentation:

a. Comprehensive study reports document experimental protocols, results, statistical analysis, and conclusions from in vivo preclinical studies.

b. Regulatory submissions summarize preclinical data for review by regulatory agencies and support the progression of immunosuppressants to clinical trials.

By following these steps in preclinical screening, researchers can comprehensively evaluate the pharmacological activity, efficacy, safety, and therapeutic potential of immunosuppressants using in vivo models, laying the groundwork for further clinical development and therapeutic translation.

In Vitro Models:

In preclinical screening of new substances for pharmacological activity, including immunosuppressants, using in vitro models involves assessing their effects on immune cell function, proliferation, activation, and cytokine production in controlled laboratory settings. Here's how immunosuppressants are involved in the preclinical screening process using in vitro models:

1. Selection of Immunosuppressants:

a. Researchers identify and select potential immunosuppressant compounds based on their known or predicted ability to modulate immune responses and inhibit specific immune cell functions.

b. Compounds may be sourced from natural products, chemical libraries, or designed through synthetic chemistry approaches.

2. Cell-Based Assays:

a. Immunomodulatory effects of immunosuppressants are evaluated using various in vitro cell-based assays, each targeting specific aspects of immune function.

b. Functional assays include T-cell proliferation assays, cytokine release assays, mixed lymphocyte reactions, and dendritic cell maturation assays to assess the effects of immunosuppressants on immune cell activation and function.

3. Immunophenotyping and Cytokine Analysis:

a. In vitro studies involve analyzing changes in immune cell populations, surface markers, and cytokine profiles in response to immunosuppressant treatment.

b. Flow cytometry, ELISA, multiplex cytokine assays, and gene expression analysis are used to quantify immune cell subsets, activation markers, and secreted cytokines in response to immunosuppressant treatment.

4. Mechanistic Studies:

a. Researchers investigate the underlying mechanisms of action of immunosuppressants in vitro, elucidating their effects on immune cell signaling pathways, gene expression profiles, and protein interactions.

b. Molecular biology techniques such as Western blotting, RT-qPCR, and immunoprecipitation are used to study molecular targets and pathways involved in immune suppression.

5. Dose-Response Relationships:

a. In vitro dose-response studies are conducted to determine the concentration-dependent effects of immunosuppressants on immune cell function, proliferation, and cytokine production.

b. Concentration-response curves and IC50 values are used to assess potency and efficacy of immunosuppressants in modulating immune responses.

6. Evaluation of Immunomodulatory Activity:

a. Immunomodulatory effects of immunosuppressants are assessed in vitro by monitoring changes in immune cell function, proliferation, activation, and cytokine production.

b. Functional assays and biomarker analysis provide insights into the mechanisms of action and therapeutic potential of immunosuppressants in vitro.

7. Safety and Toxicity Assessment:

a. In vitro studies assess the safety and toxicity of immunosuppressants by examining their effects on immune cell viability, proliferation, and apoptosis.

b. Toxicological endpoints such as cell morphology, membrane integrity, and metabolic activity are evaluated to identify potential risks and safety concerns associated with immunosuppressant treatment.

8. Optimization of Drug Candidates:

a. In vitro screening assays inform the optimization of lead compounds by guiding structure-activity relationship (SAR) studies and medicinal chemistry efforts.

b. Structure-activity relationships elucidated from in vitro data help refine compound design and enhance immunosuppressive potency, selectivity, and pharmacokinetic properties.

9. Data Analysis and Interpretation:

a. Researchers analyze and interpret in vitro data to assess the immunosuppressive activity, efficacy, and mechanism of action of compounds.

b. Statistical analysis, dose-response modeling, and comparison with control groups are used to quantify treatment effects and draw conclusions from preclinical screening studies.

10. Reporting and Documentation:

a. Comprehensive study reports document experimental protocols, results, statistical analysis, and conclusions from in vitro preclinical studies.

b. Regulatory submissions summarize preclinical data for review by regulatory agencies and support the progression of immunosuppressants to further preclinical or clinical development stages.

By following these steps in preclinical screening, researchers can comprehensively evaluate the pharmacological activity, efficacy, safety, and therapeutic potential of immunosuppressants using in vitro models, providing valuable insights into their potential for clinical translation and therapeutic applications.

Other Animal Alternative Models:

In preclinical screening of new substances for pharmacological activity, including immunosuppressants, researchers may employ various alternative animal models alongside traditional in vivo models to assess their effects on the immune system and their potential therapeutic applications. Here's how immunosuppressants are involved in the preclinical screening process using alternative animal models:

1. Zebrafish Models:

a. Zebrafish embryos and larvae provide a genetically tractable model for studying immune responses and drug effects in vivo.

b. Immunomodulatory compounds, including immunosuppressants, can be administered to zebrafish embryos to assess their effects on immune cell development, inflammation, and infection responses.

2. Drosophila melanogaster (Fruit Fly) Models:

a. Drosophila models offer a cost-effective and genetically manipulable system for studying innate immune responses and host-pathogen interactions.

b. Immunomodulatory compounds, such as immunosuppressants, can be tested in fruit flies to assess their effects on immune cell function, antimicrobial peptide production, and resistance to infections.

3. Caenorhabditis elegans (Roundworm) Models:

a. C. elegans provides a simple multicellular organism for studying innate immune responses, stress signaling, and host-microbe interactions.

b. Immunomodulatory compounds, including immunosuppressants, can be evaluated in nematodes to investigate their effects on immune cell activation, pathogen clearance, and longevity in response to infection or stress.

4. Galleria mellonella (Wax Moth) Larvae Models:

a. G. mellonella larvae serve as an alternative model for studying innate immune responses and evaluating drug efficacy in vivo.

b. Immunomodulatory compounds, such as immunosuppressants, can be administered to wax moth larvae, and their effects on immune cell activation, microbial clearance, and survival can be assessed to screen for potential therapeutic agents.

5. Patient-Derived Organoid Models:

a. Patient-derived organoids, generated from primary cells or induced pluripotent stem cells (iPSCs), recapitulate tissue architecture and function in vitro.

b. Immunomodulatory compounds, including immunosuppressants, can be screened in patient-derived organoids to evaluate their effects on tissue-specific immune responses, inflammation, and disease pathology in a personalized context.

6. Humanized Mouse Models:

a. Humanized mouse models, engrafted with human immune cells or tissues, provide a platform for studying human-specific immune responses and evaluating immunosuppressants in vivo.

b. Immunomodulatory compounds, including immunosuppressants, can be administered to humanized mice to assess their effects on human immune cell engraftment, function, and interactions with host tissues in a humanized immune environment.

7. Computational Models and In Silico Approaches:

a. Computational models, such as quantitative systems pharmacology (QSP) models and in silico simulations, complement experimental approaches by predicting drug effects on immune responses and host-pathogen interactions.

b. Immunomodulatory compounds, including immunosuppressants, can be screened in silico to prioritize lead compounds, optimize dosing regimens, and predict their efficacy and safety profiles before experimental validation.

By leveraging these alternative animal models and experimental approaches alongside traditional in vivo studies, researchers can gain valuable insights into the pharmacological activity, efficacy, and safety of immunosuppressants, accelerating the drug discovery and development process while reducing reliance on traditional animal models.

Computational Models:

1. Molecular Docking and Virtual Screening:

a. Computational modeling techniques are used to predict the interaction of potential immunosuppressants with target molecules involved in immune regulation.

b. Molecular docking simulations and virtual screening methods identify candidate compounds with favorable binding properties and potential immunomodulatory effects.

In summary, preclinical screening of new substances for immunosuppressive activity involves a combination of in vivo, in vitro, and animal alternative models, as well as computational approaches. These methods provide insights into the efficacy, mechanisms of action, and safety profiles of potential immunosuppressants, facilitating their further development for clinical use.

IMMUNOSTIMULANTS:

In preclinical screening of new substances for pharmacological activity, including potential immunostimulants, researchers employ a variety of methods to evaluate their efficacy, safety, and mechanisms of action. Here's how these substances are assessed using in vivo, in vitro, and other animal alternative models:

In Vivo Models:

In preclinical screening of new substances for pharmacological activity, immunostimulants play a crucial role in assessing their effects on the immune system and their potential therapeutic applications. Here's how immunostimulants are involved in the preclinical screening process using in vivo models:

1. Selection of Immunostimulants:

a. Researchers identify and select potential immunostimulant compounds based on their ability to enhance immune responses and activate specific immune cell functions.

b. Compounds may be sourced from natural products, chemical libraries, or designed through synthetic chemistry approaches.

2. Disease Models and Therapeutic Efficacy:

a. Immunostimulants are evaluated in relevant in vivo disease models to assess their therapeutic efficacy in enhancing immune function and combating infectious diseases, cancer, or autoimmune disorders.

b. Animal models recapitulate key aspects of human diseases, allowing researchers to assess the impact of immunostimulants on disease progression, pathogen clearance, and overall health outcomes.

3. Immune Response Assessment:

a. In vivo studies involve analyzing changes in immune cell populations, cytokine profiles, and inflammatory markers in response to immunostimulant treatment.

b. Techniques such as flow cytometry, ELISA, and immunohistochemistry are used to quantify immune cell subsets, activation markers, and secreted cytokines in tissues and blood samples.

4. Immunophenotyping and Functional Assays:

a. Immunostimulants are assessed for their ability to enhance immune cell function, proliferation, and cytokine production in vivo.

b. Functional assays may include T-cell proliferation assays, natural killer (NK) cell activity assays, and cytokine release assays to characterize the immunostimulatory properties of compounds.

5. Evaluation of Antigen-Specific Immune Responses:

a. Immunostimulants are tested for their ability to enhance antigen-specific immune responses, including antibody production, T-cell activation, and memory cell formation.

b. Animal models of vaccination or infectious disease are used to assess the adjuvant effects of immunostimulants in boosting immune responses to specific pathogens or vaccine antigens.

6. Pharmacokinetic and Pharmacodynamic Analysis:

a. Researchers study the pharmacokinetics of immunostimulants in vivo, including absorption, distribution, metabolism, and excretion (ADME) properties.

b. Pharmacodynamic analysis involves evaluating the relationship between drug exposure and immune response enhancement, including dose-response relationships and time-course effects.

7. Safety and Toxicity Evaluation:

a. Preclinical studies assess the safety and toxicity of immunostimulants to determine their potential adverse effects on vital organs, immune function, and overall health.

b. Toxicological assessments include examining organ histopathology, serum biomarkers, and physiological parameters to identify potential risks and safety concerns associated with long-term treatment.

8. Mechanistic Studies:

a. Researchers investigate the underlying mechanisms of action of immunostimulants in vivo, elucidating their effects on immune cell signaling pathways, antigen presentation, and cytokine production.

b. Molecular biology techniques such as Western blotting, RT-qPCR, and immunoprecipitation are used to study molecular targets and pathways involved in immune stimulation.

9. Optimization of Dosing Regimens:

a. In vivo studies help optimize dosing regimens for immunostimulants, including determining the appropriate dose, frequency, and duration of treatment to achieve maximal immune enhancement while minimizing adverse effects.

b. Pharmacokinetic-pharmacodynamic modeling and simulation guide dose selection and regimen optimization based on preclinical data.

10. Data Analysis and Interpretation:

a. Researchers analyze and interpret preclinical data to assess the immunostimulatory activity, efficacy, and safety of compounds in vivo.

b. Statistical analysis, data visualization, and comparison with control groups are used to quantify treatment effects and draw conclusions from preclinical screening studies.

In summary, immunostimulants are evaluated in preclinical screening using in vivo models to assess their effects on immune function, cytokine production, and disease outcomes. In vivo preclinical studies provide valuable insights into the immunostimulatory properties of compounds and inform their progression to further preclinical or clinical development stages.

In Vitro Models:

In preclinical screening of new substances for pharmacological activity, immunostimulants are essential agents that can enhance immune responses. In vitro models are crucial tools in assessing the effects of immunostimulants on immune cell function and cytokine production. Here's how immunostimulants are involved in the preclinical screening process using in vitro models:

1. Selection of Immunostimulants:
   a. Researchers identify potential immunostimulant compounds based on their ability to activate immune cells and enhance immune responses.
   b. Compounds may be derived from natural products, chemical libraries, or designed synthetically.

2. Cell-Based Assays:
   a. Immunostimulant effects are evaluated using various in vitro cell-based assays.
   b. Functional assays include proliferation assays, cytokine release assays, and phagocytosis assays, among others, to assess the activation and function of immune cells in response to immunostimulant treatment.

3. Immunophenotyping and Cytokine Analysis:
   a. Changes in immune cell populations and cytokine secretion profiles are analyzed following treatment with immunostimulants.

b. Techniques such as flow cytometry and ELISA are commonly used to quantify immune cell subsets and cytokine levels, respectively.

4. Activation of Immune Signaling Pathways:

a. Immunostimulants activate specific signaling pathways within immune cells.

b. Molecular biology techniques such as Western blotting and RT-qPCR are employed to study the activation of signaling molecules and gene expression changes induced by immunostimulants.

5. Antigen Presentation and T-Cell Activation:

a. Immunostimulants can enhance antigen presentation by antigen-presenting cells (APCs) and promote T-cell activation.

b. Co-culture assays with dendritic cells and T cells are used to assess the ability of immunostimulants to enhance antigen-specific T-cell responses.

6. Adjuvant Activity:

a. Immunostimulants often serve as adjuvants in vaccine formulations to enhance the immune response to antigens.

b. In vitro studies assess the adjuvant activity of immunostimulants by measuring antigen-specific antibody production and T-cell activation in response to vaccination.

7. Dose-Response Relationships:

a. In vitro dose-response studies are conducted to determine the optimal concentration range of immunostimulants for enhancing immune cell function.

b. Concentration-response curves are generated to assess the potency and efficacy of immunostimulants in activating immune responses.

8. Mechanistic Studies:

a. Researchers investigate the underlying mechanisms of action of immunostimulants in vitro.

b. Studies focus on elucidating the molecular pathways involved in immune cell activation and cytokine production induced by immunostimulant treatment.

9. Safety Assessment:

a. In vitro studies assess the safety profile of immunostimulants by examining their cytotoxic effects on immune cells.

b. Toxicological endpoints such as cell viability and apoptosis are evaluated to identify potential adverse effects of immunostimulant treatment.

10. Data Analysis and Interpretation:

a. Researchers analyze and interpret in vitro data to assess the immunostimulatory activity, efficacy, and safety of compounds.

b. Statistical analysis and comparison with control groups are used to quantify treatment effects and draw conclusions from preclinical screening studies.

In summary, in vitro models are valuable tools for evaluating the immunostimulatory properties of compounds and informing their progression to further preclinical or clinical development stages. These models provide insights into the mechanisms of action, dose-response relationships, and safety profiles of immunostimulants, facilitating the identification of promising candidates for immunotherapy and vaccine development.

Other Animal Alternative Models:

In preclinical screening of new substances for pharmacological activity, including immunostimulants, researchers may utilize various alternative animal models alongside traditional in vivo models to assess their effects on the immune system and their potential therapeutic applications. Here's how immunostimulants are involved in the preclinical screening process using alternative animal models:

1. Zebrafish Models:

a. Zebrafish embryos and larvae provide a transparent and genetically tractable model for studying immune responses and drug effects in vivo.

b. Immunostimulants can be administered to zebrafish embryos to assess their effects on immune cell development, inflammation, and infection responses.

2. Drosophila melanogaster (Fruit Fly) Models:

a. Drosophila models offer a cost-effective and genetically manipulable system for studying innate immune responses and host-pathogen interactions.

b. Immunostimulants can be tested in fruit flies to assess their effects on immune cell function, antimicrobial peptide production, and resistance to infections.

3. Caenorhabditis elegans (Roundworm) Models:

a. C. elegans provides a simple multicellular organism for studying innate immune responses, stress signaling, and host-microbe interactions.

b. Immunostimulants can be evaluated in nematodes to investigate their effects on immune cell activation, pathogen clearance, and longevity in response to infection or stress.

4. Galleria mellonella (Wax Moth) Larvae Models:

a. G. mellonella larvae serve as an alternative model for studying innate immune responses and evaluating drug efficacy in vivo.

b. Immunostimulants can be administered to wax moth larvae, and their effects on immune cell activation, microbial clearance, and survival can be assessed to screen for potential therapeutic agents.

5. Patient-Derived Organoid Models:

a. Patient-derived organoids, generated from primary cells or induced pluripotent stem cells (iPSCs), recapitulate tissue architecture and function in vitro.

b. Immunostimulants can be screened in patient-derived organoids to evaluate their effects on tissue-specific immune responses, inflammation, and disease pathology in a personalized context.

6. Humanized Mouse Models:

a. Humanized mouse models, engrafted with human immune cells or tissues, provide a platform for studying human-specific immune responses and evaluating immunostimulants in vivo.

b. Immunostimulants can be administered to humanized mice to assess their effects on human immune cell engraftment, function, and interactions with host tissues in a humanized immune environment.

7. Computational Models and In Silico Approaches:

a. Computational models, such as quantitative systems pharmacology (QSP) models and in silico simulations, complement experimental approaches by predicting drug effects on immune responses and host-pathogen interactions.

b. Immunostimulants can be screened in silico to prioritize lead compounds, optimize dosing regimens, and predict their efficacy and safety profiles before experimental validation.

By leveraging these alternative animal models and experimental approaches alongside traditional in vivo studies, researchers can gain valuable insights into the pharmacological activity, efficacy, and safety of immunostimulants, accelerating the drug discovery and development process while reducing reliance on traditional animal models.

Computational Models:

1. Molecular Docking and Virtual Screening:

a. Computational modeling techniques are used to predict the interaction of potential immunostimulants with target molecules involved in immune regulation.

b. Molecular docking simulations and virtual screening methods identify candidate compounds with favorable binding properties and potential immunostimulatory effects.

In summary, preclinical screening of new substances for immunostimulatory activity involves a combination of in vivo, in vitro, and animal alternative models, as well as computational approaches. These methods provide insights into the efficacy, mechanisms of action, and safety profiles of potential immunostimulants, facilitating their further development for clinical use.

GENERAL PRINCIPLES OF IMMUNOASSAY

A. Theoretical basis and optimization of immunoassay:

Immunological assays, or immunoassays, are powerful techniques used to detect and quantify specific molecules in biological samples based on the interaction between an antigen and an antibody. These assays are widely used in research, clinical diagnostics, and pharmaceutical development. The theoretical basis and optimization of immunoassays involve several key components:

Theoretical Basis of Immunoassays:

1. Antigen-Antibody Interaction:

a. Immunoassays rely on the specific binding between an antigen (the target molecule) and an antibody (the detection molecule).

b. This interaction forms the basis of the assay's specificity, as antibodies are highly selective for their target antigens.

2. Signal Generation:

a. After the antigen-antibody binding, a signal is generated to indicate the presence and quantity of the target molecule.

b. This signal can be generated through various methods, including enzymatic reactions, fluorescence, chemiluminescence, or radioactivity.

3. **Detection and Quantification:**

   a. The signal generated is detected and quantified using appropriate instrumentation.

   b. The intensity of the signal is proportional to the concentration of the target molecule in the sample.

Optimization of Immunoassays:

1. **Selection of Antibodies:**

   a. Choosing highly specific and sensitive antibodies is crucial for the success of an immunoassay.

   b. Monoclonal antibodies, which recognize a single epitope, are often preferred for their consistency and specificity.

2. **Sample Preparation:**

   a. Proper sample preparation is essential to ensure accurate and reproducible results.

   b. Steps such as sample dilution, centrifugation, and filtration may be necessary to remove interfering substances and optimize assay performance.

3. **Optimization of Assay Conditions:**

   a. Various parameters, including antibody concentration, incubation time, temperature, and buffer composition, need to be optimized to maximize assay sensitivity and specificity.

   b. Optimization experiments, such as titration assays and checkerboard assays, help determine the optimal conditions for each immunoassay.

4. **Calibration Standards:**

   a. Calibration standards containing known concentrations of the target molecule are essential for quantification.

    b. Calibration curves are generated by plotting signal intensity against standard concentrations, allowing for the interpolation of unknown sample concentrations.

5. Signal Detection:

    a. Selecting the appropriate detection method and instrumentation is critical for the sensitivity and accuracy of the immunoassay.

    b. Detection methods may include colorimetric assays, fluorescence assays, chemiluminescence assays, or radioimmunoassays, depending on the specific requirements of the assay.

6. Data Analysis:

    a. Proper data analysis techniques, such as curve fitting and statistical analysis, are used to interpret assay results accurately.

    b. Software tools may be employed to analyze raw data, calculate concentrations, and generate standard curves.

7. Quality Control:

    a. Quality control measures, including the use of controls, replicate samples, and validation experiments, are implemented to ensure assay reliability and reproducibility.

    b. Regular monitoring of assay performance and adherence to standard operating procedures (SOPs) are essential for maintaining assay quality.

By understanding the theoretical principles underlying immunoassays and optimizing experimental parameters, researchers can develop robust assays capable of accurately detecting and quantifying target molecules in biological samples. This optimization process ensures the reliability and reproducibility of immunoassay results, making them invaluable tools in various scientific and clinical applications.

HETEROGENEOUS AND HOMOGENOUS IMMUNOASSAY SYSTEMS:

Heterogeneous and homogeneous immunoassay systems are two broad categories of immunoassays that differ in their approach to detecting and quantifying target molecules. Each system has distinct advantages and limitations, making them suitable for different applications. Here's a detailed comparison of heterogeneous and homogeneous immunoassays:

Heterogeneous Immunoassays:

1. Principle:

   a. Heterogeneous immunoassays involve multiple steps and separation of bound and unbound components.

   b. The target molecule (antigen) in the sample binds to an immobilized capture molecule (typically an antibody) on a solid phase (e.g., microplate, membrane).

   c. After washing away unbound substances, a detection molecule (e.g., labeled antibody, enzyme, or fluorescent probe) is added to generate a measurable signal.

2. Types:

   a. **Enzyme-Linked Immunosorbent Assay (ELISA):** In ELISA, an enzyme-conjugated secondary antibody generates a colorimetric or fluorescent signal upon binding to the antigen-antibody complex.

   b. **Western Blot**: Western blotting involves electrophoretic separation of proteins followed by transfer to a membrane and detection with labeled antibodies.

   c. **Immunohistochemistry (IHC)**: IHC detects antigens in tissue sections using labeled antibodies and visualizes them under a microscope.

3. Advantages:

   a. **High specificity and sensitivity**: Separation of bound and unbound components reduces background noise.

b. **Wide dynamic range**: Suitable for detecting a broad range of analyte concentrations.

c. **Flexibility**: Compatible with various detection labels and formats.

4. Limitations:

a. **Longer assay times**: Multiple steps, including washing and incubation, increase assay duration.

b. **Labor-intensive**: Requires manual or automated handling of multiple reagents and washing steps.

c. **Potential for non-specific binding**: Solid-phase surfaces may lead to nonspecific binding of interfering substances.

Homogeneous Immunoassays:

1. Principle:

a. Homogeneous immunoassays are single-step assays where the reaction takes place in a homogeneous solution.

b. They rely on signal modulation upon antigen-antibody binding without the need for separation steps.

c. Signal generation can occur due to changes in fluorescence, luminescence, or energy transfer between labeled molecules.

2. Types:

a. **Fluorescence Polarization Immunoassay (FPIA)**: FPIA measures changes in the rotational movement of fluorescently labeled molecules upon antigen-antibody binding.

b. **Time-Resolved Fluorescence Resonance Energy Transfer (TR-FRET)**: TR-FRET utilizes energy transfer between donor and acceptor fluorophores to generate a signal.

c. **AlphaScreen:** AlphaScreen relies on chemiluminescent or fluorescent signals produced by the proximity of donor and acceptor beads conjugated to antibodies.

3. Advantages:

a. **Rapid results**: Single-step assays reduce assay time and complexity.

b. **Minimal sample manipulation**: No requirement for washing or separation steps.

c. **Reduced matrix effects**: Homogeneous assays are less prone to interference from sample components.

4. Limitations:

a. **Lower sensitivity**: Homogeneous assays may have higher background noise due to the absence of separation steps.

b. **Limited dynamic range**: Suitable for detecting analytes within a narrow concentration range.

c. **Limited flexibility**: Less adaptable to different detection labels and formats compared to heterogeneous assays.

In summary, heterogeneous immunoassays offer high specificity and sensitivity but require multiple steps and longer assay times. On the other hand, homogeneous immunoassays provide rapid results and simplified workflows but may have lower sensitivity and limited dynamic range. The choice between heterogeneous and homogeneous immunoassay systems depends on the specific requirements of the assay, including sensitivity, assay time, and sample matrix complexity.

IMMUNOASSAY METHODS EVALUATION:

Evaluating immunoassay methods is crucial to ensuring their accuracy, reliability, and suitability for specific applications. Several key parameters are assessed during the evaluation process to determine the performance characteristics of immunoassays. Here's a detailed overview of immunoassay method evaluation:

1. Analytical Sensitivity:

a. **Limit of Detection (LOD):** The lowest concentration of analyte that can be reliably detected by the assay.

b. **Limit of Quantification (LOQ):** The lowest concentration of analyte that can be accurately quantified with acceptable precision and accuracy.

c. **Dynamic Range:** The range of analyte concentrations over which the assay provides accurate and linear measurement.

2. Analytical Specificity:

a. **Cross-reactivity**: The extent to which the assay detects structurally similar molecules (cross-reactants) in addition to the target analyte.

b. **Selectivity:** The ability of the assay to specifically detect the target analyte in the presence of potentially interfering substances.

3. Precision:

a. **Intra-Assay Precision**: The consistency of results within a single assay run, typically assessed by measuring replicates of the same sample.

b. **Inter-Assay Precision**: The consistency of results between different assay runs, typically assessed by measuring replicates of the same sample across multiple runs.

4. Accuracy:

a. **Recovery:** The percentage of the known concentration of analyte that is detected by the assay when added to a sample matrix.

b. **Comparison to Reference Methods**: Comparison of assay results to those obtained using established reference methods to assess accuracy and agreement.

5. Linearity:

a. **Linearity of Dilution**: The ability of the assay to provide results that are proportional to the dilution of samples with known concentrations.

b. **Calibration Curve**: Construction of a calibration curve by plotting measured signal against known concentrations of analyte to assess linearity over the dynamic range of the assay.

6. Robustness and Reproducibility:

a. **Effect of Variations in Assay Conditions**: Evaluation of the impact of changes in assay parameters (e.g., incubation time, temperature, reagent concentrations) on assay performance.

b. **Inter-laboratory Reproducibility**: Assessment of the consistency of assay results when performed by different operators or in different laboratories.

7. Stability:

a. **Reagent Stability**: Evaluation of the stability of assay reagents (e.g., antibodies, enzymes, substrates) under various storage conditions.

b. **Sample Stability**: Assessment of the stability of samples during storage and handling to ensure accurate measurement of analyte concentrations.

8. Matrix Effects and Interference:

a. **Effect of Sample Matrix**: Evaluation of the impact of different sample matrices (e.g., serum, plasma, urine) on assay performance.

b. **Interference Testing**: Assessment of potential interference from endogenous substances or medications present in samples.

9. Clinical Utility:

a. **Clinical Validity**: Evaluation of the assay's ability to accurately measure analyte concentrations in clinical samples and its correlation with disease status or therapeutic response.

b. **Clinical Utility**: Assessment of the assay's usefulness in clinical decision-making and patient management.

10. Regulatory Compliance:

a. **Compliance with Regulatory Guidelines**: Evaluation of whether the assay meets regulatory requirements for accuracy, precision, and reliability (e.g., FDA, CLIA).

Validation:

a. **Validation Studies**: Comprehensive validation studies are conducted to demonstrate the performance characteristics of the assay, typically following established guidelines and protocols (e.g., CLSI, FDA guidelines).

By systematically evaluating these parameters, researchers and assay developers can assess the performance and reliability of immunoassay methods, ensuring their suitability for specific diagnostic, research, or therapeutic applications. Validation studies provide essential evidence of assay performance, guiding decision-making regarding assay selection and implementation in clinical or research settings.

PROTOCOL OUTLINE:

Creating a detailed protocol outline is essential for ensuring that experiments are conducted systematically and consistently. A well-written protocol provides clear instructions for each step of the procedure, enabling researchers to replicate the experiment accurately. Here's an outline of the key components of a protocol, along with detailed explanations:

1. Title:

a. Concise and descriptive title that summarizes the purpose of the experiment.

2. Introduction:

a. Background information explaining the rationale and significance of the experiment.

b. Literature review summarizing relevant previous studies and findings.

3. Materials:

a. List of all materials and reagents required for the experiment, including equipment, chemicals, and biological samples.

4. Methods:

a. **4.1 Experimental Design:**
   - Description of the overall experimental design, including treatment groups, controls, and replicates.

b. **4.2 Sample Preparation:**
   - Detailed instructions for preparing samples, including collection, storage, and any necessary processing steps.

c. **4.3 Assay Procedure:**
   - Step-by-step instructions for performing the assay, including reagent preparation, incubation conditions, and measurement techniques.

d. **4.4 Data Analysis:**
   - Explanation of how data will be collected, processed, and analyzed.
   - Description of statistical methods and software used for data analysis.

5. Quality Control:

a. Procedures for quality control checks to ensure the reliability and accuracy of the results.

b. Criteria for acceptability of results and actions to be taken in case of deviations or anomalies.

6. Safety Considerations:

a. Guidelines for handling hazardous materials, including chemicals, biological samples, and equipment.

b. Personal protective equipment (PPE) requirements and safety precautions to minimize risks to personnel.

7. Troubleshooting:

a. Troubleshooting tips for common issues or challenges that may arise during the experiment.

b. Strategies for identifying and resolving technical problems effectively.

8. Expected Results:

    a. Description of the anticipated outcomes of the experiment based on previous knowledge and hypotheses.

    b. Examples of expected data or results, including graphs, tables, or figures.

9. References:

    a. Citations of relevant literature sources, including research articles, protocols, and textbooks.

    b. Acknowledgment of contributions from other researchers or institutions.

10. Appendices:

    a. Supplementary information, such as protocols for specific techniques, detailed procedures for data analysis, or additional resources.

Writing Tips:

    a. Use clear and concise language, avoiding jargon or unnecessary technical terms.

    b. Organize the protocol into logical sections with headings and subheadings for easy navigation.

    c. Include diagrams, illustrations, or photographs to clarify complex procedures or equipment setups.

    d. Provide step-by-step instructions with precise measurements, timings, and temperatures for each procedure.

    e. Review and revise the protocol carefully to ensure accuracy, clarity, and completeness before implementation.

By following this detailed outline and incorporating specific instructions for each step, researchers can create well-structured protocols that facilitate the reproducibility and reliability of experimental results.

OBJECTIVES OF IMMUNOASSAY:

The objectives of immunoassays are multifaceted, reflecting their diverse applications in research, clinical diagnostics, pharmaceutical development, environmental monitoring, and food safety. Here's a detailed overview of the objectives of immunoassays:

1. Detection and Quantification of Target Molecules:

a. **Specificity**: Immunoassays aim to selectively detect and quantify target molecules (analytes) within complex biological or environmental samples.

b. **Sensitivity:** Immunoassays should be sensitive enough to detect low concentrations of analytes, even in the presence of interfering substances.

2. Biomarker Discovery and Validation:

a. **Identification:** Immunoassays facilitate the discovery of novel biomarkers associated with disease, physiological processes, or exposure to environmental toxins.

b. **Validation:** Immunoassays are used to validate candidate biomarkers by confirming their presence and quantifying their levels in biological samples.

3. Disease Diagnosis and Monitoring:

a. **Diagnostic Tests**: Immunoassays are employed as diagnostic tests to detect the presence of disease-specific biomarkers or pathogens in patient samples.

b. **Prognostic and Predictive Testing**: Immunoassays provide prognostic information and aid in predicting disease outcomes or response to treatment.

4. Therapeutic Drug Monitoring:

a. **Drug Levels:** Immunoassays are used to measure drug levels in patient samples to optimize dosage regimens, ensure therapeutic efficacy, and prevent toxicity.

b. **Compliance Monitoring**: Immunoassays help monitor patient compliance with medication regimens by measuring drug concentrations in biological fluids.

5. Pharmaceutical Development:

a. **Drug Development**: Immunoassays play a critical role in pharmaceutical research and development by assessing the pharmacokinetics, pharmacodynamics, and immunogenicity of drug candidates.

b. **Bioanalytical Assays**: Immunoassays are used to quantify drug concentrations, antibody responses, and biomarker levels in preclinical and clinical studies.

6. Environmental and Food Safety:

a. **Contaminant Detection**: Immunoassays are utilized to detect environmental pollutants, toxins, pesticides, and foodborne pathogens in water, soil, food, and agricultural products.

b. Regulatory **Compliance: Immunoassays help ensure compliance with regulatory** standards and monitor adherence to safety regulations in environmental and food industries.

7. Research and Basic Science:

a. **Functional Studies**: Immunoassays enable researchers to investigate the function, localization, and regulation of proteins and other biomolecules in biological systems.

b. **Screening Assays**: Immunoassays are employed in high-throughput screening assays to identify potential drug targets, therapeutic agents, or biomarkers.

8. Point-of-Care Testing (POCT):

a. **Rapid Diagnostics**: Immunoassays are adapted for use in point-of-care testing devices to provide rapid and convenient diagnosis or monitoring of diseases in clinical settings, remote locations, or resource-limited settings.

9. Epidemiological Surveillance:

a. **Disease Monitoring**: Immunoassays are employed in epidemiological studies to monitor disease prevalence, transmission dynamics, and population immunity levels.

b. **Outbreak Investigation**: Immunoassays help identify outbreaks, trace the spread of infectious diseases, and assess the effectiveness of control measures.

10. Personalized Medicine:

a. **Patient Stratification**: Immunoassays contribute to personalized medicine by identifying biomarkers that can stratify patients into subgroups based on disease subtype, prognosis, or treatment response.

b. **Targeted Therapies**: Immunoassays aid in selecting appropriate therapies tailored to individual patients based on their molecular profiles and disease characteristics.

Overall, the objectives of immunoassays encompass a broad range of applications aimed at advancing scientific knowledge, improving healthcare outcomes, ensuring public health and safety, and supporting drug discovery and development efforts.

PREPARATION OF IMMUNOASSAY:

The preparation of an immunoassay involves several key steps aimed at ensuring the proper functioning of the assay and accurate detection and quantification of the target analyte. Here's a detailed overview of the preparation process:

1. Selection of Antibodies and Reagents:

a. Choose highly specific and sensitive antibodies that recognize the target analyte with minimal cross-reactivity.

b. Select appropriate labels or detection systems (e.g., enzymes, fluorescent dyes, radioisotopes) based on the detection method and instrumentation available.

c. Ensure the availability of quality-controlled reagents, including buffers, blocking agents, substrates, and standards.

2. Coating of Solid Support (for Solid-phase Assays):

a. If using a solid-phase assay (e.g., ELISA), coat the surface of microplates, membranes, or beads with capture antibodies or antigens.

b. Optimize coating conditions, including antibody concentration, coating buffer composition, and incubation time, to achieve maximal binding efficiency and uniform coating.

3. Preparation of Standards and Controls:

a. Prepare a series of standard solutions with known concentrations of the target analyte to generate a calibration curve for quantification.

b. Include positive and negative controls to monitor assay performance and validate results.

4. Optimization of Assay Conditions:

a. Conduct pilot experiments to optimize assay conditions, including antibody concentrations, incubation times, temperatures, and washing steps.

b. Perform titration assays to determine the optimal concentrations of antibodies, detection reagents, and sample dilutions.

5. Blocking and Incubation:

a. Block nonspecific binding sites on the solid support with blocking agents such as bovine serum albumin (BSA), milk, or casein.

b. Incubate the coated surface with blocking solution to minimize background signal and nonspecific interactions.

c. Incubate samples, standards, and controls with detection antibodies or labeled reagents to facilitate specific binding to the target analyte.

6. Washing and Removal of Unbound Components:

a. Wash the solid support thoroughly between incubation steps to remove unbound antibodies, antigens, or detection reagents.

b. Use appropriate washing buffers and wash protocols to minimize background noise and maximize signal-to-noise ratio.

7. Signal Generation and Detection:

a. Add substrates, fluorophores, or other detection reagents that generate a measurable signal upon binding to the labeled detection antibodies or reagents.

b. Incubate the assay for the appropriate duration to allow signal development.

c. Employ appropriate instrumentation (e.g., spectrophotometer, plate reader, fluorescence reader) to measure the signal intensity.

8. Data Analysis and Interpretation:

a. Generate a calibration curve using standard solutions with known concentrations to quantify the target analyte in unknown samples.

b. Analyze assay results using appropriate software or calculation methods to determine analyte concentrations.

c. Compare sample measurements to the calibration curve and controls to validate results and ensure assay accuracy.

9. Quality Control and Validation:

a. Include quality control measures, such as replicate samples, intra- and inter-assay controls, and validation experiments, to ensure assay reliability and reproducibility.

b. Monitor assay performance using control samples and assess parameters such as precision, accuracy, linearity, and sensitivity.

10. Documentation and Reporting:

a. Record all experimental procedures, reagent preparations, and assay results in a detailed laboratory notebook or electronic record.

b. Prepare a comprehensive report summarizing the assay protocol, optimization steps, validation results, and interpretation of data.

By following these detailed steps, researchers can prepare immunoassays effectively, optimizing assay conditions, ensuring assay reliability, and generating accurate and reproducible results for the detection and quantification of target analytes.

IMMUNOASSAY FOR DIGOXIN AND INSULIN:

Immunoassay for Digoxin:

1. Introduction:

   a. **Background:** Digoxin is a medication used to treat heart failure and certain types of irregular heartbeats. Immunoassays for digoxin are used to monitor therapeutic drug levels in patient serum or plasma.

2. Materials:

   a. Digoxin standards
   b. Digoxin-specific antibodies (both capture and detection antibodies)
   c. Blocking agent (e.g., bovine serum albumin)
   d. Enzyme-conjugated secondary antibody (e.g., anti-mouse IgG-HRP)
   e. Substrate solution (e.g., TMB)
   f. Stop solution (e.g., sulfuric acid)
   g. Wash buffer (e.g., phosphate-buffered saline with Tween-20)
   h. Microplates or tubes for assay setup
   i. Plate reader for measuring absorbance

3. Protocol:

Coating:

   a. Coat microplate wells with digoxin-specific capture antibodies.
   b. Block nonspecific binding sites with a blocking agent.

Standards and Samples:

a. Prepare digoxin standards of known concentrations.

b. Dilute patient serum or plasma samples appropriately.

Incubation:

a. Incubate standards, samples, and controls with digoxin-specific detection antibodies conjugated to an enzyme (e.g., horseradish peroxidase).

Washing:

a. Wash the microplate wells to remove unbound substances and minimize background noise.

Signal Generation:

a. Add substrate solution to the wells and incubate for a specific time to allow enzymatic reaction.

b. Add stop solution to terminate the reaction.

Measurement:

a. Measure the absorbance of each well using a plate reader at the appropriate wavelength.

b. Construct a standard curve using absorbance values of standards and interpolate sample concentrations.

Quality Control:

a. Include control samples of known digoxin concentrations to monitor assay performance.

b. Validate assay results based on precision, accuracy, and linearity.

Immunoassay for Insulin:

1. Introduction:

a. Background: Insulin is a hormone that regulates blood sugar levels. Immunoassays for insulin are used to measure insulin concentrations in serum or plasma for diabetes management and research purposes.

2. Materials:

a. Insulin standards

b. Insulin-specific antibodies (both capture and detection antibodies)

c. Blocking agent (e.g., milk)

d. Enzyme-conjugated secondary antibody (e.g., anti-rabbit IgG-HRP)

e. Substrate solution (e.g., TMB)

f. Stop solution (e.g., sulfuric acid)

g. Wash buffer (e.g., phosphate-buffered saline with Tween-20)

h. Microplates or tubes for assay setup

i. Plate reader for measuring absorbance

3. Protocol:

Coating:

a. Coat microplate wells with insulin-specific capture antibodies.

b. Block nonspecific binding sites with a blocking agent.

Standards and Samples:

a. Prepare insulin standards of known concentrations.

b. Dilute patient serum or plasma samples appropriately.

Incubation:

a. Incubate standards, samples, and controls with insulin-specific detection antibodies conjugated to an enzyme (e.g., horseradish peroxidase).

Washing:

a. Wash the microplate wells to remove unbound substances and minimize background noise.

Signal Generation:

a. Add substrate solution to the wells and incubate for a specific time to allow enzymatic reaction.

b. Add stop solution to terminate the reaction.

Measurement:

a. Measure the absorbance of each well using a plate reader at the appropriate wavelength.

b. Construct a standard curve using absorbance values of standards and interpolate sample concentrations.

Quality Control:

a. Include control samples of known insulin concentrations to monitor assay performance.

b. Validate assay results based on precision, accuracy, and linearity.

Conclusion:

a. The immunoassay procedures outlined above provide a systematic approach to detect and quantify digoxin and insulin in biological samples. Optimization of assay conditions and thorough validation are essential to ensure accurate and reliable results for clinical and research applications.

LIMITATIONS OF ANIMAL EXPERIMENTATION AND ALTERNATE ANIMAL EXPERIMENTS

Animal experimentation has long been a mainstay in preclinical screening of new substances for pharmacological activity, but it comes with several limitations, including ethical concerns, species differences, and cost. Here's a detailed exploration of these limitations along with alternative animal experiments and models:

Limitations of Animal Experimentation:

1. **Ethical Concerns:**

    a. Animal experimentation raises ethical issues related to the use of sentient beings for research purposes, particularly regarding animal welfare and suffering.

    b. Ethical considerations have led to increased scrutiny of animal research practices and calls for the development and adoption of alternative methods.

2. **Species Differences:**

a. Variability in physiology, metabolism, and immune responses between animal species and humans can limit the translatability of preclinical findings to human outcomes.

b. Species-specific differences in drug metabolism, pharmacokinetics, and toxicity profiles may result in misleading or inaccurate predictions of drug efficacy and safety.

3. Cost and Time Intensive:

a. Animal studies are resource-intensive, requiring significant time, funding, and infrastructure for housing, care, and maintenance of animals, as well as skilled personnel for experimental procedures.

b. Long study durations and large sample sizes are often necessary to achieve statistically significant results, increasing costs and time-to-market for new drugs.

4. Complexity and Variability:

a. Biological complexity and variability inherent in animal models can confound experimental results, leading to inconsistencies and difficulties in data interpretation.

b. Factors such as genetic variability, environmental influences, and inter-animal variability contribute to challenges in reproducibility and reliability of preclinical studies.

5. Limited Predictive Value:

a. Despite extensive use, animal models may have limited predictive value for human responses, particularly in complex diseases and multi-factorial conditions.

b. Failures in translating promising results from animal studies to clinical success in humans highlight the limitations of relying solely on animal models for drug development.

Alternative Animal Experiments and Models:

1. In Vitro Models:

a. Cell culture-based assays and organoid systems offer controlled environments for studying cellular responses to drug candidates, providing valuable insights into mechanisms of action and toxicity.

b. High-throughput screening assays using cell lines or primary cells enable rapid evaluation of compound libraries and identification of lead candidates.

2. Organ-on-a-Chip Technology:

a. Organ-on-a-chip platforms mimic physiological functions of human organs in vitro, allowing for more accurate representation of tissue-level responses to drug treatments.

b. These microfluidic devices offer opportunities for studying drug metabolism, toxicity, and efficacy in human-relevant models.

3. Humanized Models:

a. Humanized animal models, such as mice with humanized immune systems or patient-derived xenograft models, incorporate human tissues or cells into animal hosts, providing more relevant platforms for studying human-specific responses.

b. Patient-derived organoids and tissue slices retain patient-specific characteristics and can be used to assess drug responses and personalized medicine approaches.

4. Computational Models:

a. In silico approaches, including molecular modeling, virtual screening, and quantitative structure-activity relationship (QSAR) modeling, offer predictive capabilities for drug activity, pharmacokinetics, and toxicity without the need for animal experimentation.

b. Systems biology and bioinformatics analyses provide insights into complex biological processes and enable integration of multi-omics data for drug discovery and development.

5. 3D Bioprinting:

a. 3D bioprinting technology allows for the fabrication of tissue constructs with spatial organization and physiological relevance, enabling the development of more realistic models for drug testing and toxicity screening.

b. Organoids and tissue-engineered constructs can recapitulate organ-level functions and disease phenotypes, providing platforms for studying drug responses in vitro.

Conclusion:

1. While animal experimentation has been a cornerstone of preclinical screening, its limitations underscore the need for alternative approaches that are more ethical, cost-effective, and predictive of human responses. Integration of in vitro models, humanized systems, computational methods, and advanced technologies holds promise for improving the efficiency and accuracy of drug discovery and development processes while minimizing reliance on animal experimentation.

EXTRAPOLATION OF IN VITRO DATA TO PRECLINICAL

Animal experimentation has long been a mainstay in preclinical screening of new substances for pharmacological activity, but it comes with several limitations, including ethical concerns, species differences, and cost. Here's a detailed exploration of these limitations along with alternative animal experiments and models:

Limitations of Animal Experimentation:

1. Ethical Concerns:

a. Animal experimentation raises ethical issues related to the use of sentient beings for research purposes, particularly regarding animal welfare and suffering.

b. Ethical considerations have led to increased scrutiny of animal research practices and calls for the development and adoption of alternative methods.

2. **Species Differences:**

   a. Variability in physiology, metabolism, and immune responses between animal species and humans can limit the translatability of preclinical findings to human outcomes.

   b. Species-specific differences in drug metabolism, pharmacokinetics, and toxicity profiles may result in misleading or inaccurate predictions of drug efficacy and safety.

3. **Cost and Time Intensive:**

   a. Animal studies are resource-intensive, requiring significant time, funding, and infrastructure for housing, care, and maintenance of animals, as well as skilled personnel for experimental procedures.

   b. Long study durations and large sample sizes are often necessary to achieve statistically significant results, increasing costs and time-to-market for new drugs.

4. **Complexity and Variability:**

   a. Biological complexity and variability inherent in animal models can confound experimental results, leading to inconsistencies and difficulties in data interpretation.

   b. Factors such as genetic variability, environmental influences, and inter-animal variability contribute to challenges in reproducibility and reliability of preclinical studies.

5. **Limited Predictive Value:**

   a. Despite extensive use, animal models may have limited predictive value for human responses, particularly in complex diseases and multi-factorial conditions.

b. Failures in translating promising results from animal studies to clinical success in humans highlight the limitations of relying solely on animal models for drug development.

Alternative Animal Experiments and Models:

1. In Vitro Models:

a. Cell culture-based assays and organoid systems offer controlled environments for studying cellular responses to drug candidates, providing valuable insights into mechanisms of action and toxicity.

b. High-throughput screening assays using cell lines or primary cells enable rapid evaluation of compound libraries and identification of lead candidates.

2. Organ-on-a-Chip Technology:

a. Organ-on-a-chip platforms mimic physiological functions of human organs in vitro, allowing for more accurate representation of tissue-level responses to drug treatments.

b. These microfluidic devices offer opportunities for studying drug metabolism, toxicity, and efficacy in human-relevant models.

3. Humanized Models:

a. Humanized animal models, such as mice with humanized immune systems or patient-derived xenograft models, incorporate human tissues or cells into animal hosts, providing more relevant platforms for studying human-specific responses.

b. Patient-derived organoids and tissue slices retain patient-specific characteristics and can be used to assess drug responses and personalized medicine approaches.

4. Computational Models:

a. In silico approaches, including molecular modeling, virtual screening, and quantitative structure-activity relationship (QSAR) modeling, offer predictive capabilities for drug activity, pharmacokinetics, and toxicity without the need for animal experimentation.

b. Systems biology and bioinformatics analyses provide insights into complex biological processes and enable integration of multi-omics data for drug discovery and development.

5. 3D Bioprinting:

a. 3D bioprinting technology allows for the fabrication of tissue constructs with spatial organization and physiological relevance, enabling the development of more realistic models for drug testing and toxicity screening.

b. Organoids and tissue-engineered constructs can recapitulate organ-level functions and disease phenotypes, providing platforms for studying drug responses in vitro.

Conclusion:

1. While animal experimentation has been a cornerstone of preclinical screening, its limitations underscore the need for alternative approaches that are more ethical, cost-effective, and predictive of human responses. Integration of in vitro models, humanized systems, computational methods, and advanced technologies holds promise for improving the efficiency and accuracy of drug discovery and development processes while minimizing reliance on animal experimentation.

EXTRAPOLATION OF IN PRECLINICAL TO HUMANS

Extrapolating in vitro data to preclinical in vivo settings in the screening of new substances for pharmacological activity involves bridging the gap between cellular responses observed in vitro and the complex interactions within living organisms. While in vitro studies offer controlled environments and mechanistic insights, they may not fully capture the physiological complexity and systemic effects seen in vivo. Here's how extrapolation is approached:

1. Understanding Mechanisms of Action:

a. In vitro studies elucidate the molecular mechanisms underlying the pharmacological activity of substances, providing valuable insights into their mode of action.

b. Knowledge of cellular pathways, receptor interactions, and downstream signaling cascades guides the design of in vivo experiments to validate these mechanisms in a physiological context.

2. Establishing Pharmacokinetic Parameters:

a. In vitro studies inform the absorption, distribution, metabolism, and excretion (ADME) properties of substances, including permeability, solubility, and metabolic stability.

b. Pharmacokinetic models and in silico predictions are used to estimate drug concentrations and exposure levels in vivo, guiding dosing regimens and route of administration.

3. Translating Efficacy and Toxicity:

a. In vitro efficacy assays assess the potency and efficacy of substances against target cells or tissues, providing preliminary evidence of pharmacological activity.

b. In vivo efficacy studies validate these findings in animal models, assessing therapeutic outcomes such as tumor regression, symptom improvement, or disease progression.

c. In vitro toxicity assays identify potential adverse effects and safety concerns, guiding the selection of doses and monitoring parameters in preclinical studies.

4. Considering Pharmacodynamic Relationships:

a. In vitro dose-response curves establish concentration-response relationships and potency estimates for substances.

b. Extrapolation to in vivo settings involves considering factors such as drug distribution, target engagement, and tissue exposure to predict in vivo efficacy at clinically relevant doses.

5. Addressing Pharmacological Variability:

a. In vitro studies may not fully capture the variability in drug responses observed across patient populations or species.

b. Preclinical in vivo models incorporate factors such as genetic variability, disease heterogeneity, and physiological differences to assess the robustness and generalizability of in vitro findings.

6. Integration of Data and Models:

a. Integration of in vitro and in vivo data through quantitative systems pharmacology (QSP) models, physiologically based pharmacokinetic (PBPK) models, and pharmacodynamic models enables holistic understanding and prediction of drug responses.

b. Model validation and refinement iteratively improve the predictive accuracy of preclinical screening approaches and facilitate decision-making in drug development.

7. Reducing Animal Use:

a. In vitro-in vivo extrapolation (IVIVE) approaches aim to minimize reliance on animal experimentation by optimizing in vitro assays, leveraging computational models, and prioritizing promising candidates for in vivo validation.

b. Alternative animal models, such as humanized mice, patient-derived xenografts, and organoid cultures, offer human-relevant platforms for preclinical assessment while reducing the need for traditional animal models.

Conclusion:

a. Extrapolation of in vitro data to preclinical in vivo settings in the screening of new substances involves a comprehensive approach that integrates mechanistic insights, pharmacokinetic considerations, efficacy and toxicity assessments, and predictive modeling. By leveraging the strengths of in vitro and in vivo methodologies while addressing their respective limitations, researchers can optimize preclinical screening strategies and accelerate the translation of promising candidates into clinical development.

Multiple Choice Questions (MCQs)

1. What is a primary objective of immunoassays in pharmaceutical development?
    A) Monitoring environmental pollutants
    B) Discovery of novel biomarkers
    C) Assessment of pharmacokinetics and pharmacodynamics
    D) Ensuring food safety

2. Which component is crucial in the preparation of immunoassays to minimize cross-reactivity?
    A) Highly specific antibodies
    B) Standard solutions
    C) Enzyme-conjugated secondary antibodies
    D) Microplates

3. What is the primary role of immunoassays in therapeutic drug monitoring?
    A) To detect environmental toxins
    B) To ensure regulatory compliance
    C) To measure drug levels in patients
    D) To identify outbreaks of infectious diseases

4. What ethical concern is associated with animal experimentation?
    A) High costs

B) Use of sentient beings for research

C) Long study durations

D) Species-specific differences

5. What is the advantage of organ-on-a-chip technology in drug development?

    A) Reduces the need for animal testing

    B) Offers high throughput screening

    C) Generates standard calibration curves

    D) Uses bovine serum albumin for blocking

6. Which assay is used for monitoring levels of digoxin?

    A) Point-of-care testing

    B) ELISA

    C) High-throughput screening

    D) Computational modeling

7. What is the significance of including control samples in an immunoassay?

    A) To measure the absorbance

    B) To monitor assay performance

    C) To coat microplate wells

    D) To block nonspecific binding sites

8. What is the purpose of a blocking agent in immunoassays?

    A) To detect the target analyte

    B) To minimize background signal

    C) To generate a measurable signal

    D) To create a calibration curve

9. What is a common use of insulin immunoassays?

    A) To detect foodborne pathogens

    B) To monitor drug compliance

    C) To measure insulin concentrations for diabetes management

    D) To identify environmental pollutants

10. Which alternative to animal experimentation involves the use of human tissues or cells to provide more relevant data?

  A) In vitro cell culture assays

  B) Humanized animal models

  C) Organ-on-a-chip technology

  D) Computational models

11. What is the primary role of antibodies in immunoassays?

  A) To enhance the immune response

  B) To bind specifically to target molecules

  C) To serve as a control

  D) To act as a buffer

12. What technique is used to measure the rotational movement of molecules in a homogeneous immunoassay?

  A) ELISA

  B) Western Blot

  C) Fluorescence Polarization Immunoassay (FPIA)

  D) Immunohistochemistry

13. Which model organism is used for studying immune responses and drug effects using a transparent and genetically tractable model?

  A) Humanized mice

  B) Zebrafish

  C) Drosophila melanogaster

  D) Caenorhabditis elegans

14. In the evaluation of immunoassay methods, what does LOD stand for?

  A) Level of Detection

  B) Limit of Dilution

  C) Limit of Detection

  D) Level of Dilution

15. Which of the following is a key advantage of heterogeneous immunoassays?

A) Faster assay times

B) No need for separation steps

C) High specificity and sensitivity

D) Simpler assay procedures

16. What is the primary advantage of using homogeneous immunoassays?

A) They require multiple washing steps

B) They provide rapid results with minimal sample manipulation

C) They use solid phases for binding

D) They are more labor-intensive

17. Which parameter is assessed to determine the lowest concentration of an analyte that can be accurately quantified with acceptable precision in immunoassays?

A) Analytical sensitivity

B) Limit of Quantification (LOQ)

C) Dynamic range

D) Analytical specificity

18. What does IC50 represent in dose-response studies?

A) The initial concentration that causes 50% response

B) The concentration that inhibits 50% of the immune response

C) The 50% increase in signal intensity

D) The maximum achievable response

19. Which assay is commonly used to study antigen presentation and T-cell activation in vitro?

A) Phagocytosis assay

B) Mixed lymphocyte reaction

C) Co-culture assay with dendritic cells and T cells

D) Cytokine release assay

20. In immunoassay optimization, what is the purpose of using calibration standards?

A) To identify potential safety concerns

B) To assess the dynamic range of the assay

C) To determine known concentrations of the target molecule for quantification

D) To validate the assay's limit of detection

Short Answer Questions

1. Why are specific and sensitive antibodies important in immunoassays?

2. What is the purpose of using a substrate solution in an immunoassay?

3. Describe the role of pharmacokinetic parameters in translating in vitro data to preclinical settings.

4. What are the benefits of using organ-on-a-chip technology in drug development?

5. How does the inclusion of patient-derived xenografts improve preclinical studies?

6. Explain the importance of blocking nonspecific binding in an immunoassay.

7. How does a standard curve assist in the quantification of analytes in immunoassays?

8. Why are ethical concerns significant in animal experimentation?

9. What is the main advantage of using computational models in preclinical drug screening?

10. Why is it important to validate immunoassay results with control samples?

11. What is the significance of signal generation in immunoassays?

12. Describe the role of a solid phase in heterogeneous immunoassays.

13. Why is cross-reactivity an important consideration in immunoassay specificity?

14. Explain the principle behind the use of fluorescent polarization in immunoassays.

15. What is the purpose of pharmacokinetic analysis in preclinical studies?

16. How do homogeneous immunoassays minimize matrix effects?

17. What is the benefit of using patient-derived organoid models in drug screening?

18. Describe the significance of linearity of dilution in immunoassay evaluations.

19. What advantages do computational models offer in the preclinical screening of immunomodulators?

20. How do regulatory compliance factors influence immunoassay development?

Long Answer Questions

1. Discuss the implications of species differences in animal experimentation and how these limitations can impact drug development.

2. Explain how in vitro and in vivo data are integrated to enhance the predictive accuracy of preclinical drug testing.

3. Describe the process and significance of therapeutic drug monitoring using immunoassays.

4. Analyze the role of high-throughput screening assays in pharmaceutical development and how they complement traditional research methods.

5. Evaluate the ethical, logistical, and scientific challenges associated with animal experimentation and propose viable alternative methods that could address these issues.

6. Discuss the advantages and limitations of using zebrafish as a model organism in the preclinical screening of immunomodulators.

7. Explain the different types of heterogeneous immunoassays and their specific applications in biomedical research.

8. Describe the process and importance of evaluating analytical specificity and precision in the development of immunoassays.

9. Analyze the impact of computational modeling on enhancing the efficiency of preclinical drug discovery.

10. Evaluate the role of high-throughput screening in the rapid identification of immunomodulatory agents.

Answer Key for MCQs

1. C) Assessment of pharmacokinetics and pharmacodynamics

2. A) Highly specific antibodies

3. C) To measure drug levels in patients

4. B) Use of sentient beings for research

5. A) Reduces the need for animal testing

6. B) ELISA

7. B) To monitor assay performance

8. B) To minimize background signal

9. C) To measure insulin concentrations for diabetes management

10. B) Humanized animal models

11. B) To bind specifically to target molecules

12. C) Fluorescence Polarization Immunoassay (FPIA)

13. B) Zebrafish

14. C) Limit of Detection

15. C) High specificity and sensitivity

16. B) They provide rapid results with minimal sample manipulation

17. B) Limit of Quantification (LOQ)

18. B) The concentration that inhibits 50% of the immune response

19. C) Co-culture assay with dendritic cells and T cells

20. C) To determine known concentrations of the target molecule for quantification